COURTHOUSES
OF THE
SECOND CIRCUIT

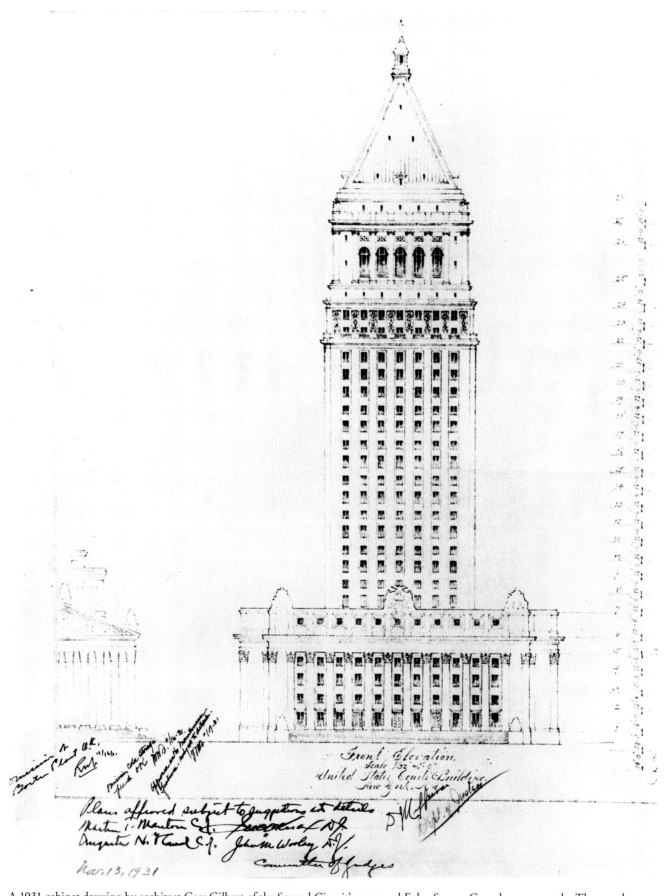

A 1931 cabinet drawing by architect Cass Gilbert of the Second Circuit's proposed Foley Square Courthouse, now the Thurgood Marshall U. S. Courthouse, with the signatures of the judges who approved the drawing appearing in the lower left.

COURTHOUSES OF THE SECOND CIRCUIT

THEIR ARCHITECTURE, HISTORY, AND STORIES

AUTHORED BY
The Federal Bar Council

with the assistance of
The Second Circuit Committee on History and Commemorative Events

EDITORS
Patricia A. McGovern and Michael P. Zweig

ASSOCIATE EDITOR
Marjorie Press Lindblom

A PUBLICATION OF
THE FEDERAL BAR FOUNDATION

AND

ACANTHUS PRESS
NEW YORK : 2015

FEDERAL BAR FOUNDATION
123 Main Street, #L100
White Plains, NY 10601

AND

ACANTHUS PRESS
48 West 22nd Street
New York, NY 10010

Copyright © 2015, Federal Bar Foundation

Every reasonable attempt has been made to identify the owners of copyright.
Errors of omission will be corrected in subsequent printings of this work.

All rights reserved. This book may not be reproduced in whole or in any part
(except by reviewers for the public press) without written permission from the publisher.

Library of Congress Cataloging-in-Publication Data

Federal Bar Council, author.

Courthouses of the Second Circuit : their architecture, history, and stories / authored by The Federal Bar Council
with the assistance of The Second Circuit Committee on History and Commemorative Events ;
editors, Patricia A. McGovern and Michael P. Zweig ; associate editor, Marjorie Press Lindblom.

pages cm

Includes bibliographical references and index.

ISBN 978-0-926494-93-0 (hardcover : alk. paper)

1. Courthouses—New York (State)—History. 2. Courthouses—Connecticut—History. 3. Courthouses—Vermont—History. 4. United States. Court of Appeals (2nd Circuit) New York (State)—History. 5. United States. Court of Appeals (2nd Circuit)—Connecticut—History. 6. United States. Court of Appeals (2nd Circuit)—Vermont—History. I. McGovern, Patricia A., 1949– editor. II. Zweig, Michael P., editor. III. United States. Court of Appeals (2nd Circuit). Committee on History and Commemorative Events. V. Title.

NA4472.N7F43 2015

725'.15—dc23

2015018675v

Printed in China

FEDERAL BAR COUNCIL

The Federal Bar Council is an organization of lawyers who practice in federal courts within the Second Circuit. The purposes of the Council since its inception in 1932 have been fourfold: to promote excellence in federal jurisprudence; to protect the administration of justice; to uphold the high professional standards of the bench and bar; and to encourage friendly relations among members of the legal profession.

FEDERAL BAR FOUNDATION

The Federal Bar Foundation is a not-for-profit corporation that supports many activities of the Federal Bar Council. The purposes of the Foundation since its founding in 1964 have included: to facilitate and improve the administration of justice; and to facilitate the cultivation and diffusion of knowledge and understanding of law and the promotion of the study of the law and the science of jurisprudence. The Foundation supports, for example, the Council's educational programs as well as publications of legal and historical interest.

CONTENTS

FOREWORD 9

PREFACE 11

ACKNOWLEDGEMENTS 13

CHAPTER CREDITS AND BIOGRAPHICAL INFORMATION 17

INTRODUCTION 21

CHAPTER ONE | 31

THE UNITED STATES COURT OF APPEALS FOR THE SECOND CIRCUIT

CHAPTER TWO | 55

THE SOUTHERN DISTRICT OF NEW YORK

CHAPTER THREE | 95

THE NORTHERN DISTRICT OF NEW YORK

CHAPTER FOUR | 121

THE EASTERN DISTRICT OF NEW YORK

CHAPTER FIVE | 149

THE WESTERN DISTRICT OF NEW YORK

CHAPTER SIX | 171

THE DISTRICT OF CONNECTICUT

CHAPTER SEVEN | 207

THE DISTRICT OF VERMONT

JUDGES 223

ENDNOTES 230

PICTURE CREDITS 250

INDEX 253

A view from the bench in the 17th-floor courtroom of the Thurgood Marshall U.S. Courthouse.

FOREWORD

P ublic architecture, Daniel Patrick Moynihan told an audience in 1967, "is the bone and muscle of democracy." What public buildings should aspire to do, he said, is to bring people together "in an experience of confidence and trust."[i] Nowhere is this insight more telling than in the architecture of our courthouses.

The inhabitants of this nation look to the judiciary to resolve their disputes. That ours is a country of civil peace reflects the role of courts in administering justice, fairly and efficiently. The courthouse is the place where people gather, where individuals playing different roles converge—the litigants, prosecutors, defense attorneys, jurors, judges, courthouse staff, the building maintenance crew. Where the courthouse is welcoming, it fosters a civility, essential to productive deliberation that characterizes our adversarial legal system. Justice Stephen Breyer in his foreword to *Celebrating the Courthouse* elegantly outlined the challenge facing successful courthouse architecture:

> How can our work better reflect several basic tenets of modern public life: first, the fact that, in our democracy, power flows from the people; second, the need to resist the technical, atomizing forces that divide us and to encourage those forces that unify and bring us together as a community; and third, the effort to prevent our government from being perceived as a hostile, alien entity, but rather to emphasize through participation that it can and should amount to no more than our nation's individual citizens themselves, each showing a "civic" face as each acts in his or her public capacity.

In the pages that follow, the Federal Bar Council has produced a splendid testament to the courthouses of the Second Circuit. These structures differ in period of construction, architectural design, and scale, reflecting the tastes of the times in which they were built. Inside the courthouses, the reader experiences the courtrooms and other public spaces unique to each building. However much they differ in design, the courthouses of the Second Circuit share much in common: they are living, functioning institutions that embody in form the activities within them, the ongoing and steadfast commitment of the Third Branch to do its work in ways that maintain the trust of those who look to it for assistance. We are all much in debt to the Federal Bar Council, especially editors Patricia McGovern and Michael Zweig and associate editor Majorie Press Lindblom, for this volume—an extraordinary undertaking melding photographs and historical narrative, educating us about the courthouses of the Second Circuit.

—Robert A. Katzmann
Chief Judge, U.S. Court of Appeals for the Second Circuit
MAY 2015

PREFACE

What are our courthouses for? Why are they made to be so much more than premises for the transaction of court business?

Courthouses are made to change us as we enter. On the steps, lawyers arm themselves for the decisive confrontations of their profession. Litigants who enter taste the approach of judgment. Jurors know that they will be doing that most unaccustomed thing: taking an oath. Witnesses search their memories and pat down their hair. And judges are reminded daily of the values they must serve.

Courthouses are designed to bring about those transformations. The site is prominent and central. The architecture is sober, stable, and conservative (usually about a quarter century behind the times). The lettering over the entrance is raised in brass or incised in stone. There are steps to mount, looking up.

Most of the people who come are reminded of their roles and responsibilities by the spaces inside. At the entry, there are (variously) broad steps, columns and pilasters, entry lobbies—all of them momentous signals. Then a courtroom; however simple, it stirs awe: the judge is elevated, the jurors are set apart, and the whole adapted to theater. The judges go to private chambers and robing rooms. The jurors are sent to deliberation rooms, which are more private still. The Clerk's Offices are open to the public, with a desk where filings are made, records are available, and what we do and accomplish is made public and manifest.

This book documents the buildings, their histories, and their stories. While often the pictures have no people in them, in considering courthouses, it is good to keep in mind those who use them, dread them, work there, and enliven them: those who win and lose there, or settle on the steps; those who turn over documents, or hide them, or eat them; those who get justice, revenge, or grief; the clients and pro se litigants; the prosecutors; the defendants, convicted and acquitted; the insider traders, the spies, the defrauders by mail and wire, the racketeers, conspirators and co-conspirators (named and unnamed); the witnesses who swear to tell the truth; the spectators, some with lunch; the jurors, the ones who serve and the ones dismissed with good excuses; the lawyers, on contingency or retainer, white-shoe or solo practice, scorched earth or sweet reason, prepared or unprepared, partners or novices, those with an entourage and bag carriers, and those without; the generations of elbow law clerks; the interns; the court reporters who get it right (and those who tactfully correct the judge's grammar); the judicial assistants; the Clerks of Court; the marshals; the judges; those who clean and maintain and polish; and the school kids and law students. They are, seen and unseen in this volume, the life in the edifice.

—Dennis Jacobs
Judge, U.S. Court of Appeals for the Second Circuit
MAY 2015

ACKNOWLEDGMENTS

On January 19, 2010, members of the Second Circuit Courts Committee of the Federal Bar Council attended a meeting of the Second Circuit Committee on History and Commemorative Events to discuss the possibility that the two committees would work together, as they sometimes had in the past, to produce a book, this time about courthouses within the Second Circuit.

At the long-ago initial meeting, then–Chief Judge Dennis Jacobs expressed enthusiasm for the project but doubted that it could be completed in its estimated time span of a year or so. While at the time we found it unusual for a federal judge to suggest that a deadline might be too tight, we have come in retrospect to appreciate the wisdom of Judge Jacobs's caution.

The production of this book has occupied the time of many people, over many years within the Federal Bar Council and the Second Circuit Committee on History and Commemorative Events. Although we name specific individuals below, any list of all those who contributed will necessarily be incomplete. We wish to acknowledge everyone who helped make production of this book possible, almost always by adding help on the project to an already full list of professional obligations.

We are particularly grateful to Circuit Executive Karen Greve Milton: she and her staff, including Christopher Cooper, Josette Jones, and Kaleena Guzman, gave freely of their valuable knowledge and expertise, helped track down information and photographs, and served as patient resources and sounding boards. We also wish to thank former Circuit Court Executive Steve Flanders for his insightful advice. Many other court personnel also provided assistance and insight, including former Southern District of New York District Executive Clifford P. Kirsch.

This book is in many ways about the work done every day by the judges of the Second Circuit in its courthouses and courtrooms. The book itself is a grateful acknowledgment of the work of each of those judges. A full list of the judges who have served each of the courts within the Second Circuit begins on page 223.

Judicial members of the Second Circuit's Committee on History and Commemorative Events provided valuable support, as did many other members of the federal judiciary. We are particularly indebted to Chief Judge Katzmann and former Chief Judge Jacobs for contributing, respectively, the book's Foreword and Preface. As referenced in notes to the text, many judges participated in interviews, both in person and by phone, and lent their support to the project in other ways. We wish to acknowledge particularly the steady interest in the project of Southern District of New York Judge P. Kevin Castel, who provided inspiration for the project at its inception, and the support of Judge Deborah A. Batts as Chair of the Second Circuit Committee on History and Commemorative Events.

The book has been a project of the Federal Bar Council's Second Circuit Courts Committee under three successive chairs, each of whom was instrumental in overseeing its progress: Vilia Hayes, Mary Kay Vyscocil, and Linda Goldstein. The contributors to each of the courthouse chapters were primarily, although not exclusively, committee members. The book would not have been possible without their diligent efforts, studious research, and fine writing.

Members of the Second Circuit Courts Committee and of the Federal Bar Council contributed in other ways as well. In addition to acting as an author, Marjorie Press Lindblom acted as Associate Editor and oversaw work with rights and permissions. This book might not have been completed without her efforts and those of her law firm Kirkland & Ellis LLP. Invaluable help in cite checking was provided by Kevin Ainsworth, Sarah Cave, Ira Matetsky, Una O'Boyle, and Matthew Schwartz. Assistance with photographs was provided by Eric Askanase, Marjorie Berman, and

Ed Pakarek. Many of the architectural descriptions in this book draw from published sources, particularly those of the General Services Administration (GSA). Their assistance with this book is gratefully acknowledged. Any errors in this volume, typographical, grammatical, or otherwise, are the responsibility of the editors.

To a large extent, photographs and illustrations give life to this book. We are enormously grateful to the photographers and artists who allowed their work to be used. We are particularly grateful to photographer Rick Kopstein, who graciously agreed to contribute his time and talent by traveling to some of the more distant parts of the Second Circuit to take courthouse photographs, to Eastern District Clerk of Court Douglas C. Palmer for permitting us to include his striking photographs of that district's courthouses, photographer Timothy Schenck, and to courthouse personnel and GSA photographers who allowed their photographs to be used. We also are very appreciative that courtroom artist Christine Cornell permitted a number of her drawings to be used in the book.

Barry Cenower, our publisher at Acanthus Press, was the consummate professional, patiently guiding us through this process, and we wish to acknowledge his varied and expert contributions.

Finally, we would like to thank the law firm of Loeb & Loeb LLP for supporting this project through the countless hours contributed by its staff. In particular, we wish to bring out from behind the scenes some of the individuals at Loeb who provided invaluable support, including Jacque Allen, Debora Garcia, Trudy Kloptosky, Shireen Kumar (research librarian), Antoinette Pepper, Juan Pla, Richard Sutherlin, Courtney Treubert, and Loeb partner Jonathan Zavin. We thank them all and most particularly Trudy Kloptosky, who patiently dealt with change after change by multiple lawyers to draft after draft of the book's chapters and, equally importantly, supported the project and helped keep it on track over its long period of gestation.

—The Editors
May 2015

The lantern of what is now the Thurgood Marshall U.S. Courthouse.

CHAPTER CREDITS AND BIOGRAPHICAL INFORMATION

CHAPTER CREDITS

Contributors for the Introduction are Marjorie Press Lindblom and Patricia A. McGovern.

Contributors for Chapter 1, The United States Court of Appeals for the Second Circuit, are Marjorie Press Lindblom, Daniel Slifkin, and Judith A. Archer.

Contributors for Chapter 2, The Southern District of New York, are Judith A. Archer, Joseph Gershman, Vilia B. Hayes, Marjorie Press Lindblom, Kathy S. Marks, Gerald A. Stein, and Mary Kay Vyskocil.

Contributors for Chapter 3, The Northern District of New York, are Anthony DiSarro, Ira B. Matetsky, Sarah O'Connell, and Gerald Silver.

Contributors for Chapter 4, The Eastern District of New York, are Mark Berman, Clifford Chen, Anthony Dean, Melisa Gerecci, and Patricia A. McGovern.

Contributors for Chapter 5, The Western District of New York, are Kevin N. Ainsworth and Patricia A. McGovern.

Contributors for Chapter 6, The District of Connecticut, are Monte E. Frank, Stewart Edelstein, Seth Lesser, Molly Guptill Manning, Craig Raabe, Michael P. Zweig, and Mary Kay Vyskocil.

Contributors for Chapter 7, The District of Vermont, are Jennifer Williams and Michael P. Zweig, with assistance on photography from Marjorie Berman.

CONTRIBUTOR BIOGRAPHICAL INFORMATION

Kevin N. Ainsworth is a partner at Mintz Levin Cohn Ferris Glovsky and Popeo, P.C., where he concentrates his practice in the area of complex commercial litigation.

Judith A. Archer is a litigation partner in the New York office of Norton Rose Fulbright US, LLP.

Marjorie Berman is a founding member of Krantz & Berman LLP, a litigation boutique serving individuals and businesses in the areas of commercial and employment disputes and white-collar criminal defense.

Mark Berman is a partner at Ganfer & Shore. Previously, he was an associate at Skadden, Arps and clerked for U.S. Magistrate Judge Michael L. Orenstein for the Eastern District of New York. Mr. Berman lectures on and has a column in *The New York Law Journal* addressing electronic discovery. He is Vice-Chair of the Commercial and Federal Litigation Section of the New York State Bar Association for 2014–2015. Mr. Berman is a 1986 graduate of Columbia College and a 1990 magna cum laude graduate of Benjamin N. Cardozo School of Law.

Anthony Dean is Counsel and a former Director at Gibbons P.C. He is president of the Eastern District Civil Litigation Fund, Inc. and a member of the Antitrust Section of the American Bar Association and the Commercial and Federal Litigation Section of the New York State Bar Association. Following graduation from Yale College and Yale Law School, he was a Fulbright

Scholar at the University of Cologne, Germany, and an associate at Cravath, Swaine & Moore.

Anthony DiSarro is Assistant Professor and Constitutional Law Chair at the United States Military Academy at West Point and of counsel to Allegaert Berger & Vogel LLP, in complex litigation.

Stewart Edelstein and *Monte E. Frank* are commercial litigation partners with Cohen and Wolf, P.C. in Connecticut.

Joseph Gershman is a litigation partner at the law firm of Rich, Intelisano & Katz, LLP. His practice focuses on commercial litigation, securities litigation and construction litigation.

Vilia B. Hayes is a litigation partner in the New York office of Hughes Hubbard & Reed LLP. Her practice focuses on commercial litigation, product liability and employment law. She is active in numerous bar associations and other professional associations and is currently the President and chair of the Executive Committee of the Federal Bar Council.

Seth Lesser is a partner with Klafter Olsen & Lesser LLP. He received his bachelor's degree with highest honors from Princeton University, a doctorate from Oxford University, and graduated magna cum laude from Harvard Law School. Since 1995, he has primarily represented plaintiffs in contingent fee litigations and has represented companies, businesses, employees, and shareholders.

Molly Guptill Manning is a staff attorney at the United States Court of Appeals for the Second Circuit and a former law clerk for U.S. Magistrate Judge Kevin Nathaniel Fox for the Southern District of New York. She is the author of the books, *When Books Went to War: The Stories that Helped Us Win World War II* and *The Myth of Ephraim Tutt* and of several legal-history pieces published in the *Federal Bar Council Quarterly*.

Kathy S. Marks is a partner at Yankwitt LLP in White Plains, New York. A former Assistant U.S. Attorney for the Southern District of New York and former Counsel to the New York State Attorney General's Medicaid Fraud Control Unit, Ms. Marks specializes in general commercial litigation, government investigations, and health care fraud.

Ira Brad Matetsky is a litigation partner at Ganfer & Shore, LLP in New York City. He is a 1984 graduate of Princeton University and a 1987 graduate of the Fordham University School of Law, where he served on the *Fordham Law Review*. He has co-edited the annual *Green Bag Almanac and Reader* and *In Chambers Opinions by the Justices of the Supreme Court of the United States*. He is a Master of the New York American Inn of Court, a New York Super Lawyer, and a past recipient of the President's Pro Bono Service Award from the New York State Bar Association.

Melisa Mayler is an associate at Thompson & Horton LLP and was previously in the commercial litigation group at Nixon Peabody LLP. Upon graduation from New York University School of Law in 2009, she clerked for U.S. Magistrate Judge Ramon E. Reyes Jr. for the Eastern District of New York.

Sarah O'Connell is a senior associate in the New York office of Norton Rose Fulbright. Her practice focuses on the representation of financial services and energy-related clients in commercial disputes.

Craig Raabe is a partner and trial lawyer at Robinson & Cole LLP. Mr. Raabe's practice involves trials of complex commercial and white-collar criminal matters.

Gerald Silver is a partner at Sullivan & Worcester LLP in New York. Mr. Silver specializes in technology litigation, including business disputes relating to IT/IP, software, Internet, privacy, and employment.

Daniel Slifkin has been a litigator with Cravath, Swaine & Moore LLP since 1991, and a partner since 1998. He is a graduate of Oxford University (B.A. 1987, B.C.L. 1988) and Harvard Law School (J.D., magna cum laude, 1991), where he was an editor of the Law Review. Mr. Slifkin is a fellow of the American Bar Foundation and a member of the ABA, NYSBA. and City Bar Association, and he serves on the Board of Americans for Oxford.

Gerald A. Stein is an attorney in the Bureau of Competition at the Federal Trade Commission, Northeast Region, which is housed in the Alexander Hamilton U.S. Custom House.

Mary Kay Vyskocil is a senior litigation partner at Simpson Thacher & Bartlett LLP, where she handles complex commercial litigation. Among other top-tier rankings, she has been listed among the Top Ten Female Litigators in the United States. Ms. Vyskocil is very active in professional organizations and community affairs, including numerous positions held by judicial appointment, and is a board member of civic and educational institutions. She is currently Vice President and a member of the Executive Committee of the Federal Bar Council.

Jennifer A. Williams is a law clerk for the Honorable Roanne L. Mann in the Eastern District of New York. Prior to that position, she worked as a litigation associate in the New York office of Loeb & Loeb LLP.

ASSOCIATE EDITOR

Marjorie Press Lindblom is of counsel with Kirkland & Ellis LLP, having retired from the partnership in 2013. During her 35 years of active commercial practice, much of her work focused on litigating disputes concerning business contracts, particularly those involving patents, computers, and scientific and engineering issues. She now serves as co-chair of the firm's pro bono management committee.

EDITORS

Patricia A. McGovern is a former Deputy General Counsel of EY and a former Regional Counsel of the U.S. Commodities Futures Trading Commission. She started her legal career as an associate at Cahill, Gordon & Reindel after graduating from New York University School of Law, where she was a member of the Law Review. She has served as a member of the Board of Directors of the City Bar Justice Center and as a director of the Federal Bar Foundation.

She first became aware of courthouses when her father took her to work with him in the Bristol County Superior Court in Massachusetts. The towered stone courthouses in Fall River and Taunton, Massachusetts that seemed like fairy tale castles to her as a child she now realizes were fine examples of late 19th-century Richardsonian Romanesque architecture. One summer while working at the Bristol County Clerk's Office, she happened upon a folder of court filings in the unsuccessful prosecution of Lizzie Borden of Fall River for allegedly murdering her parents with an ax and she immediately discovered the lure of courthouse stories.

Michael P. Zweig is a senior litigation partner at Loeb & Loeb LLP in New York City. He is a graduate of Cornell University and New York University School of Law. His litigation practice is concentrated in the area of entertainment and media law, as well as employment- and commercial-related disputes. His interests include architecture, photography, and outdoor activities of all kinds and involvement as a director in several not-for-profit organizations. He is the author of the Entertainment Litigation chapter in the federal practice treatise Business and Commercial Litigation in the Federal Courts and a director of the Federal Bar Foundation.

In early 2009, at a meeting of the Federal Bar Council's Second Circuit Courts Committee, he and Pat McGovern innocently raised their hands to volunteer to explore an idea involving a courthouse photography book. The rest, as they say, is history.

COURTHOUSES OF THE SECOND CIRCUIT

UNITED STATES COURT OF APPEALS FOR THE SECOND CIRCUIT
Thurgood Marshall U.S. Courthouse (Manhattan)

SOUTHERN DISTRICT OF NEW YORK
Thurgood Marshall U.S. Courthouse (Manhattan)
Daniel Patrick Moynihan U.S. Courthouse (Manhattan)
Charles L. Brieant Jr. Federal Building and U.S. Courthouse (White Plains)
Alexander Hamilton U.S. Custom House (Manhattan)

NORTHERN DISTRICT OF NEW YORK
James T. Foley U.S. Courthouse and Post Office (Albany)
James M. Hanley Federal Building and U.S. Courthouse (Syracuse)
Binghamton Federal Building and U.S. Courthouse (Binghamton)
Alexander Pirnie U.S. Courthouse and Federal Building (Utica)

EASTERN DISTRICT OF NEW YORK
Theodore Roosevelt U.S. Courthouse (Brooklyn)
Conrad B. Duberstein U.S. Bankruptcy Courthouse (Brooklyn)
Alfonse M. D'Amato U.S. Courthouse and Federal Building (Central Islip)

WESTERN DISTRICT OF NEW YORK
Kenneth B. Keating Federal Building (Rochester)
Robert H. Jackson U.S. Courthouse (Buffalo)

DISTRICT OF CONNECTICUT
Richard C. Lee U.S. Courthouse (New Haven)
Abraham A. Ribicoff Federal Building and U.S. Courthouse (Hartford)
Brien McMahon Federal Building and U.S. Courthouse (Bridgeport)

DISTRICT OF VERMONT
Rutland U.S. Courthouse and Post Office (Rutland)
Brattleboro U.S. Post Office and Courthouse (Brattleboro)
Burlington Federal Building (Burlington)

INTRODUCTION

By reason of its business, its bench, and its bar, the United States Court of Appeals for the Second Circuit has commonly been recognized as one of the nation's most influential and prestigious courts. Its decisions have reach and authority, and it has been characterized both as "the nation's leading commercial court" and "the second most important court in the nation."[1]

Courthouses of the Second Circuit looks at the Second Circuit and its district courts and, more particularly, at the courthouses, past and present, in which judges have sat and cases have been heard. It describes 19 courthouses in use today within the circuit, as well as earlier buildings these courts once called home. These structures range from some of the earliest federal courthouses in the nation, to newly built, contemporary ones. Although this book does not attempt to comprehensively survey litigation within the circuit, it briefly describes some of the historic cases litigated in its courtrooms. Because the first sitting of any U.S. court took place within the Second Circuit, and because of the significance of its cases, a study of its courthouses reveals, to a surprising degree, the nation's history and civic life.

Today, the Second Judicial Circuit comprises 13 federal courts: the U.S. Court of Appeals for the Second Circuit itself, as well as the district courts and bankruptcy courts for the Districts of Connecticut and Vermont and for the Southern, Northern, Eastern, and Western Districts of New York. All in all, the circuit encompasses some 13 circuit judgeships, 62 district court judgeships, 26 bankruptcy court judgeships, and 47 magistrate judgeships, as well as nine senior circuit judges and 45 senior district judges who continue to play an active role in these courts.

But the Second Circuit was not always as it is today. Some background on how it came into existence sets the stage for exploring its courthouses. And to help place the architecture of the Second Circuit's courthouses in context, this introduction also includes a brief overview of the development of federal courthouse architecture.

THE EARLY FEDERAL COURT SYSTEM AND THE CREATION OF COURTS OF APPEALS

Aside from a short-lived court created in 1801 and disbanded in 1802, no circuit judgeships existed in what is now the Second Circuit until 1869, and the circuit court of appeals was created only in 1891. Before that, Supreme Court justices "rode circuit," serving on trial and appellate panels together with district court judges.

Article III of the Constitution left it to Congress to create courts other than the Supreme Court: "The judicial Power of the United States shall be vested in one supreme Court and in such inferior Courts as the Congress may from time to time ordain and establish." With the Judiciary Act of 1789 (introduced in the First Congress as Senate Bill 1), Congress created district courts in each of the 11 states that had then ratified the Constitution, with a single judgeship in each. Notably, Vermont was not included, since it had split off from New Hampshire and New York and did not join the United States until 1791.

President George Washington appointed former New York City Mayor James Duane as District Judge for the District of New York and Richard Law as District Judge for the District of Connecticut. On November 3, 1789, the United States District Court for New York held its first session. Based on the Judiciary Act, the Districts of New York and New Jersey would have been tied as the "first" federal courts, since they were both supposed to meet on the first Tuesday of November 1789, but the New Jersey judge fell ill and his court's first session was postponed.[2]

When Vermont joined the Union in 1791, Congress established the state as a single judicial district. President Washington appointed Nathaniel Chipman its first district court judge in 1791.

At their inception, the district courts had only limited jurisdiction: federal crimes where the punishment did not exceed a whipping of "thirty stripes," a fine of not more than $100, or a prison term of six months, as well as admiralty and maritime cases and a few other types of suits involving federal statutes or foreign consuls, or where the United States was a party.[3] In the early years of the federal government, the district courts' caseload depended largely on the volume of admiralty suits.

In the 1789 Judiciary Act, Congress created three circuit courts—for the Eastern, Middle, and Southern Circuits. New York and Connecticut were assigned to the Eastern Circuit. But Congress deliberately did not create any circuit-court judgeships. Rather, the six justices of the Supreme Court were required to "ride circuit": by law, two Supreme Court Justices held circuit-court sessions in each district twice each year, with the local district judge also sitting as a member of the circuit court. Two or more jurists were required for hearing circuit-court cases.

In sharp contrast to today's court of appeals, the circuit court in the early years primarily served as a trial court. The circuit court had jurisdiction over all civil suits in law or equity where the parties were of diverse citizenship and the amount in controversy exceeded $500, and over all serious crimes or offenses under federal law. The circuit court also could hear appeals from decisions of district judges, although in those cases the district judge was not allowed to vote as a panel member but was permitted only to "assign the reasons" for his decision.[4] For much of the 19th century, district judges were likely to devote more time to their duties on the circuit courts than to the business of their own district courts.

The original 1801 Judiciary Act did not specify how the circuit assignments should be made, so at its first meeting the Supreme Court decided that the circuits would be allocated based on the home states of the Justices. Chief Justice John Jay of New York and Associate

Justice William Cushing of Massachusetts became the first Justices assigned to the Eastern Circuit, which included Massachusetts, New Hampshire, Connecticut, New York, and later Vermont.[5] Thus at its inception, the entire federal judiciary in what is now the Second Circuit included only two full-time judges—one district judge each in Connecticut and New York—and two Supreme Court Justices who each spent part of their time riding circuit in the region.

Perhaps not surprisingly, the Supreme Court Justices detested their circuit-riding duties, and they repeatedly asked Congress to relieve them of that responsibility.[6] As Senator Gouverneur Morris later remarked, candidates for the Supreme Court required "less the learning of a judge than the agility of a post-boy."[7] Yet not until 1891 were Supreme Court Justices finally freed of their circuit-riding duties.

The first time that a "Second Circuit" came into being was with the Judiciary Act of 1801, signed into law just three weeks before the end of President John Adams's term. The Act was an early attempt to reform the federal judicial system, but it was too enmeshed in the partisan divide between the Federalist and Republican forces to provide lasting change. The Act created six circuits in place of three and provided for 16 circuit judges, including three in what is now the Second Circuit.[8] In the 17 days that elapsed from the law's signing on February 13, 1801, until his term ended, President Adams made more than 90 judicial and legal appointments, including naming judges in the newly created positions in the Second Circuit: Egbert Benson of New York as Chief Judge, Oliver Wolcott Jr. of Connecticut, and Samuel Hitchcock of Vermont.[9] As part of the group of "midnight judges," each was nominated on February 18, 1801, and confirmed on February 20, 1801, by the Federalist-majority Congress, before President Thomas Jefferson took office on March 4.

Jefferson saw the midnight judges' appointment as part of a Federalist attempt to control the judiciary. Unlike the unfortunate justice of the peace who had not received his commission before Adams's term expired and who was made famous in *Marbury v. Madison*,[10] all of the newly appointed Second Circuit judges promptly received their commissions and took office. But the Republican Congress quickly undid the new judicial appointments with a March 8, 1802 Act that restored the federal judiciary to its previous status and in the process did away with the short-lived Second Circuit Court as of July 1, 1802.[11]

Almost immediately, that same Congress re-created those circuits, albeit without circuit judges, through the Judiciary Act of 1802.[12] The designation of the "Second Circuit" in that Act did little more, however, than to group together the states of Connecticut, New York, and Vermont for purposes of assigning a Supreme Court Justice to preside over the circuit-court sessions in those states. That Act even specified that the presiding justice should be the senior Associate Justice then residing in the Fifth Circuit—Bushrod Washington, a nephew of George Washington—presumably because none of the then-sitting Supreme Court justices were from the area encompassed by the Second Circuit.

More than 60 years passed before enactment of the Judiciary Act of 1869, which marked the beginning of a new era, creating the first permanent judgeships for each of the nine existing circuits. Each circuit judge had the same powers as the Justice of the Supreme Court assigned to that circuit. Lewis Bartholomew Woodruff, a judge on the New York Court of Appeals, was appointed in the Second Circuit.[13] Circuit-court sessions could be held by the Supreme Court Justice or the circuit- or district-court judge sitting either alone or in tandem, and the circuit-riding duties of the Supreme Court Justice were cut back to require attendance at only one term of the circuit court in each district of the circuit every two years. The circuit courts remained primarily trial courts, however, and they continued to be based in each district rather than having jurisdiction over the circuit as a whole.

In the decades following the Civil War, Congress expanded the jurisdiction of the federal courts, and federal caseloads mushroomed, leading to lengthy delays at all levels.¹⁴ In 1887 Congress authorized an additional judgeship for the Second Circuit to help relieve some of the burden. Finally, with the "Evarts Act" of 1891, named after Senate Judiciary Committee Chairman William Evarts of New York, Congress undertook the most important restructuring of the federal court system since the Judiciary Act of 1789: it permitted the Supreme Court, for some categories of cases, to decide which cases it would hear; gave final appellate jurisdiction to the newly created circuit courts of appeals in all cases not heard by the Supreme Court; created an additional circuit judgeship in each of the circuits; and finally relieved the Supreme Court Justices of the burden of riding circuit and sitting as trial court and intermediate appellate judges.¹⁵ Thus the Second Circuit Court of Appeals could be said to be born in 1891.

The system differed from today's, however. Three judges were required to sit on each appeal, but the Second Circuit was the only circuit with that many judges. The Supreme Court Justice assigned to the circuit and the district-court judges within the circuit were also eligible to sit as members of the appeals court (although not in cases they had presided over as trial judges), and in most circuits that had to occur as a matter of course. Somewhat confusingly, the existing circuit courts were not disbanded but retained their trial-court jurisdiction for 20 more years, until the passage of the Judicial Code of 1911.¹⁶ Gradually over the 19th century, Congress had expanded the jurisdiction of the district courts, especially in the area of noncapital criminal cases. The district courts became the primary trial courts in the federal system with the elimination of the circuit courts as trial courts.

Over the years, the work of the district courts in New York grew. To accommodate that growth, the original District of New York was, over time, ultimately separated into four separate districts. First, in 1812, Congress passed an act authorizing a second judgeship for the District of New York.¹⁷ Matthias Burnett Tallmadge, who had succeeded John S. Hobart as District Judge in 1805, continued to serve in the first position, while William Peter Van Ness, a protégé of Aaron Burr and his second in the duel with Alexander Hamilton, was appointed to fill the new position.¹⁸ Until the 20th century, this was the last time more than one judge was assigned to any district court in the Second Circuit. Notably, the Act provided that if the judges disagreed, the senior judge's opinion would prevail, and that only the senior district judge would serve on the circuit court.¹⁹

Shortly into Van Ness's tenure, animosity arose between him and Tallmadge, ultimately leading to the division of the District of New York into two districts.²⁰ On April 9, 1814, Congress officially split the original District of New York into the Northern and Southern Districts of New York.²¹ The law specified that Van Ness should remain as the district judge in the Southern District, but it also assigned him to sit in the Northern District when Judge Tallmadge was unable to do so. The Southern District of New York has traditionally traced its lineage to the original District of New York, viewing itself as the "mother court" in light of this history.

In 1865 the Eastern District of New York was created, when President Abraham Lincoln approved an Act of Congress removing the counties of Kings, Queens (including what is now Nassau County), Richmond, and Suffolk from the Southern District's jurisdiction. The division gave the Eastern District and the Southern District concurrent jurisdiction over the waters of New York Harbor. In May 1900, Congress carved the 17 westernmost counties of New York from the Northern District of New York to create a new Western District of New York.²²

COURTHOUSE ARCHITECTURE AND THE COURTS OF THE SECOND CIRCUIT

United States courthouses play a role akin to that of secular churches. Functioning as sites for the administration of justice, the buildings are also themselves imposing public structures that anchor the communities in which they are situated. "Architecture is inescapably a political art for it reports faithfully for ages to come what the political values of a particular age were," wrote Senator Daniel Patrick Moynihan.[23] And so it is, especially for courthouses.

But in the earliest days of the Second Circuit, federal architects had no opportunity to reflect the values of their age in courthouses. In these early days, no courthouses within the Second Circuit or elsewhere in the nation had been purpose-built to serve the federal courts. Instead, during the late 18th and early 19th centuries, federal courts sat in rented space in buildings neither built nor owned by the federal government. Not until the 19th century did the federal government begin a building program. First, the Department of the Treasury, which collected customs duties and administered the hospital fund for seamen, assumed responsibility for constructing buildings to house these operations. Treasury's role grew to include the construction of other government buildings, such as post offices that included courtrooms for the federal courts.[24]

During the 1850s, expansion of the federal government and of the nation's urban areas led to more federal buildings across the nation including courtrooms. In 1852 the Secretary of the Treasury established the Bureau of Construction, later to be known as the Office of the Supervising Architect, to help manage and unify the growing federal building program. Ammi B. Young became the first government architect appointed to the position of "Supervising Architect." He remained Supervising Architect until 1861, when building projects stopped due to the Civil War.[25] The Second Circuit's first federal courthouse and post office, in Windsor, Vermont, was designed by Young.

In 1866, following the Civil War, Alfred B. Mullett became Supervising Architect. Mullet oversaw the design of elaborate federal buildings in a grand Second Empire style, based on French architecture during the reign of Emperor Napoleon III (1852–1870). The buildings were meant to express the power, stability, and graciousness of the federal government.[26] One such Mullet-designed building, a granite and marble U.S. Courthouse and Post Office at Broadway and Park Row (now demolished), was opened in 1878 and housed proceedings of the Second Circuit Court of Appeals and the Southern District of New York, until the two courts moved to what is now known as the Thurgood Marshall U.S. Courthouse[27] on January 21, 1936. The Mullet Post Office (as it was called) has been described as one of "the most opulent expressions of Second Empire France as interpreted in America."[28]

The financial panic of 1873 and the depression that followed caused a change in the federal building program. The grand, ornate, and expensive-looking Second Empire style no longer suited the times. It was replaced by a less decorative Romanesque Revival style characterized by massive rough-textured stone walls, rounded arches, and square towers. Courthouses in this style are sometimes called "Richardsonian" Romanesque after the work of Henry Hobson Richardson, whose Allegheny Courthouse in Pittsburgh exemplified the style with rich arched stonework. As one architectural critic describes it, the stone of the Allegheny Courthouse "creates a sort of wrapping for a distinctly civic building, yet one with the romance of an abstract sort of distant past, a certain gloom and mystery."[29]

This style was widely used for courthouses built during the 1880s and well into the 1890s. A stunning example is found in the Eastern District's first permanent home, the U.S. Post Office and Courthouse Building in Brooklyn, built in 1892 and now the Conrad B. Duberstein U.S. Bankruptcy Courthouse. In the Western District, the U.S. Post Office and Courthouse in Rochester, now Rochester City Hall, was built in the Romanesque style, as were the U.S. Post Office and Courthouse in Auburn in the Northern District and several other early courthouses within the Second Circuit.

During this period, private architects led by the American Institute of Architects expressed the view that the federal buildings designed under the Supervising Architect were overly repetitive in design yet cost more to build than privately designed buildings. A bill was passed in 1893, sponsored by Missouri Congressman John C. Tarsney, allowing public buildings to be designed by private architects through design competitions. In the same year, the World's Columbian Exposition of 1893—commonly remembered as the Chicago World's Fair—made a profound impression on both private and public architecture. The event was housed in a great visionary white "city" of plaster. Its Renaissance Revival, neoclassical architecture was identified with the École des Beaux-Arts in Paris, a leading institution for the training of architects at the time. The Beaux-Arts ideal espoused acceptance of modern innovation, reconciling these improvements with what its creators judged to be the best designs of the past. The Beaux-Arts architects welcomed collaboration with painters, sculptors, and other artists and craftspeople.

Beaux-Arts architecture was deemed appropriate to civic architecture and quickly applied to courthouses.[30] Two of the Second Circuit's enduring courthouses were designed by private architects after the Tarsney Act and show the influence of architectural trends that emerged from the Chicago World's Fair. They are the Alexander Hamilton U.S. Custom House at Bowling Green in Manhattan, designed by Cass Gilbert and now home to the Southern District Bankruptcy Court, and the Richard C. Lee U.S. Courthouse in New Haven, Connecticut, designed by James Gamble Rogers. The Lee courthouse was the last federal building designed under the Tarsney Act before its 1912 repeal.[31] The Courthouse and U.S. Post Office Building in Brattleboro, Vermont, built in 1917, with its Renaissance Revival style, also shows the wide influence of the Chicago World's Fair.

The federal building program was temporarily halted during World War I. But the Great Depression of the 1930s spawned a major new wave of federal building. The Keyes-Elliott Bill of 1930, an amendment to the 1926 Public Buildings Act, permitted private architectural firms to compete for certain federal projects until 1934, when the amendment lapsed. The federal building program was seen as a tool to spur the economy by providing work to unemployed construction workers, artists, and others. Federal funds were lavished upon public buildings, both to help localities and as a symbol of nationalism.

During the administration of President Franklin D. Roosevelt, the Office of the Supervising Architect was renamed the Office of Public Works. The Second Circuit greatly benefited from the Depression-era building program. In the Northern District, the James T. Foley U.S. Courthouse and Post Office was built in Albany, and the Federal Building and U.S. Courthouse was built in Binghamton. In the Western District, the Michael J. Dillon U.S. Courthouse was built in Buffalo. In the District of Vermont, a new U.S. Courthouse was built in Rutland. A new courthouse for the Second Circuit Court of Appeals and the Southern District, now the Thurgood Marshall U.S. Courthouse, opened in Manhattan's Foley Square in 1936, although planning for the courthouse and its design by architect Cass Gilbert had preceded the Depression years.

The Beaux-Arts tradition in courthouse design persisted throughout the Depression. With time, however, the designs were often stripped down to simpler line and form, divested of historically imitative elements. In a style sometimes referred to as "starved classicism," white masonry and the rhythm of wall and window evoked vestigial columns. Courthouse architecture of this type combined classical proportions with Art Deco detailing, as seen in the Binghamton Federal Building and U.S. Courthouse. Also used were the streamlined forms of Art Moderne, exemplified in the Second Circuit in the Western District's Michael J. Dillon U.S. Courthouse in Buffalo, New York, and in the James T. Foley U.S. Courthouse and Post Office in Albany.

Many buildings integrated sculptural details depicting their intended civic activities. For example, a frieze running along three sides of the Foley Courthouse in Albany depicts the building's three functions: post office, custom house, and courthouse. For the post office, scenes show delivery of mail; for the custom house, the delivery of goods; for the court, trial proceedings. At the Thurgood Marshall U.S. Courthouse, four carved medallions sit above the corners of the front cornice, showing founding thinkers of Western tradition: Demosthenes, Moses, Plato, and Aristotle. Civic art was commissioned for the courthouses under the Treasury Relief Art Project, such as murals in the Rutland Courthouse depicting memorable scenes in Vermont history.

Courthouse building was in abeyance during World War II while the administration focused on wartime demands. The General Services Administration (GSA), created by President Truman in 1949, became responsible for all federal building procurement and management. The 1960s and 1970s brought renewed growth in federal projects, including courthouse construction. During this period, more severe modernism began to hold sway over courthouse design. The modern style, which had first made its appearance in the 1950s, soon became the dominant form. Examples in the Second Circuit include the Brien McMahon Courthouse in Bridgeport, Connecticut; the Abraham A. Ribicoff Federal Building and U.S. Courthouse in Hartford, Connecticut; the Federal Building, U.S. Post Office, and Courthouse in Burlington, Vermont; the James M. Hanley Federal Building in Syracuse; and the Kenneth B. Keating Federal Building in Rochester, New York. Plain and cool, the style featured smooth, unadorned surfaces, "expanses of marble panels, marble or terrazzo floors, smooth plaster and windowless courtrooms, paneled in flush sheets of mahogany, walnut, and other woods." It substituted function and economy for formal, hierarchical interior space.[32]

The philosophy of the modern movement favored clearing sites and starting over, echoing aspects of the era's Marshall Plan of 1948–1952. The movement disfavored preserving historic structures. In New Haven, this philosophy led to a long struggle between GSA and the federal judiciary over whether the historic Richard C. Lee U.S. Courthouse would be razed or preserved. The judiciary and the preservation movement prevailed, and the Lee courthouse remains standing today. Today's trend favoring historic preservation recognizes historic courthouses as major monuments to be preserved.

Federal architecture in the modern style sometimes met with criticism from the architectural community and others. The Task Force on Federal Architecture of the National Endowment of the Arts found that, during the time when this style prevailed, federal architecture declined. Modern courthouses were sometimes found lacking by those who used them. Judges reported that courtroom designs divorced from the traditions of the past made courtroom proceedings confusing, because it was hard for the public to "read" the authority of court personnel.[33] GSA later acknowledged that while modern architecture at its best could produce striking contemporary designs, economy and efficiency were sometimes the stronger driving forces during this period than architectural distinction.[34]

At the same time, a quiet revolution was beginning in courthouse architecture, spurred by Daniel Patrick Moynihan, whose "Guiding Principles of Federal Architecture" served as a manifesto for late 20th- and early 21st-century courthouse construction.[35] Moynihan authored his "Guiding Principles" as Assistant Secretary of Labor in 1961 and over the next three decades pushed for their implementation in federal building programs. The principles provided that public buildings should be provided in "an architectural style and form that is distinguished and which will reflect the dignity, enterprise, vigor and stability of the American National Government"; that an official style should be avoided; and that the leading architects of the day should be involved. "Design must flow from the architectural profession to the Government and not vice versa," Moynihan wrote. "It should be our object," he wrote, "to meet the test of Pericles' evocation to the Athenians . . . 'we do not imitate—for we are a model to others.'"[36]

The Guiding Principles were first included in the report of the Ad Hoc Committee on Federal Office Space of 1962, approved by President John F. Kennedy in 1963, and subsequently pressed by Moynihan during the Johnson administration and under Richard Nixon, for whom Moynihan served as urban advisor. When Moynihan entered the Senate in 1977, his first committee appointment was to the Committee on Environment and Public Works, where, as his influence grew, he continued to press the Guiding Principles. They became widely embraced by architects and others, including Justice Stephen Breyer, who, while Chief Judge of the United States Court of Appeals for the First Circuit, helped put them into practice as a member of the architect selection committee for a new federal courthouse in Boston.[37]

The Moynihan Guiding Principles of Federal Architecture now underlie the Design Excellence Program adopted by the GSA in 1992. The program encourages "design that embodies the finest contemporary American architectural thought" while encouraging regional traditions.[38] Among new steps implemented as part of the Design Excellence Program are the requirement that courthouse architects be chosen through juried competitions and the implementation of Design Excellence Awards. In 1990 the GSA began a 10-year, $10 billion project to build 50 to 60 new federal courthouses. During that time, five new courthouses were built in the Second Circuit.

Moynihan's Guiding Principles have influenced and benefited these contemporary courthouses, all of which have been designed by leading architects of their time in widely differing, visually arresting styles. The courthouses include the Eastern District's Alfonse M. D'Amato U.S. Courthouse in Central Islip, designed by architect Richard Meier, and its Theodore Roosevelt U.S. Courthouse in Brooklyn, designed by Argentine American architect Cesar Pelli; the Western District's Robert H. Jackson U.S. Courthouse in Buffalo, designed by Kohn, Pederson, Fox; the Southern District's Charles L. Brieant Jr. Federal Building and U.S. Courthouse in White Plains, designed by Skidmore, Owings and Merrill; and, fittingly, the Daniel Patrick Moynihan U.S. Courthouse at Foley Square in Manhattan, also designed by Kohn, Pederson, Fox.

In several of these contemporary courthouses, a play of forms and light that descends from the architectural philosophy of Le Corbusier epitomizes the majesty of the federal justice system and welcomes the community into the building. The design of the Jackson courthouse in Buffalo "expresses the dignity and transparency of the federal judicial system" through dramatic use of glass, including a glass-enclosed pavilion where all the words of the U.S. Constitution are etched in the facade. The D'Amato courthouse welcomes the community with a grand, multistory atrium.

Contemporary courthouses have been designed not only as symbols of justice and to embrace their communities, but also with practical attention to workloads that would have seemed unimaginable in the early federal court era of "one district, one judge." The list of practical features that courthouses must have is long. It includes courtrooms, judicial chambers, robing rooms, public space, secured facilities for prisoners, waiting areas for witnesses, cafeterias, public restrooms, libraries, administrative offices, storage, and maintenance facilities. Courthouses must have adequate acoustics, provide barrier-free access, and embrace technology, and increasingly they must consider security as an integral and crucial design element.[39]

Two other contemporary GSA programs have influenced the look of today's federal courthouses: the First Impressions and the Art in Architecture Programs. The First Impressions Program extends the GSA Design Excellence principles into the public space of existing federal courts, including updating lobbies and redesigning plazas. Work was done on the plaza of the James M. Hanley Federal Building in Syracuse in 2007 as part of this program.

The Art in Architecture Program oversees the commissioning of artworks for new federal buildings nationwide. GSA dedicates one-half of 1 percent of the estimated construction costs of federal buildings to commissioning the artists, who are selected by a panel of art professionals, civic and community representatives, and the project architects and design team members. With the sponsorship of Art in Architecture Program, artists such as Raymond Kaskey, Sol LeWitt, Maya Lin, Robert Mangold, Patsy Norvell, Lisa Scheer, and Frank Stella have created magnificent art works that now grace courthouses within the Second Circuit.

COURTHOUSES
OF THE
SECOND CIRCUIT

CHAPTER ONE

THE UNITED STATES COURT OF APPEALS FOR THE SECOND CIRCUIT

The U.S. Court of Appeals for the Second Circuit, the appellate court for the federal district courts in New York, Connecticut, and Vermont, has long been viewed as one of the most important courts in the United States. Over the past century it has played an influential role in developing and refining American jurisprudence, ruling on some of the nation's most significant cases. It continues in that role today, sitting in the Cass Gilbert-designed Thurgood Marshall U.S. Courthouse on Manhattan's Foley Square.

The Second Circuit as we know it today met for the first time on June 16, 1891. (See Introduction for a history of how the Second Circuit evolved.) For the first 45 years of its existence, the Second Circuit sat in the Courthouse and Post Office, a controversial building opened in lower Manhattan in 1878 and considered by some as the height of French Second Empire style and by others as an architectural eyesore. It was a massive structure rising to 195 feet in height with frontages of 279 feet on the north narrowing to 144 feet on the south—the largest building project that had ever been undertaken by the federal government outside the District of Columbia. During these years, the Second Circuit grew from two judgeships to five, increased the number of cases it heard, ruled on subjects ranging from admiralty to obscenity, and began developing its reputation as the nation's pre-eminent commercial court.[1]

Opposite: The Cass Gilbert-designed U.S. Courthouse at 40 Foley Square, now the Thurgood Marshall U.S. Courthouse, as it looked when it opened in 1936.

The south-facing entrance of the massive Mullett Courthouse and Post Office showing the building's ornamental cupola.

THE MULLETT COURTHOUSE AND POST OFFICE

The Courthouse and Post Office where the Second Circuit first sat was designed by supervising Architect Alfred B. Mullett in vigorous French Second Empire style, and was often referred to as the Mullett Post Office. Each of the structure's two multi-windowed granite and marble frontages boasted its own monumental entrance portico, with end pavilions containing circular stairwells placed at each of the building's four corners. During construction, the Post Office Department's demand for greater working space led to a fourth story being added to the building, making it one of the tallest buildings in the city at the time, as well as one of the largest. Above the fourth story was an additional level, tucked beneath the slate-covered mansard roof. The roof was studded with dormers, and the building also sported a pair of bulbous domes on its north and south frontages, with the southern one crowned with an ornamental cupola.

Inside, the post office took up most of the ground-floor level and shared the second floor with the district and circuit courtrooms, which were placed on the north side of the building overlooking City Hall Park. Handsomely appointed with classical detailing, each courtroom measured 70 by 40 feet and extended upward for 60 feet through the third-floor level to an ornate beamed ceiling. Judges' chambers, the U.S. Attorney's office, and a law library were located on the third and fourth floors. The building also housed federal offices.[2]

From its earliest days, the Mullett Courthouse and Post Office was often mired in controversy. As it was built, many expressed outrage over its ever-escalating

Fig. 2.—THE UNITED STATES COURT, POST OFFICE BUILDING, NEW YORK CITY.

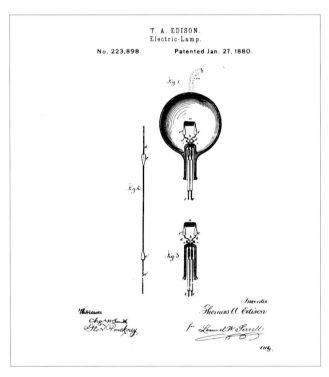

Top: The second-floor courtrooms within the Mullett Courthouse and Post Office extended upward for 60 feet through the third-floor level to an ornate beamed ceiling. *Bottom*: Thomas A. Edison's patent No. 223,898 for the use of a carbon filament in a vacuum in the incandescent light bulb, illustrated here in a filing with the U.S. Patent Office, was upheld in an 1892 Second Circuit decision.

cost, more than $8.5 million before it was finally completed. Others viewed its overweening size as an affront to the diminutive New York City Hall nearby. An early commentator wrote, "The Mullett Post Office has always been an architectural eyesore, and has, from the first, been unsatisfactory to the Postal Service and Federal Courts beneath its roof."[3]

By 1903, the Second Circuit Court of Appeals was the busiest in the nation, and its workload was steadily increasing. A new judgeship had been added in 1902, and dozens of visiting judges assisted with the work of the Second Circuit beginning in 1913, after Congress passed legislation authorizing the Chief Justice of the United States to assign district judges on certification of need to do so by the senior judge of the circuit.[4] In 1923 the court issued 250 opinions and disposed of an additional 72 cases.

Because New York had emerged as a mercantile and seaport center, its district courts became prominent admiralty courts and the Court of Appeals for the Second Circuit became the leading appellate admiralty court in the nation. By the late 19th century the Second Circuit also had begun to gain its enduring reputation as a leader in deciding commercial disputes. Some have speculated that it was the knowledge of mercantile customs and practices developed in admiralty cases that first led to the Second Circuit's becoming a great commercial court.[5]

As New York became a center for invention and industry, the Court of Appeals for the Second Circuit became a center for the development of patent law. In a case brought by Edison Electric Light Co., the court engaged in a detailed discussion of the development of the incandescent light bulb and affirmed the decision of the trial-level circuit court that Edison's patent, which claimed the use of a carbon filament in a vacuum, was not obvious and had been infringed.[6] The court also heard a number of appeals involving the Wright brothers' patent on an airplane and whether it included the use of an aileron—each time either reversing the lower court's injunction against claimed infringement or staying entry

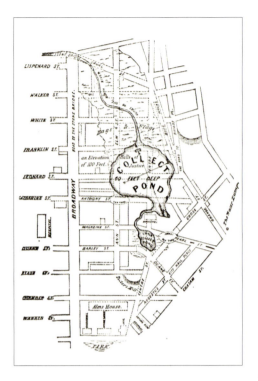 

Left: Collect Pond, located on the border of the Five Points District near what later became known as Foley Square, was once the source of New York City's water supply. Today, Collect Pond Park occupies part of the pond's original site. *Above*: *History of the City of New York* shows this image of an early steamboat trial on Collect Pond.

of an injunction. As a result, the unlicensed aircraft that used an aileron remained in production through July 1917, when, as a wartime measure, the federal government required the parties to contribute the patents to a low-royalty licensing pool.[7]

In the early 20th Century as Wall Street developed into a world financial center, the Second Circuit began to be called upon to decide complex issues of securities law; Justice Blackmun called it "the 'Mother Court' in this area of law".[8] The initiation of federal regulation of the economy during the New Deal similarly led to a number of high-profile cases in the Second Circuit Court of Appeals while it remained in the Mullett Courthouse and Post Office.

In 1934 the Second Circuit issued what would come to be regarded as a landmark obscenity ruling, affirming a decision by Southern District Judge John M. Woolsey that permitted James Joyce's *Ulysses* to be brought into the United States after the book's seizure by the customs service. The case set forth for the first time a test for obscenity based on the work as a whole, rather than on isolated passages. Ironically, the Second Circuit panel—consisting of Judges Manton and Learned and Augustus Hand—had intended its opinion not to be memorable: Judges Learned and Augustus Hand thought that the *Ulysses* case was already receiving far too much attention and decided that "the opinion affirming Woolsey's ruling should, if at all possible, contain 'not a single quotable line,'" accordingly assigning the job of writing it to Augustus Hand rather than the more naturally quotable Learned.[9] It was one of the many cases in which a Second Circuit ruling set the parameters of debate on the scope of First Amendment protection.

White-collar crime made an early entry in the annals of Second Circuit jurisprudence after Charles W. Morse was indicted and found guilty of looting the Mercantile National Bank, having used more than 70 brokerage houses to conceal his theft. The Second Circuit reversed convictions on 12 counts of submitting false reports to the Comptroller of the Currency, but the remaining three counts were enough to send Morse to prison for 15 years. Two years later, President Taft pardoned Morse because he was suffering from a fatal illness, only to have him make a remarkable recovery as soon as he was free.[10]

The Five Points District shown in this stereopticon image surrounded the site where the Foley Square courthouse was built. A dangerous slum in the 19th century, the area remained beset by poverty into the early 20th century.

THE THURGOOD MARSHALL U.S. COURTHOUSE

In 1936 the Second Circuit moved to its first—and, except for a period of temporary residency during renovations—only dedicated courthouse home, the Cass Gilbert–designed building known since 2003 as the Thurgood Marshall U.S. Courthouse on Manhattan's Foley Square, in what was formerly the former Five Points district. Thurgood Marshall U.S. Courthouse was the first U.S. federal building to be built solely for use as a courthouse, rather than as a multi-function federal building.

As early as 1912, Congress had considered a proposal to build a new federal building on the site of the former Five Points district. The Five Points district was infamous as one of the poorest and most dangerous slums in the world, first accommodating many breweries and tanneries, then a massive prison called the Tombs, and then livestock slaughterhouses.[11] Charles Dickens described the area in lurid prose after an 1842 visit: "This is the place: these narrow ways, diverging to the right and left, and reeking everywhere with dirt and filth. Such lives as are led here, bear the same fruits here as elsewhere. The coarse and bloated faces at the doors have counterparts at home and all the wide world over. Debauchery has made the very houses prematurely old."[12] In even earlier days the area had been partially covered by Collect Pond, once a source of New York City's water supply.[13]

At the turn of the 20th century, the Five Points area had lost its nefarious reputation, but it remained poor, with nondescript buildings. By the mid-1920s, the location—just a few blocks northeast of City Hall—had spurred the area's renaissance as a civic center, and in April 1926 Foley Square was named after Thomas F. Foley, a saloonkeeper and prominent district leader of the political group Tammany Hall.[14]

In 1928 Congress authorized funds to acquire land southwest of City Hall Park for what was planned to be a combined federal court and post office, but by 1930, the U.S. Treasury Department gave in to pressure by the federal courts to have their own building. A deal was worked out for the U.S. Treasury to pay the City $2.45 million for the Foley Square site, northeast of the park, for the federal courthouse, plus $5.0 million for the previously approved site to the southwest. In turn, the City paid the U.S. Treasury $7.45 million to demolish the Mullett Post Office and to return that site—located inside City Hall Park—to the City.[15]

The next year, Congress authorized spending up to $8.25 million on the construction of the new courthouse, part of the dramatic increase in funding for public buildings after the onset of the Great Depression that spurred a wave of courthouse construction, including new courthouses in the Second Circuit. The federal courthouse at Foley Square was one of the largest projects outside the District of Columbia undertaken as part of this building program.

In 1931 the Treasury Department commissioned Cass Gilbert to design the courthouse at Foley Square to house the Second Circuit, the United States District Court for the Southern District of New York, and other related offices.[16] Gilbert was a prominent architect of the time—in New York City alone he had already designed both the U.S. Custom House, a building in the

Beaux-Arts style that opened in 1907, and the 57-story Woolworth Building, a Gothic Revival skyscraper that was tallest in the world when it opened in 1913. Shortly after receiving the commission for the New York courthouse, Gilbert was also asked to design the nation's Supreme Court Building. The Supreme Court project was completed first, in 1935, but neither courthouse was finished until after Gilbert's death in 1934. Gilbert's son Cass Gilbert Jr. supervised the final phases of construction of the courthouse at Foley Square. The new Foley Square courthouse opened on January 21, 1936.

In 2001 President Bush signed Public Law 107-33, rededicating the courthouse at Foley Square in honor of Justice Thurgood Marshall, the first African American Supreme Court Justice, who had sat on the Second Circuit Court of Appeals from 1961 to 1965. At the April 14, 2003 dedication ceremony, Second Circuit Judge Ralph K. Winter Jr. told a story that took place while Marshall was serving his initial interim appointment to the Second Circuit during the turbulent civil-rights era of the 1960s. As Judge Winter told it, Marshall arrived for a group photo while the other judges were waiting for an electrician to fix a blown courthouse fuse; a secretary for one of the judges mistook Marshall for the electrician. Marshall, one of the most successful lawyers of the 20th century prior to taking the bench, did not appear to take offense. Instead, he used the mistake to educate his law clerk on how certain trade unions were not open at the time to African Americans, saying: "Boy, that woman must be crazy if she thinks I could become an electrician."[17]

THURGOOD MARSHALL
(1908–1993)

President John F. Kennedy nominated Thurgood Marshall to the Second Circuit in 1961. After a group of southern senators held up his confirmation, Marshall received a recess appointment and was confirmed the following year. Marshall previously had served as chief counsel at the NAACP, where he won 29 of the 32 cases he argued before the United States Supreme Court. President Lyndon Johnson appointed Marshall as the first African American U.S. Solicitor General in 1965, and then as the first African American Associate Justice of the Supreme Court in 1967. Justice Marshall served on the Supreme Court until October 1991.

At the NAACP and then the NAACP Legal Defense and Education Fund, Marshall successfully litigated a series of civil-rights cases that challenged the "separate but equal" doctrine established in *Plessy v. Ferguson*.[18] One of his first cases, *Murray v. Pearson,* struck down the segregation policy of the University of Maryland School of Law, Marshall's hometown law school.[19] (Because of the school's policy, Marshall had attended Howard University School of Law, graduating in 1933.) In 1954 Marshall argued *Briggs v. Elliot,* one of five consolidated cases reported under the name *Brown v. Board of Education of Topeka* that ended legal segregation in public schools.[20] (The companion case titled *Brown v. Board of Education* was argued by Marshall's NAACP colleague and later Southern District Judge Robert L. Carter).[21]

While on the Supreme Court, Marshall was well known for his powerful dissenting opinions, especially in cases where the Court upheld application of the death penalty, such as *Ake v. Oklahoma*.[22] He also issued influential dissents in *San Antonio School District v. Rodriguez* (arguing that the property-tax system used by Texas to finance public education was unconstitutional); *Milliken v. Bradley* (disagreeing with the Court's conclusion that suburbs could not be used to desegregate inner-city schools); and *Regents of the University of California v. Bakke* (arguing for a legal standard that would allow educational institutions broad discretion to engage in affirmative action).[23] Justice Marshall died in early 1993.

THE COURTHOUSE EXTERIOR

The courthouse was built on a small, irregularly shaped lot of less than one acre facing Foley Square, shoehorned between the hexagonal six-story New York State Supreme Court Building, then known as the New York County Courthouse (1926) to the

The July 20, 1932 groundbreaking for the new Foley Square Courthouse with then senior judge Martin T. Manton at the controls of a massive steam shovel.

northeast; the 40-story Municipal Building (1914) to the immediate southwest; the Hall of Records, which houses the Surrogate's Court (1911), nearby; and St. Andrews Roman Catholic church to the south.[24] Farther to the southwest, across Centre Street, are New York City Hall (1811) and the historic Tweed Courthouse (1881), and to the east and across Pearl Street, tucked behind the New York Supreme Court Building, lies the much newer Daniel Patrick Moynihan U.S. Courthouse (1994). All of the 20th-century courthouses except the Surrogate's Court are in the Five Points area.[25]

The Thurgood Marshall U.S. Courthouse is the largest and most distinctive example of federal architecture built by the Treasury Department during the expanded public-works program of the 1930s, surpassing even the Supreme Court in size. Construction of the courthouse began in July 1932 and lasted for three and a half years. It was among the first federal skyscrapers ever constructed and one of the last neoclassical office buildings in New York.[26]

The building has two main sections: one neoclassical, with a seven-story base that fills most of the site, and the other a 590-foot tower that rises 37 stories, with 30 occupied stories and capped by a gold-leafed pyramid crowned by an open lantern.[27] The exterior other than the pyramid is finished in Minnesota granite in an off-white color, mottled with peach and gray. The building as a whole encompasses 761,798 square feet.[28]

The seven-story building that forms the base begins at the southwest portion of the site, adjacent to the tower. It then wraps around the tower to parallel Centre Street on the front (northwest) and Pearl Street on the northeast side of the site, from there curving back toward the south and eventually back to the southeast side of the tower, forming three courtyards in the process. The front of the building, facing Centre Street, is reminiscent of the classic Federal style seen in Washington, D.C. and other U.S. cities. Its monumental granite staircase leads to the portico, which is created by 10 four-story, unfluted Corinthian columns with pedestals at each end and topped by a horizontal cornice

Foley Square U.S. Courthouse, now known as the Thurgood Marshall U.S. Courthouse, as it appeared from the back while under construction in September 1934.

The lantern of what is now the Thurgood Marshall U.S. Courthouse, shown under construction in June 1935.

The pyramid of what is now the Thurgood Marshall U.S. Courthouse, shown under construction in May 1935.

that obscures the fifth floor. "United States Courthouse" is carved into the area just above the columns—a helpful means of distinguishing the building from its similar state-courthouse neighbor. Although a casual observer might not notice the four carved medallions that sit above the corners of the front cornice in line with the sixth-floor windows, they represent founding thinkers of the Western tradition: Demosthenes, Moses, Plato, and Aristotle, in order from north to south. The Corinthian columns are echoed in pilasters (projecting vertical elements) that continue along the southern portion of the building until it meets the tower, and along the northeast Pearl Street side for five window bays. On the remainder of the seven-story building's exterior, projecting but unornamented pilasters alternate with window bays. The curve of the building in its eastern section, combined with the reduction in ornamentation, make that portion of the building look something like the apse of a Romanesque church.

While Gilbert undoubtedly intended the seven-story edifice to be of a similar scale as its sibling state courthouse next door, he also appears to have designed the tower section of the building to be part of the New York City skyline. The use of a skyscraper for a federal building was a significant departure from the accepted norm of the time for federal architecture.[29] The square tower, roughly 100 feet on each side, is set well back from and, not surprisingly, parallel to the front of the building. But the odd angles of the seven-story section mean that the two are parallel only at the main entrance, and what appears at first to be a straightforward lining up of the tower and base instead presents an ever-changing relationship as the observer moves around the building. Indeed, from many angles it is not obvious from street level whether the tower is part of the same structure as the lower section.

The exterior of the tower is a simple, repetitive shaft from where it emerges from the base at floor seven, through the 22nd floor. Horizontal elements denote each of the next three floors, and a setback starting at the 25th floor marks the library, which is a two-story space with high arched windows separated by deep pilasters. At the 27th floor, a heavy cornice forms the base of another deep setback, with large granite urns on the

Four medallions at the corners of the courthouse's front cornice depict founding thinkers of the Western tradition, including Demosthenes *(left)* and Aristotle *(right)*.

corners and a heavy granite railing on all sides. The pyramidal roof starts at the 31st floor, with a large dormer window on each side emphasizing the scale of the top portion of the building, and smaller dormer windows, barely visible from the ground, admitting light into the pyramid. The pyramid continues to what the architectural drawings describe as the 38th floor and terminates at an observation platform, surmounted by a small open lantern. The pyramid and the lantern are finished with gold-glazed terra-cotta tiles.

Although the courthouse certainly qualifies as monumental, its architecture has not been universally praised. In an October 1934 *New Yorker* column, critic Lewis Mumford called the courthouse, before the building was even complete, "the supreme example of pretentiousness, mediocrity, bad design and fake grandeur," and he particularly objected to what he viewed as the odd coupling of the tower and the base.[30] Not content to limit his criticism to a single building, Mumford also described Gilbert as "one of the worst monumental architects America has ever produced." But users of the courthouse disagree. Responding to Mumford's 1934 assessment, Second Circuit Judge Dennis Jacobs wrote in 2001, "Take it from me—I go there every day, and I sit in the court of appeals courtroom: it is real grandeur, and real grandeur has never been out of style for long."[31] The courthouse was given landmark status by the New York Landmarks Preservation Committee in 1975 and added to the National Register of Historic Places in 1987.[32] The application for the latter recognition noted both the architectural and historical significance of the building, describing it as embodying "the restrained Neoclassicism that had become the preferred idiom for federal buildings during the 1920s," and also reflecting the shift in Gilbert's work to more conservative designs toward the end of his career.[33]

THE COURTHOUSE INTERIOR

The interior of the building is as grand as the exterior, with the lobby following classical Beaux-Arts principles.[34] At the entrance to the building, the high ceiling of the portico dramatically steps down to the 14-foot height of the vestibule, with a corresponding reduction in width and length. The restriction in the height and size of the vestibule serves to emphasize the importance of the next room, the Main Lobby, which is the building's principal public space. The ceiling of the main floor increases to 30 feet, and once again the space opens up so that the room is correspondingly wider and longer. The lower-ceilinged elevator lobby, which is cen-

The Thurgood Marshall U.S. Courthouse tower in 2013, with the Freedom Tower under construction in the background.

The Main Lobby of Thurgood Marshall U.S. Courthouse as it looked when the courthouse reopened in January 2013 after infrastructure upgrades and repairs.

tered on the portico and vestibule, likewise emphasizes the Main Lobby's size, as do the lower-ceilinged corridors that extend from the sides of the Main Lobby. The floor and walls are of veined white marble, in a warmer tone on the walls. The primary ornamentation in the Main Lobby is the ceiling, which is divided into square bays that in turn are subdivided into three square panels in each direction. A large white chrysanthemum with gilded highlights is centered in each panel, with the background color of the chrysanthemums alternating between a soft peacock blue and crimson. The chrysanthemums are identical to those used in the Supreme Court Building, which Gilbert was designing at the same time. A Greek key pattern decorates the lines defining the bays, with smaller chrysanthemums at the junctions of the coffers. In the center of three of the seven bays, six-foot bronze lanterns, each holding 16 light bulbs, hang from the center of a chrysanthemum. Variations on the decorative ceiling scheme established in the main hall appear throughout the rest of the building.

Bronze detailing around the doors and directory does not appear on the original drawings but apparently was chosen by the designer of the metalwork, using images of plants and animals as metaphors. The architects who prepared the Historic Structures Report suggest, for example, that the use of the dolphin, whose name comes from the Greek for "womb," is intended to show that we were born of one womb and thus all created equal. The use of an owl presumably signifies wisdom; an olive branch, peace; and oak leaves and acorns, strength. More subtly, the architects use wheat to suggest cultivation and truth, combined with a grasshopper and the word "meta," which together show that change is integral to growth. The historic-structure report provides no explanation for the use of seahorses, although it does suggest that the letters A, E, and O, which surround the owls, stand for *American, Earth, and Ocean*.[35]

Clockwise from upper left: A composite shows the Main Lobby's dazzling ceiling panels with their gilded chrysanthemums. Bronze detailing inside the courthouse uses images of plants and animals as metaphors for qualities such as wisdom that are important to the administration of justice. A combination of the word "meta" together with a grasshopper and wheat in the bronze detailing was intended to suggest that change is integral to growth. One of three six-foot bronze lanterns in the Main Lobby, each holding 16 light bulbs.

As originally designed, the building contained an elegant courtroom for the Second Circuit, as well as district court courtrooms, with the Second Circuit being literally the highest court, on the 17th floor of the tower. This courtroom, which has been characterized as "one of the finest public rooms in Manhattan,"[36] is both larger (with five window bays) and more elaborately decorated than those of the three-windowed district courts. The tower courtrooms and the three ceremonial courtrooms in the base contain many original features, including wood-paneled walls with fluted Ionic pilasters set between colossal round arches.[37]

A private elevator for judges was incorporated into the original design when it became apparent that the building site would not provide enough space to allow a judge's chambers to adjoin each courtroom.[38] On the 25th floor, the double-height library features large ceiling beams supported by brackets painted with stenciled leaves, and the high, arched windows provide dramatic views of the Manhattan skyline.[39]

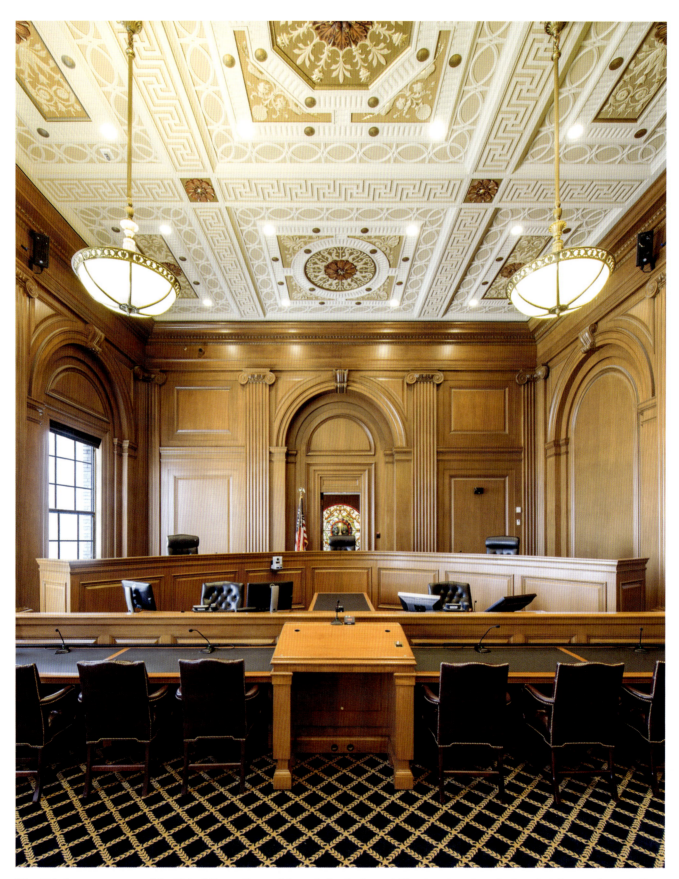

The 17th floor courtroom of the United States Court of Appeals for the Second Circuit as it appeared when the Thurgood Marshall U.S. Courthouse reopened in January 2013.

On January 21, 1936, when the Second Circuit moved into the Foley Square Courthouse, there were five authorized appellate judgeships, held (in order of appointment) by Martin T. Manton, Learned Hand, Thomas Walter Swan, Augustus N. Hand, and Harrie Brigham Chase. Four of those judges had distinguished careers on the court. Manton, the senior judge at the time of the move, later earned the dubious distinction of becoming the first federal judge ever to be indicted, convicted, and sentenced to prison for corruption—based on his taking large gifts and loans from parties in cases before the court. Shamelessly, Manton argued in his petition for certiorari that "it serves no public policy for a high judicial officer to be convicted of a judicial crime, for [it] tends to destroy the confidence of the people in the court."[40] In later years, Second Circuit judges have found Manton's conduct an unthinkable breach of his responsibilities and have had mixed reactions concerning whether it should be erased from legal annals or highlighted as a cautionary tale. For years, law clerks in the Second Circuit were admonished by their judges not to cite Manton opinions. But Southern District Judge Charles L. Brieant had different ideas, displaying Judge Manton's portrait in his chambers as a reminder of the fallibility of judges.[41]

Not long after the move to the new courthouse, Learned Hand assumed the role of Chief Judge (called "senior circuit leader" until the official position was created in 1948), a position he held from 1939 to 1951. Appointed to the Second Circuit in 1924 after 15 years of distinguished service on the Southern District bench, Learned Hand served on the Second Circuit for the next 38 years. He was widely respected by his fellow jurists and the public alike[42] and, although he was bypassed for a seat on the Supreme Court several times, he was sometimes called "the Tenth Justice" and the "heir to [Oliver Wendell] Holmes' triple crown of jurist, philosopher and poet of liberty."[43] Respected for his work across multiple disciplines, and praised for his thoughtful and probing approach to cases,[44] he also became widely known to the American public. In 1944, two weeks before the allied invasion of Normandy, he gave an "I Am an American Day" speech in Central Park attended by over a million people. Disclaiming an ability to define "the spirit of liberty" he nonetheless offered instead his "faith" that:

> The spirit of liberty is the spirit which is not too sure that it is right; the spirit of liberty is the spirit which seeks to understand the mind of other men and women; the spirit of liberty is the spirit which weighs their interests alongside its own without bias; the spirit of liberty remembers that not even a sparrow falls to earth unheeded; the spirit of liberty is the spirit of Him who, near two thousand years ago, taught mankind that lesson it has never learned but never quite forgotten; that there may be a kingdom where the least shall be heard and considered side by side with the greatest. And now in that spirit, that spirit of an America which has never been, and which may never be; nay, which never will be except as the conscience and courage of Americans create it; yet in the spirit of that America which lies hidden in some form in the aspirations of us all; in the spirit of that America for which our young men are at this moment fighting and dying ….

The speech was excerpted in the following week's issue of *The New Yorker* in "Talk of the Town," quoted in full a few weeks later by *The New York Times* Sunday magazine and reprinted again in *Life* magazine and *Reader's Digest*.[45] Eight years later, *The Spirit of Liberty* was used as the title of a book of Hand's essays that became a surprise best seller.

The Hand court exercised significant influence in the fields of admiralty, copyright, patent, trademark, antitrust, tax, laws affecting aliens, and the First Amendment. Having earlier struck down congressional efforts to regulate wages and hours in the poultry industry in *United States v. Schechter Poultry* (1935), shortly after moving to the new courthouse the Hand

The 17th floor lobby of the courthouse leading to the courtroom of the United States Court of Appeals for the Second Circuit.

court issued one of the first decisions upholding New Deal legislation.[46] The American Newspaper Guild had filed charges with the National Labor Relations Board (NLRB), alleging that the Associated Press engaged in unfair labor practices under the National Labor Relations Act. Finding that the relationship between an employer and employee in the news business affected interstate commerce, the court held that the statute was therefore within Congress's power to regulate and enforced the NLRB's order to reinstate an employee with back wages.

The court upheld the constitutionality of New Deal legislation again when North American Company attacked an order of the Securities and Exchange Commission, issued under the Public Utility Holding Company Act of 1935, limiting the company's operation and requiring it to reorganize and divest subsidiaries. The Second Circuit affirmed the SEC order, finding the Act's provision within the power of Congress under the commerce clause because ownership of securities of operating companies is related to interstate commerce.[47] The Supreme Court affirmed both cases.

In an influential antitrust case decided in 1945, the Second Circuit was given the singular honor of being authorized by Congress to sit as the court of last resort in lieu of the Supreme Court.[48] The government had charged Alcoa with monopolization in violation of Section 2 of the Sherman Antitrust Act, but the district court dismissed the complaint after a lengthy trial. By statute at that time, the normal route of appeal for government antitrust cases was directly to the Supreme Court. But four Justices disqualified themselves, which meant that the Supreme Court lacked a quorum.[49] It therefore "transferred the case to a special docket and postponed further proceedings in it until such time as there was a quorum of Justices qualified to sit in it."[50]

46 | CHAPTER ONE

Rather than wait for that to happen, Congress amended the statute to require the Supreme Court to certify such a case to the appropriate regional circuit court of appeals, to be heard by the chief judge and two next most senior judges, with no further possibility of appeal—which meant that the Second Circuit was assigned the case.[51] Chief Judge Learned Hand wrote the opinion, joined by Judges Swan and Augustus Hand. The court reversed the lower court's dismissal, finding Alcoa to be an illegal monopoly based on its long-term overwhelming dominance in the industry. It established a new approach to monopolization, holding that if a defendant charged with a violation of Section 2 has market control, the defendant bears the burden of demonstrating that it could not avoid having a monopoly. As Hand summarized the purpose of the statute, Congress "did not condone 'good trusts' and condemn 'bad' ones; it forbad[e] all."[52] The ruling, later effectively adopted by the Supreme Court, established a new standard for determining whether a monopoly power constituted illegal monopolization and left little room for "innocent" monopolization.[53]

During this period former SEC Chairman Jerome Frank spearheaded the court's leading role in the development of securities law. Judge Frank, joined by Judges Swan and Chase, issued *Fischman v. Raytheon Manufacturing Co.*, the first appellate opinion holding that the Securities Exchange Act of 1934 and SEC Rule 10b-5 gave a private cause of action to those who relied on false and misleading statements in a registration statement.[54] This decision became a key precedent that spawned an era of private securities law litigation and was ultimately ratified by later Supreme Court decisions.[55]

The court's influence was not limited to business decisions, but frequently extended to the pressing issues, political and otherwise, of the times. In the *Dennis* case, 11 leaders of the American Communist Party were convicted under the Smith Act for conspiring to advocate overthrowing the U.S. government by force; defendants challenged the application of the Smith Act on First Amendment grounds. The Second Circuit, in an opinion written by Learned Hand and joined by Judges Swan and Chase, upheld the conviction and adopted a version of the "clear and present danger" test that involved balancing the gravity and probability of the "evil" sought to be prevented, against the free-speech rights invaded. The Supreme Court affirmed.[56]

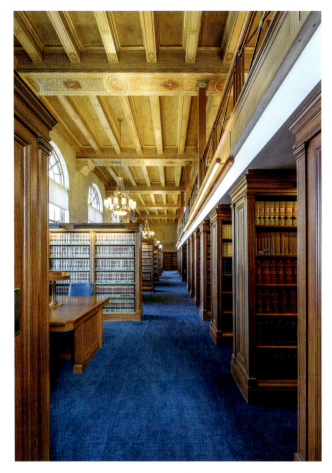

The 25th floor library shown just before Thurgood Marshall U.S. Courthouse reopened in January 2013.

Judge Irving R. Kaufman, Chief Judge of the Second Circuit between 1973 and 1980, has written that, for him, appearing before this eminent group as a young lawyer, was, "a thrilling and somewhat terrifying experience."[57] After Hand's tenure as Chief Judge ended in 1951, the role was taken on successively by Judges Swan, Chase and Charles E. Clark. Clark, who was appointed to the Second Circuit by Franklin Delano Roosevelt in 1939 and took the Chief Judgeship in 1954, set about improving matters of judicial administration, which had not been a focus for the Second

Details of the interior of the Thurgood Marshall U.S. Courthouse.

Circuit's prior chief judges. Hand, in particular, had a disdain for administration, judicial conferences, and other matters of routine maintenance. Under Clark's leadership the Second Circuit revived the circuit conference and the judicial council, instituted at least occasional en banc hearings (which had been disfavored by Hand), drafted new rules for the court of appeals, and helped relieve congestion in the Southern and Eastern Districts. Before his appointment to the court, Clark had been Dean of Yale Law School as well as the principal architect of the first Federal Rules of Civil Procedure. He was a strong supporter of civil liberties, and his disagreements with Jerome Frank, also a Roosevelt appointee, were notable in Second Circuit rulings for many years. Frank was a devout legal realist able to understand and rely on disciplines outside the law and averse to overly strict compliance with legal rules. A prolific writer with an influence on the Supreme Court, Frank was especially concerned with rules of procedure involving criminal defendants. In *United States v. Johnson*, for example, 20 years before *Gideon v. Wainwright*, Judge Frank took the position in dissent that the Sixth Amendment requires that trial counsel be appointed for indigent criminal defendants and that the federal *in forma pauperis* statute requires that a trial transcript be supplied for an appeal.[58]

Succeeding Clark as Chief Judge was J. Edward Lumbard, who was appointed to the court in 1955 and served as Chief Judge from 1959 to 1971. Lumbard focused on increasing the efficiency of case disposition in the Second Circuit and was responsible for instituting the practice of studying cases in advance of oral argument and announcing decisions from the bench in straightforward cases. He also put forward a plan to expedite criminal trials and appeals.

One of the first environmental-law cases was decided during Judge Lumbard's tenure as Chief Judge. Scenic Hudson Preservation Conference petitioned the court to set aside orders of the Federal Power Commission (FPC), which had granted a license to Consolidated Edison to construct a pump-storage hydroelectric project. The court set aside the licensing order, finding that the preservation conference had standing to sue on behalf of the public interest and holding that the FPC failed to compile a sufficient record, failed to make a study of possible alternatives, and ignored relevant factors, including a study identifying the beauty and historical significance of the project location.[59] The opinion was important for its recognition of the duty of federal agencies to give weight to ecological as well as economic factors in reaching decisions affecting the environment, and for its enlargement of standing to sue for those seeking to intervene on behalf of a public interest in noneconomic values. The case was not finally resolved until nearly 15 years later, when a settlement was reached and Consolidated Edison dropped the plan for its facility. This case helped launch the environmental-law movement that led to the Environmental Protection Act and other environmental laws and litigation.

In one of its rare en banc decisions, nearly contemporaneous with the 1971 Attica prison uprising, the Second Circuit considered a prisoners' rights case in 1971 that raised what the court itself described as "important questions concerning the federal constitutional rights of state prisoners which neither Supreme Court precedent nor our own past decisions have answered," and for which "[t]he sparse authority from other courts is for the most part either inconclusive or conflicting."[60] Judge Irving R. Kaufman, writing for the majority and reversing the lower court in part, held that while the prisoner's lengthy placement in solitary confinement did not violate the Eighth Amendment's prohibition on cruel and unusual punishment, due process required a hearing and other fact finding before imposition of serious discipline (although complete trial-type procedures were not required).[61] The decision also held that the prisoner could not be punished for possessing political and other writings, and that the prison might open and read a prisoner's incoming and outgoing mail but was limited in what it could delete from that mail; many years later, the court placed further restrictions on a prison's ability to read a prisoner's mail.[62]

Henry J. Friendly held the Chief Judgeship from 1971 to 1973. Friendly had an extraordinary 26-year career as a judge, writing substantially more majority opinions than any other member on that court, and he was widely praised for his careful approach to fact and probing analysis of the law. Judge John Minor Wisdom is quoted as having said of him, "except for the giants (Holmes, Brandeis and Cardozo) and possibly Learned Hand, no federal appellate judge had commanded more respect. . . ."[63] His impact was felt across multiple legal disciplines, especially in administrative and securities regulation, and also in corporate law, tax, creditors' rights, torts, criminal law and procedure, and First Amendment law. He was a prolific scholar, writing on subjects of statutory interpretation, the Fourteenth Amendment, administrative law and agency reform, and federal courts and federal jurisdiction. Notably, he was a strong supporter of abolishing federal diversity jurisdiction.

One of the most famous decisions during Friendly's tenure as Chief Judge was the Pentagon Papers case.[64] On Sunday, June 13, 1971, *The New York Times* began publication of a series of articles based on a classified Defense Department study of the war in Vietnam, which had been obtained illegally. The U.S. government sought a permanent injunction against publication of the series—the first time the federal government had sought to impose a prior restraint on a major newspaper.[65] On June 15, 1971 after holding an evidentiary hearing, newly appointed District Court Judge Murray Gurfein refused to grant the injunction on First Amendment grounds, although he had earlier granted a temporary restraining order.[66] (For more detailed discussion of the proceedings in the Southern District see Chapter 2.) The Second Circuit held argument on the case en banc the following Tuesday, June 22, and issued its opinion on June 23. The one-paragraph per curiam, en banc decision remanded the case to the district court to permit the government to make a showing that disclosure of the study posed a grave and immediate threat to national security. Three of the eight active judges dissented and would have affirmed the district court, denying the injunction. The Supreme Court granted certiorari on June 25 (before the district court had held the hearing mandated by the Second Circuit), heard argument on June 26, and issued its decision on June 30—17 days after publication of the first article—ruling in favor of *The New York Times* and reversing the Second Circuit.[67]

In 1973, Judge Irving R. Kaufman succeeded Judge Friendly as Chief Judge of the Second Circuit. While on the District Court for the Southern District of New York, Judge Kaufman had been the trial judge in the Rosenberg case (see Chapter 2) and had sentenced Julius and Ethel Rosenberg to the death penalty, a controversial decision that was viewed by some as the defining moment of his career. As chief judge he sought to modernize appellate procedure and improve court administration. Decisions during his era as chief judge focused on First Amendment issues, civil rights, environmental protection and other major issues. He was also widely respected by former clerks for being a marvelous teacher.[68] During this period, the Second Circuit continued in the forefront of First Amendment law, recognizing for example the role of "neutral reportage" in rejecting a libel claim against *The New York Times* in *Edwards v. National Audubon Society*.[69] The opinion, authored by Chief Judge Kaufman, held that the press could report accusations made by a responsible, prominent organization like the National Audubon Society (such as the one made by the Aubudon Society in *Edwards* that certain scientists involved in bird counts were "paid liars") regardless of the reporters' views about their validity, when it was newsworthy that such charges had been made.

The Second Circuit also continued its role in the development of antitrust law. In *Berkey Photo*, described by the Second Circuit panel as "one of the largest and most significant private antitrust suits in history," the court addressed the question of whether a monopolist could compete on the merits with rivals or whether Section 2 of the Sherman Act imposed a special duty on monopolists to refrain from competing with its smaller rivals because of its dominant position.[70] Berkey Photo, both a competitor and customer of Kodak, brought suit alleging that Kodak violated the Sherman Antitrust Act and claiming that Kodak's monopoly caused it to lose sales and pay excessive prices to Kodak for film, paper, and equipment. Many but not all of the charges arose from Kodak's simultaneous introduction in 1972 of the "Pocket Instamatic" camera and Kodacolor II film. Although the court, in an opinion by Chief Judge Kaufman, reversed the judgment entered on a jury verdict against Kodak, it remanded the case for retrial and held that even where monopoly power is legitimately acquired, the monopolist violates Section 2 of the Act if such power is wielded "to prevent or impede competition."

In 1980 Judge Kaufman was succeeded as Chief Judge by Wilfred Feinberg, known as a "judge's judge: thoughtful and incisive while at the same time modest, meticulous, and restrained."[71] The Second Circuit's decision on school prayer in *Brandon v. Board of Education* was among many notable decisions issued during this period. In *Brandon* the court held that students' rights under the First Amendment's Free Exercise Clause were not violated by the school board's refusal to allow voluntary communal prayer meetings in public schools and that authorization of voluntary prayer would have violated the Establishment Clause: "The sacred practices of religious instruction and prayer, the Framers foresaw, are best left to private institutions— the family and houses of worship."[72]

Second Circuit Chief Judges since the 1980s have included James L. Oakes, Thomas J. Meskill, Jon O. Newman, Ralph K. Winter, John M. Walker Jr., Dennis Jacobs and the judge serving in that position today, Chief Judge Robert A. Katzmann. In this modern era, the court has continued to blaze trails in commercial law, constitutional law and other areas. For example, continuing its role as a prominent court in the development of antitrust law, the court in 2003 affirmed the district court's ruling that credit-card companies Visa and MasterCard had violated Section 1 of the Sherman Act by prohibiting their member banks from issuing American Express and Discover cards, explaining that the agreements among credit-card consortium members were "far from being 'presumptively legal'" but instead were "exemplars of the type of anticompetitive behavior prohibited by the Sherman Act."[73]

No recounting of the role of the Second Circuit can do more than scratch the surface. In addition to the cases and areas of law touched upon here, the Second Circuit has issued influential rulings concerning such matters as copyright, fair use, the National Prohibition Act, sovereign immunity, international law, habeas corpus, search and seizure, the Federal Tort Claims Act, Title VII of the Civil Rights Act of 1964, the Clean Water Act, the doctrine of federalism, the right to sue for fourth amendment violations committed by federal agents and many, many more.[74]

RENOVATIONS

Prior to 1974, poor records were kept of changes made to the courthouse building, although it appears that at least some of the offices and chambers had been revised by then.[75] Starting in 1974, the building interior was substantially changed when the U.S. Attorney's Office left the courthouse and the vacated space was remodeled to provide additional courtrooms, judges' chambers, and office space.

By the early 21st century, the building was showing its age. The water fountains were wrapped in plastic due to concern over possible leakage of lead and copper from the pipes. The 30th floor had been abandoned after water damage, the ceiling of the 25th-floor library leaked, and on the 17th floor a water pipe had burst, flooding a judicial robing room. Only the base of the building had central air conditioning, and temperatures in the tower were often too high for the window air conditioners to bring under control. These conditions, combined with other leaks and mildew, meant that at least 20 percent of the building was no longer habitable.[76] In November 2006, the building was

Top: Repair work in progress on the Thurgood Marshall U.S. Courthouse pyramid. *Bottom:* Paintwork in progress on the 15th floor appellate courtroom, originally used as a courtroom by the district court.

closed for a major renovation to upgrade and replace its mechanical, electrical, and plumbing systems and to install a modern HVAC system.

During the renovation, the Second Circuit moved into the nearby Daniel Patrick Moynihan U.S. Courthouse, just off Foley Square. Some judges' chambers were created in space formerly occupied by the Probation Office, and as a temporary measure, Second Circuit judges who had their primary chambers out of town used the smaller spaces assigned to visiting judges. The $317 million infrastructure upgrade, designed by the architecture firm Beyer Blinder Belle, updated the building's infrastructure and repaired its granite facades and pyramidal roof. In November 2012, the Second Circuit returned to the Thurgood Marshall courthouse, which reopened to the bar and the public on January 7, 2013.[77] The courthouse has 45 chambers for circuit, district, and magistrate judges and 23 courtrooms, including three large ceremonial courtrooms located on the first, third, and fifth floors. This most recent infrastructure upgrade and renovation guarantees that judges, lawyers, litigants, and the public will continue to work at and access the Thurgood Marshall U.S. Courthouse for generations to come.[78]

The refurbished courthouse is an appropriate home for one of the busiest and most productive courts in the nation. In 1937, the year after the move to the current courthouse, the court issued 714 dispositions. In 1968 that number rose to over a thousand. In fiscal 2012 the court terminated more than 5,700 filings.[79] During that period the number of judges on the Second Circuit increased to six in 1938, nine in 1961, 11 in 1978, and finally 13 in 1984.[80] The court's cases continue to include ground-breaking decisions, such as the court's recent decisions in *ACLU v. Clapper* concerning electronic surveillance and in *United States v. Newman*, clarifying the law of insider trading.[81]

Cass Gilbert's extraordinary courthouse has, since its first opening, been the working home of judges and lawyers of extraordinary character. Among them, three Second Circuit judges have gone on to the Supreme Court: John Marshall Harlan II, who was appointed to the Second Circuit in 1954 and served for only one year before being nominated to the Supreme Court; Thurgood Marshall, who served on the Second Circuit from 1961 to 1965, when he was appointed U.S. Solicitor General, and who was nominated to the Supreme Court in 1967; and most recently Sonia Sotomayor, who served on the Second Circuit from 1998 to 2009, when she was nominated to the Supreme Court.

Thurgood Marshall U.S. Courthouse is notable not only as the site of momentous judicial rulings and the workplace of distinguished judges, but also as a place where promising young lawyers begin their careers by serving as law clerks—learning lessons that shape their professional lives. Many former clerks to judges on the Court of Appeals for the Second Circuit now practice in the courts of the Second Circuit or have gone on to other distinguished careers such as serving as law professors, law school deans, politicians and judges—including Chief Justice Roberts of the United States Supreme Court, who served as a law clerk for Judge Friendly from 1979 to 1980.

For all those who use the courthouse, it remains, as Judge Jacobs has written, an ennobling environment: "This building reminds lawyers what they owe the court and the law, it reminds litigants what they owe to the rule of law, and it reminds judges what they owe to everybody."[82] Today, judges of the United States Court of Appeals for the Second Circuit Court continue to hear appeals in the courthouse's magnificently restored 17th floor courtroom: some are everyday litigation and others, ground-breaking cases that will continue to influence U.S. jurisprudence and history.

CHAPTER TWO

THE SOUTHERN DISTRICT OF NEW YORK

On November 3, 1789, the United States Court for the District of New York, predecessor to the Southern District of New York and all other New York district courts, held its first session, presided over by District Judge and former New York City Mayor James Duane. Established under the Judiciary Act of 1789, it was the earliest operating federal court in the nation, predating by several weeks the first meeting of the Supreme Court of the United States.[1]

For the first 200 years of its existence, the Southern District of New York and its predecessor, the District of New York, functioned out of one courthouse, often, in the early days, in rented space in locations ranging from a merchant's exchange to a theater to a private home. The expansion in the number of cases heard by the court, and the resulting expansion in the number of judges, led by the late 20th century to spreading the court functions among the four main courthouses that serve the Southern District today: the Thurgood Marshall U.S. Courthouse, home of the Second Circuit Court of Appeals as well as the Southern District; the Daniel Patrick Moynihan U.S. Courthouse, which serves as the main courthouse for the Southern District; the Charles L. Brieant Jr. U.S. Courthouse in suburban White Plains; and the Alexander Hamilton U.S. Custom House in New York City, used by the United States Bankruptcy Court of the Southern District.

Opposite: Clockwise from upper left, Thurgood Marshall U.S. Courthouse; Daniel Patrick Moynihan U.S. Courthouse; Alexander Hamilton U.S. Custom House; Charles L. Brieant Jr. U.S. Courthouse.

The New York Royal Exchange, sometimes called the Merchant's Exchange or the Exchange. The District Court for the District of New York held its first session in the building's second floor public meeting room.

THE DISTRICT OF NEW YORK AND ITS EARLY SITES FOR HOLDING COURT

The District of New York's first quarters were in the second-floor public meeting room of the New York Royal Exchange, sometimes also referred to as the Exchange, or Merchant's Exchange (erected 1752–1754 at the foot of Broad Street in New York City).[2] Eighty-six years passed before the district court occupied a place purpose-built for its usage.

THE ROYAL EXCHANGE

The building that first housed the court was a two-story structure used by merchants to transact business, designed by architect John Watts.[3] It "stood upon brick stilts, or arches, at the lower end of Broad Street in a line with Water Street ... a very curious structure, for its ground floor was open on all sides, and in tempestuous weather the merchants who gathered there for business found it extremely uncomfortable. It had a second story which was enclosed and consisted of a single room."[4]

Given the court's limited jurisdiction at that time, it is perhaps not surprising that at the court's first session, "nothing was done, and there was nothing to do but read the Judge's commission and admit to the bar of the new Court such gentlemen as chose to attend."[5] Among these was Aaron Burr, future Vice President of the United States and arch foe of Alexander Hamilton and the Federalists. Not until five months later, in April 1790, would the court hear its first case, *United States of America v. Three Boxes of Ironmongery, & Co.*, a customs case involving the determination and assessment of duty.[6]

FEDERAL HALL (FORMERLY OLD CITY HALL)

In 1791, after only two years at the Royal Exchange, the district court moved to Federal Hall, at the northeast corner of Wall and Nassau Streets and at the north end of Broad Street. Originally built in 1699–1700 by an unknown architect to serve as New York's City Hall, the building had been used for a variety of civic functions, served the British during the Revolutionary War "as the place of the main guard," and even functioned as the City Prison, prior to being extensively redesigned and enlarged by architect Pierre Charles L'Enfant in 1788 to accommodate the two houses of Congress established by the newly ratified U.S. Constitution.[7] Renamed Federal Hall at the time of the redesign, it was the first example of the Federal style of architecture in the United States.

As can be gleaned from historical descriptions and drawings, the redesigned Federal Hall was a grand edifice—sufficiently grand that on April 30, 1789, General Washington was inaugurated as the first President of the United States on its second-floor open gallery.[8] The long side of the building's rectangular main section fronted Broad Street. Its ground-floor portico featured four massive pillars in the center and two large rectangular openings on either side, with arches at either end so that it "formed an open arcade over the foot pavement."[9] The ground-floor design was echoed on the upper level, with four central Doric columns in front of an open gallery, crowned by a pediment, and two tall rectangular windows on either side of the center.

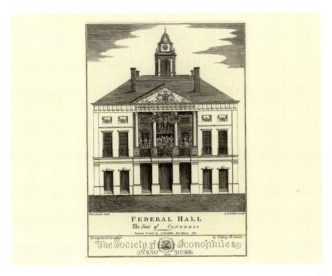 

Between 1791 and 1811, the district court met at Federal Hall shown, on the left, in a reproduction of a 1790 engraving of George Washington's inauguration drawn by Peter Lacour and engraved by Amos Doolittle and, on the right, in a colorized reproduction of a 1798 drawing.

An eagle was carved into the pediment, and 13 stars in the entablature over the portico, with tablets over the windows carved with 13 arrows and an olive branch.[10] The roof was punctuated by four chimneys and topped by a fanciful cupola. The building after L'Enfant's redesign was widely praised for its grandeur, although that opinion was not universal: one commentator described it as a "long building surmounted by an ugly cupola … [v]amped up, rechristened, shining resplendent with new paint."[11] Contemporary descriptions of its interior during the time that Congress met in Federal Hall describe the elegant chambers for the House and Senate (on the lower and upper floors, respectively), but the interior was renovated again in 1791 to accommodate the district court and New York State Legislature.[12]

Following the federal government's 1790 move to Philadelphia, Federal Hall again became home for New York's municipal government, which would serve as the District of New York's landlord for the next 63 years. The district court remained in Federal Hall until 1811. Neither of the first two homes of the district court survives: the Merchant's Exchange was demolished, apparently in 1799, and Federal Hall was torn down in 1812.[13]

During the district court's early years in the Royal Exchange and Federal Hall, not much happened of note: "During Judge Duane's five-year tenure as District Judge, only 378 final orders were entered; all concerned admiralty or customs matters and none, apparently, was seriously contested."[14]

In 1794 Duane was succeeded by former Congressman John Laurance, who in turn resigned in 1796 upon his election as U.S. Senator from New York. The first reported case heard by the Supreme Court out of the District of New York arose during Judge Laurance's term, when the Attorney General of the United States sought a mandamus against him for refusing to issue a warrant for the arrest of a French sea captain who had apparently abandoned his ship.[15] Laurance had strictly construed the terms of a treaty that required "an exhibition of the register of the vessel, or ship's roll," refusing to issue the warrant absent that evidence. The Supreme Court unanimously found that in doing so Laurance was acting in a judicial capacity, and that they therefore had no power to compel him to decide otherwise.

Judge Laurance was succeeded by Robert Troup, who served only from December 10, 1796, to April 1798 and then returned to private practice. John S. Hobart was appointed next, beginning his tenure at age 65 and serving until his death in February 1805.[16] During the tenure of Judges Troup and Hobart, admiralty

Engraving showing City Hall and its park as it appeared in the 19th century, viewed from the south.

cases increased in number and importance.[17] One particularly notable case was *Talbot v. Seeman*, involving the *Amelia*, a ship owned by merchants from Hamburg, Germany, that was first captured by the French and then seized by an American ship.[18] The case was politically explosive: the United States was in a low-grade naval conflict with France under Napoleon, and Congress had passed several statutes authorizing the seizure of armed French vessels, but it had not officially declared war.[19] Judge Hobart awarded the American captain half the value of the ship and its cargo, and the appeal was argued to the Circuit Court by political foes Aaron Burr, representing the Hamburg merchant, and Alexander Hamilton, on behalf of Captain Talbot. When the Circuit Court overturned the ruling, the case went to the Supreme Court, where the oral argument lasted for four days. Justice Marshall's opinion neatly balanced the political issues: he awarded one-sixth of the vessel's value as salvage, finding that the right to salvage derived from an implied contract; he also simultaneously bolstered the Federalists by recognizing the existence of the quasi-war and supported the Republican (or "Democratic-Republican") position that only Congress had the right to declare war.

NEW YORK CITY HALL

In 1811, after 20 years of residency at Federal Hall, the District and Circuit Courts were moved to the newly built New York City Hall, designed by architects John McComb Jr. and Joseph Francois Mangin, on the former city common (renamed City Hall Park) east of Broadway below Chambers Street. Of the various buildings housing the United States Court for the District of New York, City Hall is the only one still standing and serving its original purpose.

City Hall was built following a design competition in 1802, which specified that all the functions of city government were to be housed under one roof, including "four court rooms, two large and two small," and "six rooms for jurors."[20] McComb and Mangin won that competition, with Mangin—whose name was left off the foundation stone—doing most of the design work and McComb supervising the construction and interior finishes.[21] McComb, whose father had worked on the old City Hall, also designed Castle Clinton in Battery Park. Mangin, who had studied architecture in his native France before coming to New York in 1795, was also the architect of the landmark St. Patrick's Old Cathedral on Mulberry Street.[22] City Hall is the only known project on which the two collaborated.[23] Construction started in 1803 and was completed in 1811.

The building, most of which is two stories, was designed in the Federal style and consists of a central pavilion with two projecting wings. French influences can be seen in the large arched windows, delicate ornamental swags, and decorative Corinthian and Ionic columns and pilasters.[24] The formal staircase sweeps up to the one-story portico at the center of the tallest, central section of the building, and the roof of the portico, with its surrounding balustrade, forms a balcony outside the five large arched windows of the Governor's Room. The diminutive attic story over that section, which originally served as the caretaker's apartment, forms a base for a domed tower, which originally was capped by a wooden statue of Justice carved by John Dixey (later destroyed by fire and replaced with a copper replica).[25] The exterior, originally clad with Massachusetts marble in the front and brownstone on the back as an economy measure, now sports more durable Alabama limestone on all sides and red Missouri granite on the basement level. During the years when the district court was in the building, City Hall was one of the tallest structures in the City, and for a small fee visitors could climb up into the cupola to admire the view.[26]

Inside the building, a grand marble staircase splits into two cantilevered sections that rise on either side of the rotunda to the second floor. The soaring space of the rotunda and its 10 fluted Corinthian columns date from the original design. That cupola was twice destroyed by fire (in 1858 and again in 1917), and therefore the coffered dome topped with an oculus (a circular window) is of more recent vintage.

The district court had been meeting in City Hall for about a year when Congress passed an Act assigning a second judgeship to the District of New York.[27] Matthias Burnett Tallmadge, who had succeeded John S. Hobart as District Judge in 1805, was to continue to serve in the first spot, while William Peter Van Ness, a protégé of Aaron Burr and his second in the duel with Alexander Hamilton, was appointed to fill the new position.

THE SOUTHERN DISTRICT OF NEW YORK AND ITS EARLY SITES FOR HOLDING COURT

Shortly into Van Ness's tenure, on April 9, 1814, Congress divided the original District of New York into two districts, the Northern and Southern Districts of New York.[28] The law specified that Van Ness should remain as the district judge in the Southern District, but he also had to sit in the Northern District when Judge Tallmadge was unable to do so. The Southern District of New York has traditionally viewed itself as the successor court to the original District of New York and thus the "Mother Court" of all New York district courts and of the nation.

COUNTY ALMSHOUSE

In 1832 the phenomenal growth of New York and the corresponding increase in size of its municipal government led to the district court and several city offices being

The Almshouse, sometimes called the "New City Hall."

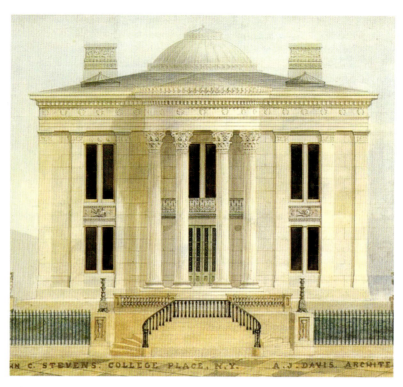

John Cox Stevens House.

moved out of City Hall and into the former County Almshouse, located behind City Hall on Chambers Street, where the Tweed-era New York Supreme Court now stands. Built in 1796–1797 by architect Robert Derry, this rudimentary three-and-a-half-story brick structure, at times somewhat euphemistically referred to as "the New City Hall," was hastily converted to government usage, with the federal courts occupying two floors of the building's east wing.[29]

During its time at the Almshouse, the District Court for the Southern District of New York came to prominence as the busiest federal court in the nation. In the early 1840s the Southern District averaged over 300 motions or cases per year. Judge Samuel Betts, who took office as District Judge in 1828 and served until 1867, oversaw the significant development of admiralty law, creating rules for claiming prizes in admiralty and publishing the first significant treatise on American admiralty-law practice.[30]

The Circuit Court for the Southern District of New York, which remained largely a trial court at that time, played a major role in the development of federal law. (See Introduction for an explanation of the circuit courts.) By the early 1840s it was adjudicating more than 130 matters per year, with District Judge Betts and a Supreme Court Justice serving as the trial judges, and by the 1850s the circuit court was handling more cases than all of the district courts in all of the southern states.[31] *Swift v. Tyson*, a case originating in the circuit court in which a New Yorker was swindled while attempting to purchase land in Maine, dealt for the first time with the question of whether the federal courts were required to follow the common-law decisions of the state courts. The judges (Betts, and Justice Thompson from the Supreme Court) disagreed on that question and certified it to the Supreme Court. Justice Story, writing for the Supreme Court, had "not … the slightest difficulty in holding" that the Judiciary Act required federal courts to follow only "rules and enactments promulgated by the legislative authority thereof, or long-established local customs having the force of laws," but not "the decisions of the local tribunals."[32] This approach, which granted federal courts an expansive role in developing federal common law, remained in effect for diversity cases for nearly a century, until it was overruled by *Erie Railroad Co. v. Tompkins* in 1938.³³

Unfortunately, Betts's place in history is also defined by his rulings in slavery cases, in which he often upheld the rights of slave owners. In the case of the *Catherine*, for example—a ship seized while on its way to Africa—Betts was faced with the interpretation of a federal law prohibiting the outfitting of ships for the slave trade. Betts was "satisfied that this vessel was chartered, fitted out and laden at Havana, with intent to be employed in the slave trade, prohibited by [this Act]."³⁴ He nevertheless decided that the ship did not violate the law because it was to be sold to noncitizens before taking on slaves. Justice Thompson, sitting in the circuit court, reversed, noting that the vessel had lumber already numbered for installing a slave deck, was equipped with 570 wooden spoons, cooking equipment for 300 people, materials to make water containers that would hold about 4,500 gallons, and more than 20 passengers who, based on written instructions found on board, were in fact crew for the return voyage, all of which led him "irresistibly to the conclusion" that the sale arrangements were "part of the contrivance to avoid the interruption of the adventure by capture."³⁵

The district and circuit courts for the Southern District of New York also took an active role in the development of patent law, along with their sister court in the Northern District. Among the cases decided in the Southern District were suits involving Charles Goodyear's patents on the vulcanization of rubber, and W. T. G. Morton's patent on an improved ether mixture for anesthesia.³⁶

After more than 20 years in the Almshouse, the district and circuit courts were suddenly forced to move on January 19, 1854, when fire completely destroyed the building. Just one week earlier, the Receiver of Taxes had written to the Board of Aldermen to complain about the dangerous condition of the building's heating flues, to no avail. The fire broke out in the afternoon and drew a large crowd of spectators who stayed for many hours; as *The New York Times* commented, "no show of pyrotechnics could have been finer."³⁷ Luckily, no important federal court documents were lost, but the court itself was left without a home.

JOHN COX STEVENS HOUSE

Almost as soon as the fire was put out at the Almshouse, *The New York Times* called for the federal government to create "a suitable building … for the accommodation of the United States Courts" rather than continue to be "dependent upon the City for the rooms they required."³⁸ Its suggestion went unheeded, however, and six weeks after the fire the district court moved into the former home of ship builder John Cox Stevens.³⁹ The white marble Greek Revival house, designed by architect Alexander Jackson Davis, was located two blocks west of City Hall Park at the intersection of Murray Street and College Place (now West Broadway). It had been hailed as one the city's finest residences when it was built in 1845.⁴⁰ Stevens, however, apparently had decided that the neighborhood was no longer fashionable enough to suit him, leaving the building available for the court. But its chambers were ill suited for use as courtrooms, and the Stevens House was vacated after a mere two years. The building was razed by Stevens in 1856 and replaced with warehouses.⁴¹

BURTON'S CHAMBERS STREET THEATRE BUILDING

Exactly when the Southern District of New York moved into its next known quarters, the former Burton's Theatre at 39–41 Chambers Street, between Broadway and

Burton's Theatre.

Centre Street across from the north end of City Hall Park, is a matter of some dispute. City directories at the time show the federal courts in the same location as the city courts, even when at least some court functions were located in Stevens House.[42] Decades later, *The New York Times* reported that "two or three years" after occupying the Stevens House "another move was made, across College Place to a number not now recalled," although that account was disputed by a prominent lawyer who recalled the court moving directly to Burton's Theatre.[43] It seems likely, however, that an interim move in fact occurred, as a two-year gap exists between the time Stevens House was razed and Burton's Theatre was leased. The city courts located in City Hall Park may have served as temporary quarters, if city directories of the time are to be believed.

What is fairly clear is that in April 1858 the U.S. government leased Burton's Theatre, began the process of altering the building for use as a courthouse as well as to provide offices for the U.S. Marshal and U.S. Attorney, and planned an opening "in grand style" to occur in December.[44] Originally built in 1827 as a public bathhouse and operated as a theater since 1844, the structure underwent extensive alterations to create separate courtrooms for the district and circuit courts on its second-floor level, each 60 feet in length and illuminated by overhead skylights. A broad corridor between the two courtrooms led to judges' chambers, a petit jury room, and the offices of the U.S. Attorney at the building's rear overlooking Duane Street.[45] The court remained in that building until 1875, and it was razed the following year.

The period immediately after the Civil War ushered in two major developments in the administration of the Southern District. In 1865 the Eastern District of New York was created, removing the counties of Kings, Queens (including what is now Nassau County), Richmond, and Suffolk from the Southern District's jurisdiction.[46] The new Eastern District was given concurrent admiralty jurisdiction with the Southern District—jurisdiction that still exists today. The new Eastern District judge was required to help out in the Southern District as needed.[47] Then, in 1869 the first permanent judgeship was created in the Second Circuit.[48] Although the circuit courts remained primarily trial courts based in each district, rather than serving as a circuit-wide court of appeals, the addition of the permanent judgeship marked the beginning of a new era of judicial administration.

THE SOUTHERN DISTRICT MOVES INTO THE MULLETT COURTHOUSE

In 1867, after more than three quarters of a century of quartering the Southern District and its accompanying circuit court in various privately owned and city buildings, the federal government obtained from the City of New York a triangular plot at the southern end of City Hall Park, on the northeast corner of Broadway and Park Row, for a building to house a new central post office and the Southern District and the Second Circuit Court of Appeals. That same year an architectural competition was held for the new building, but its 52 competitors failed to produce a satisfactory design. Five of the competitors, including noted architects Richard Morris Hunt and Napoleon LeBrun, were then invited to collaborate on a new effort, with their work to be overseen by Alfred B. Mullett, the recently appointed Supervising Architect of the Treasury Department. Criticizing their work as both too expensive and riddled with inefficiencies, Mullett prepared his own simplified treatment of the project, thereby effectively appropriating the commission for himself. Congress repeatedly delayed allocating funds for construction of the new courthouse, and it was not until 1869 that ground was finally broken.[49] The monumental courthouse built from Mullett's design is described in Chapter 1.

The 61-year residency at the Mullett Post Office marked a time of immense change for the Southern District of New York. In the early years, admiralty business dominated, and the judges tried cases in their capacity as judges at the trial-level circuit court. Most

The Mullett Courthouse and Post Office at the south of City Hall Park viewed from the north with its surrounding buildings, including the Woolworth Building.

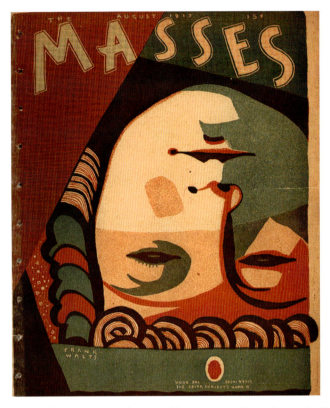

Left: The Masses, a socialist monthly, was the subject of an early First Amendment case. *Right:* The controversial illustration *Conscription* in the August 1917 issue of *The Masses* was one of the reasons that the U.S. Postmaster General sought to bar the issue from the mails.

decisions were brief and per curiam, with only a small number of signed opinions and even fewer dissents.

Change came with the creation of the Second Circuit Court of Appeals in 1891 and the later abolition of the old circuit trial court in 1911. The passage of the Bankruptcy Act of 1898 greatly increased the number of cases heard by the Southern District, and Congress authorized additional judgeships to deal with the increasing numbers of cases filed in the court: starting with one judge at the time of the move to the Mullett Post Office in 1875 (Judge Samuel M. Blatchford), one judgeship was added each year in 1903, 1906, and 1909.[50] Among the additional judges appointed to handle the court's crowded docket was the eminent jurist Learned Hand, who was named to the seat created in 1909.[51]

During that same time, admiralty matters continued as a primary focus of the court's work. Most notable were two that arose from historic passenger-ship disasters, the sinking of the *Titanic* on April 15, 1912, and the torpedoing by Germany of the Cunard liner *Lusitania* on May 7, 1915. After four years of litigation, the *Titanic* case was resolved by settlement, with the claimants receiving payment of $665,000, and shortly afterward Judge Julius M. Mayer signed a decree absolving the White Star Line of blame in the ship's sinking.[52] In the *Lusitania* litigation, some 67 actions filed in several courts by passengers and survivors of the victims were consolidated into a single proceeding before Judge Mayer. The trial began on April 17, 1918, and involved the examination of 40 witnesses and the reading of pre-trial testimony given by many more. Judge Mayer issued his decision in August of that year, determining that neither the Cunard line nor the *Lusitania*'s master, Captain Will Turner, was negligent, and that fault for the ship's sinking "lay in the illegal act of the Imperial German Government … violating a cherished human rule observed, until this war, by the bitterest antagonists."[53]

First Amendment–related litigation, particularly in connection with the 1918 amendments to the Espionage Act, also became a notable aspect of the Court's work during and after World War I. Judge Mayer imposed harsh sentences on some antiwar activists, including Emma Goldman, but during the trial of Scott Nearing and the American Socialist Society he gave the defense wide latitude to explain their views, resulting in Nearing's (but not the Society's) acquittal.[54] Perhaps the most influential of the First Amendment cases from the district court, even though it was reversed, was Judge Learned Hand's opinion in the *Masses* case.[55] Founded in 1911 as an illustrated socialist monthly, *The Masses* mixed contributions from visual artists such as John French Sloan with those from political radicals such as John Reed and Louise Bryant and also included the work of major American writers, such as Carl Sandburg, Jack London, Upton Sinclair, and Sherwood Anderson. The U.S. Postmaster General had decided to prevent mailing of the August 1917 issue of *The Masses* because of its antiwar sentiments, pointing to the illustration "Conscription" by Henry Glintenkamp, among other things. The publisher sued, and Hand granted a preliminary injunction against the Postmaster General, finding that the Espionage Act prohibited only direct incitement to violence. His opinion balanced the value of free speech against the state's interest in preserving unity in time of war and concluded that the value of free speech was preferable to the value of silencing criticism of the war effort. While the Second Circuit stayed the injunction and later reversed, the Supreme Court, in the long run, adopted a view of the First Amendment much closer to that advocated by Hand.[56]

During the 1920s, two temporary judgeships (later made permanent) and three permanent judgeships were added to the district court roster to deal with the caseloads arising from the huge surge in organized-crime activity following passage in 1919 of the National Prohibition Act, also known as the Volstead Act. Two more judgeships were added in 1936, so that the number of judges jumped from four to six in 1922, nine in 1929, and 11 by the time of the move out of the Mullett Post Office.[57]

Toward the end of the court's tenure in the Mullett building, overcrowding had worsened to such a degree that several cases were heard in rented quarters in the Woolworth Building across the street where Judge Learned Hand also had his chambers. *The New York Times* had long endorsed the construction of a new courthouse, characterizing Mullett's design as poor both artistically and functionally.[58] But not until 1936 were the federal courts able to leave their antiquated home for new quarters at what is now the Thurgood Marshall U.S. Courthouse on Foley Square. Three years later, what was to some the worst building in New York was demolished and replaced by an access ramp for the Brooklyn Bridge. Ironically, in the years since its destruction, Mullett's Courthouse and Post Office building has been acknowledged as an exceptional example of the architecture of its period and lamented as a lost landmark of New York.

THE SOUTHERN DISTRICT IN TODAY'S COURTHOUSES

In 1936 the Southern District of New York (along with the Second Circuit Court of Appeals) moved to the U.S. Courthouse at 40 Foley Square now known as the Thurgood Marshall U.S. Courthouse. That courthouse, whose architecture is described in Chapter 1, remains one of its primary homes today.

THE THURGOOD MARSHALL U.S. COURTHOUSE

Since 1936, the Southern District of New York has heard some of the country's most prominent cases on a variety of issues in the Thurgood Marshall U.S. Courthouse. Well-known cases include espionage and terrorism trials, other major criminal prosecutions, important First Amendment cases, and celebrity cases—and this list only hints at the scope and breadth of the litigation that has come before the judges of the Southern District.

Courtroom 110 in Thurgood Marshall U.S. Courthouse has been the site of many famous trials ranging from Julius and Ethel Rosenberg's historic espionage trial and Alger Hiss's prosecution for perjury to the more recent prosecution of Martha Stewart for obstruction of an agency investigation.

Espionage and Terrorism

During the height of the Cold War and the Red Scare, the House Committee on Un-American Activities (HUAC) focused its investigations on real and suspected Communists in positions of actual or supposed influence in the United States. The Justice Department wanted to indict former State Department official Alger Hiss for espionage, but the three-year statute of limitations had long since expired. To get around that obstacle, in December 1948 Hiss was called before a New York grand jury and asked whether he had ever given government documents to *Time* editor and acknowledged Soviet spy Whittaker Chambers, and whether he had ever seen Chambers after the winter of 1936. Hiss answered no to both questions and was indicted on two counts of perjury.

The first trial against Hiss, begun on May 31, 1949 before District Judge Samuel H. Kaufman, ended in a mistrial five weeks later. In a second trial, Judge Henry W. Goddard presided; on January 20, 1950, the jury returned a verdict of guilty, and Judge Goddard sentenced Hiss to five years in jail. Later that year, the Second Circuit Court of Appeals affirmed Hiss's conviction.[59]

On March 6, 1951, the espionage trial of Julius and Ethel Rosenberg and Morton Sobell began before U.S. District Judge Irving R. Kaufman, in courtroom 110. The same prosecutor who had won the Alger Hiss conviction, U.S. Attorney Irving Saypol, told the jury that "the evidence will show that the loyalty and allegiance of the Rosenbergs and Sobell were not to our country but to Communism, Communism in this country and Communism throughout the world."[60] The defendants, according to the prosecution, had stolen and turned over to their co-conspirators "sketches and descriptions of secrets concerning atomic energy and sketches of the very bomb itself."[61] Julius and Ethel Rosenberg testified in their own defense, but to no avail. On March 29, 1951, the jury found all the defendants guilty of conspiracy to commit espionage. When he sentenced the Rosenbergs to death, Judge Kaufman declared that he considered the Rosenbergs' crime to be "worse than murder."[62] The Rosenbergs were executed on June 19, 1953.

Then–Assistant U.S. Attorney Roy Cohn assisted in the prosecution, examining co-conspirator and prosecution witness David Greenglass. Ironically, Cohn was subsequently tried in the same courthouse three times by longtime Manhattan U.S. Attorney Robert Morgenthau for a variety of alleged swindles.[63] Most famously, in a 1969 trial for bribery and conspiracy before Judge Inzer B. Wyatt, Cohn delivered his own closing statement when his lawyer was admitted into St. Vincent's Hospital the night before with symptoms of a heart attack.[64] Cohn was more fortunate than the Rosenbergs—he was acquitted.

Since the 1990s, the U.S. Attorney's Office for the Southern District of New York has investigated and successfully prosecuted a wide range of international and domestic terrorism cases, including the bombings of the World Trade Center and U.S. embassies in East Africa in the 1990s. On February 26, 1993, Ramzi Yousef and Eyad Ismoil drove a bomb-laden van onto the B-2 level of the parking garage below the north tower of the World Trade Center. They then set the bomb's timer to detonate minutes later. At approximately 12:18 p.m. that day, the bomb exploded, killing six people, injuring more than a thousand others, and causing widespread fear and more than $500 million in property damage.[65]

The following March, four men—Mahmud Abouhalima, Ahmad Mohammad Ajaj, Nidal Ayyad, and Mohammad A. Salameh—were tried and convicted of charges that included conspiracy, explosive destruction of property, and interstate transportation for the

Top: Former State Department official Alger Hiss was convicted of perjury in a trial before Judge Henry W. Goddard. As a Congressman, Richard Nixon pursued Hiss as a secret communist based on testimony before the House Committee on Un-American Activities; the truth of the charge has been debated for many years. *Bottom*: Julius and Ethel Rosenberg, separated by a heavy wire screen, as they leave the Foley Square courthouse after being found guilty on charges of conspiracy to commit espionage.

The 1997 trial of Ramzi Yousef for his role in the 1993 World Trade Center bombing, with Judge Kevin T. Duffy presiding, shown in a drawing by Christine Cornell.

bombing.[66] Yousef, who had been indicted in March 1993, was not apprehended until nearly two years later, when U.S. authorities received a tip from a confidential informant that he could be found in Islamabad, Pakistan. Investigators linked Ismoil to the bombing after the first trial, and he was indicted later in 1994, apprehended in Jordan in July 1995, and extradited to the United States.[67] A superseding indictment also charged Yousef and two others with plotting to plant bombs aboard a dozen U.S. commercial aircraft that were timed to go off as the planes were flying over the Pacific. Trial on those charges proceeded before Judge Kevin T. Duffy from May 29, 1996, through September 5, 1996, and resulted in all three defendants' conviction. Yousef and Ismoil's trial on charges relating to the World Trade Center bombing began before Judge Kevin T. Duffy on July 15, 1997 and concluded on November 12, 1997, when the jury found both defendants guilty on all counts.

At his sentencing on January 8, 1998, Yousef showed no remorse, stating, "Yes, I am a terrorist and I am proud of it."[68] Judge Duffy sentenced Yousef and Ismoil to a total of 240 years of imprisonment for the World Trade Center bombings and Yousef to an additional term of life imprisonment for the airline bombing charges, to be served consecutively. More than 10 years after the bombing, the Second Circuit affirmed those convictions.[69]

Other terrorism trials prosecuted by the U.S. Attorney's Office in the Southern District of New York at the Thurgood Marshall U.S. Courthouse include the 1995 trial in which 10 defendants, among them Omar Adel Rahman, also known as the "Blind Sheikh" associated with a mosque in Brooklyn, New York, were convicted of plotting to blow up the World Trade Center, United Nations headquarters, and various bridges, tunnels, and landmarks in and around New York City. The Southern District was also the forum for the indictment of Osama Bin Laden and the Embassy Bombings Trial, arising out of the August 1998 bombings of the U.S. embassies in Kenya and Tanzania. Four defendants were convicted of conspiring to murder Americans worldwide after a nearly four-month trial in early 2001.[70]

Other Criminal Cases

In addition to traitors and terrorists, many notable criminals, including politicians, mobsters, and drug dealers, have been prosecuted in the Thurgood Marshall U.S. Courthouse. In 1965 James Marcus began his political career in New York City. Starting as a lowly unpaid volunteer for Mayor Lindsay's campaign, Marcus eventually climbed his way up the political ladder and into the heart of Lindsay's administration.[71] In the fall of 1966, Marcus became NYC's Water Commissioner, and the next summer Lindsay announced Marcus as the head of the new Environmental Protection Administration.[72] But before the appointment took effect, Marcus was exposed as "the personal political patsy of a Cosa Nostra gangster, Antonio ('Tony Ducks') Corallo."[73] In December 1967, Marcus and Corallo were indicted by a federal grand jury for conspiracy.[74]

Though Marcus pled guilty before the trial, Tony Ducks Corallo did not go down without a fight. He was convicted and the Second Circuit affirmed, with Judge Medina stating:

> And so the sorry story of the corruption of a public official comes to a close. We see politicians hovering in the background, a labor leader as the master of ceremonies and underworld characters weaving a web of intrigue in the midst of secrecy and stealth. These sinister figures chisel in on one another in the fixing of their respective shares of the loot, and finally submit to the power of one who wanted his share "from off the top." This record reeks with proof of the guilt of every one of those whom the jury found guilty as charged.[75]

A string of Southern District prosecutions against mob defendants is sometimes credited with having broken the influence of organized crime. Judge Pierre Leval

This magazine cover is said to have led to the prosecution of drug kingpin Leroy "Nicky" Barnes and 11 of his associates. From *The New York Times*, June 5, 1977. © 1977 The New York Times.

presided over the "pizza connection" case involving New York mafia kingpin Salvatore Catalano, in which the jury convicted 18 men of over 100 acts of racketeering. The trial was one of the longest in history for the federal courts, beginning on September 30, 1985, and ending March 2, 1987.[76]

In 1977 *The New York Times Magazine* released an article about renowned drug lord Leroy "Nicky" Barnes. Dubbing him "Mr. Untouchable," the feature article pictured a smug Barnes next to the tagline "This is Nicky Barnes. The police say he may be Harlem's biggest drug dealer. But can they prove it?"[77] It is said that the photo of Nicky Barnes so offended President Jimmy Carter that he launched a full-scale DEA investigation into the renowned drug lord's business.[78] The following year, "Mr. Untouchable" and 11 of his associates were indicted, and he was convicted after a 10-week trial before Judge Henry F. Werker.[79] Barnes's sentence: life in prison without parole.

The first publication by *The New York Times* of what became known as the Pentagon Papers. From *The New York Times*, June 13, 1971. © 1971 The New York Times.

Barnes appealed, asserting that the trial court's use of an "anonymous" jury—the failure to disclose background information about jurors and the failure to inquire into prospective jurors' ethnic backgrounds—compromised his right to a fair trial. On April 25, 1979, in a decision written by Judge Leonard P. Moore, the Second Circuit affirmed the conviction and refused to grant Barnes a new trial, seeking in its ruling to strike a balance between the need to protect jurors' privacy during voir dire and defendants' ability to make peremptory challenges.[80]

First Amendment

In 1959 Grove Press, a publisher of literary works, decided to publish an unexpurgated version of Lady Chatterley's Lover, as part of a campaign to establish First Amendment protection of works of literary merit. The Postmaster General ruled that the book was "obscene and non-mailable," and the publisher sued in the Southern District. District Judge Frederick van Pelt Bryan first rejected the government's assertion that the court had to defer to the post office decision, finding that the relevant statute did not give the Postmaster General discretion to determine whether a book was obscene. Describing the case as the first time since the Second Circuit's 1934 landmark decision on James Joyce's *Ulysses* that the court was called upon to decide a federal obscenity charge against a book of comparable literary stature, Judge Bryan ruled that to be obscene, "the dominant effect of the book must be an appeal to prurient interest—that is to say, shameful or morbid interest in sex. Such a theme must so predominate as to submerge any ideas of 'redeeming social importance' which the publication contains." After finding that the book was not, by that standard, obscene, Judge Bryan added his view of the First Amendment: "It is essential to the maintenance of a free society that the severest restrictions be placed upon restraints which may tend to prevent the dissemination of ideas. It matters not whether such ideas be expressed in political pamphlets or works of political, economic or social theory or criticism, or through artistic media. All such expressions must be freely available."[81]

Another Southern District judge delivered a ringing endorsement of First Amendment values when on June 16, 1971, the United States sought a restraining order against publication by *The New York Times* of a series about Vietnam based on highly classified documents obtained by Daniel Ellsberg that would come to be known as the Pentagon Papers. The *Times* had begun the series in its prior Sunday edition under the deliberately unexciting headline "Vietnam Archive: Pentagon Study Traces 3 Decades of Growing U.S. Involvement."

The government's application for an injunction was randomly assigned to Judge Murray I. Gurfein, a Nixon appointee who had been sworn in the week before; it was the first case he heard as a judge. Years later, one of the lawyers for *The New York Times* recalled that Judge Lawrence W. Pierce, sworn in the same day as Judge Gurfein, had later told him "that every night since that day in June 1971 when Gurfein drew the Pentagon Papers case, he got down on his knees to thank God that it had not happened to him."[82]

After issuing an unprecedented four-day temporary restraining order—which the *Times* obeyed—and conducting a hearing on the merits, Judge Gurfein ended the historic case's first chapter by denying the government's application for an injunction, in an opinion that included strong statements about the value of a free press:

> The security of the nation is not at the ramparts alone. Security also lies in the value of our free institutions. A cantankerous press, an obstinate press, a ubiquitous press must be suffered by those in authority in order to preserve the even greater values of freedom of expression and the right of the people to know.[83]

As discussed in Chapter 1, the historic case would also occupy the attention of the Second Circuit before its ultimate resolution before the United States Supreme Court.

Celebrity Cases

The Southern District of New York, home to its fair share of celebrities, has also seen its fair share of celebrity cases, including the first trial involving paparazzi.

Ron Galella is considered by many to be the most famous paparazzo of all time.[84] Photographing the famous earned Galella his own sort of celebrity status and inspired an HBO documentary titled *Smash His Camera*.[85] In 1968 Galella began pursuing his favorite subject: Jacqueline Kennedy Onassis.[86] His pursuit eventually landed him in front of District Judge Irving B. Cooper—a President Kennedy appointee—facing claims based on "violations of [Onassis's] common law, statutory, and constitutional rights of privacy and intentional infliction of emotional distress, assault, harassment and malicious prosecution."[87]

After sitting through a six-week trial that compiled a massive 4,716-page record, Judge Cooper rejected Galella's First Amendment arguments and issued a permanent injunction against him.[88] On July 5, 1972, Galella was ordered to stay 100 yards away from Onassis's home and her children's school, 75 yards away from the Kennedy children, and 50 yards away from Onassis herself.[89] In 1973 Galella made it abundantly clear that he had no intention of leaving his celebrated target alone when he landed himself in court again, this time in front of the Second Circuit. Galella challenged the lower court's ruling, alleging that the district court's refusal to allow a jury trial despite an untimely request resulted in a denial of due process.[90] Delivering the opinion of the court, Circuit Judge J. Joseph Smith wrote: "Galella fancies himself as a 'paparazzo' (literally a kind of annoying insect, perhaps roughly equivalent to the English 'gadfly').

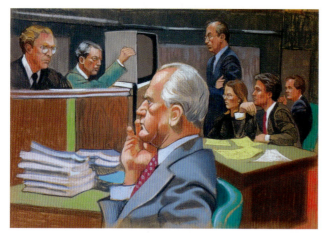

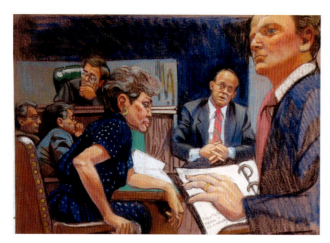

Top: Woody Allen outside the Daniel Patrick Moynihan U.S. Courthouse after settling for $5 million a "right of celebrity" claim based on the unauthorized use of his image. Photo John Marshall Mantel/*The New York Times*/Redux. *Middle:* Testimony before Judge Pierre N. Leval in General William Westmoreland's claim for libel against CBS based on the documentary "The Uncounted Enemy: a Vietnam Deception," shown in a drawing by Christine Cornell. *Bottom:* Testimony before Judge John M. Walker Jr. in Leona Helmsley's jury trial for tax evasion, shown in a drawing by Christine Cornell.

Paparazzi make themselves as visible to the public and obnoxious to their photographic subjects as possible."[91] Then, swatting away Galella's claim with a wave of his hand, he affirmed the district court's ruling: "Injunctive relief is appropriate. Galella has stated his intention to continue his coverage of defendant as she is newsworthy, and his continued harassment even while the temporary restraining orders were in effect indicate that no voluntary change in his technique can be expected."[92]

John Lennon, Beatles member and writer of famous songs such as "Imagine," "Lucy in the Sky with Diamonds," and "Strawberry Fields Forever," is known for his musical genius and also for his radical politics and antiwar activism. In 1972 his antiwar sentiments brought him into conflict not only with the U.S. Immigration and Naturalization Services, but also with President Nixon himself.[93]

In March 1972, Lennon's application for a renewed visa to the United States was refused on the basis of a 1968 marijuana-possession conviction in England, and he was ordered to leave the country the following year.[94] Instead of doing so, Lennon fired back at the government with a suit of his own, claiming that the real reason behind the deportation proceedings was fear that he would participate in demonstrations that might be embarrassing to the Nixon administration.[95] As the case progressed, the Watergate scandal broke, and Nixon resigned in August 1974.

Riding the Watergate scandal waves, *Rolling Stone* published an article in Lennon's defense titled "Justice for a Beatle: The Illegal Plot to Prosecute and Oust John Lennon."[96] The article started a media frenzy, exposing the government's true motives for prosecuting Lennon—fear of his influence over the American public.[97] On October 7, 1975, the saga came to a close as Judge Irving R. Kaufman delivered a decision barring the U.S. immigration office from deporting Lennon.[98] In his opinion Judge Kaufman acknowledged the unusual circumstances of the case and declared that "the courts will not condone selective deportation based upon secret political grounds."[99]

Martha Stewart surrounded by U.S. Marshals. Associated Press Bebeto Matthews.

The court has also had multiple occasions to address the "right of celebrity," deciding, for example, that Cary Grant was entitled to make a claim against a magazine that superimposed his head on the torso of a model in an article about different clothing styles, but that he would have to prove that the photograph was used for advertising or for purposes of trade. It also held that under California law, the Marx Brothers' right of publicity continued after their deaths. In the 1980s Woody Allen established that he was entitled to an injunction preventing a lookalike from pretending to be him in advertisements; the same Woody Allen sued American Apparel in 2008 for using his image without permission on billboards in New York City and Los Angeles. The 2008 case settled on the first day of trial (at the Daniel Patrick Moynihan U.S. Courthouse) for a then-record sum of $5 million.[100] Celebrities are no strangers to the Court in other contexts, either, as exemplified by J. K. Rowling's copyright actions against a would-be infringer and copyright claimant concerning her Harry Potter books (Rowling won both). Libel cases were brought by Gen. William C. Westmoreland against CBS for a television documentary that dealt with intelligence estimates of enemy strength during the Vietnam War (settled post-trial), and by former Israeli Minister of Defense Ariel Sharon against *Time* magazine for an article that suggested that he encouraged the murder of Palestinian refugees by a Lebanese political party. *Time* prevailed, although the special verdict form made clear that the jury found the article defamatory and untrue. Another suit against basketball great Isaiah Thomas based on sexual harassment settled post-trial.[101]

In a case sometimes viewed as emblematic of 1980s greed, Leona Helmsley, the self-proclaimed "queen" of the Helmsley hotels and wife of billionaire Harry Helmsley, was sentenced to 18 months in prison and fined $7.1 million after a trial for tax evasion that featured testimony from a string of disgruntled Helmsley contractors and employees, including, memorably, a housekeeper who quoted Helmsley as saying "We don't pay taxes, only the little people pay taxes."[102]

Television personality, cookbook author, and lifestyle expert Martha Stewart was sentenced in July 2004 to five months in prison, five months in home confinement, and two years' probation, along with a $30,000 fine, for lying to investigators about her sale of ImClone Systems stock in late 2001. In March 2004, after a highly publicized five-week jury trial before Judge Miriam Goldman Cedarbaum, Stewart had been found guilty of conspiracy, obstruction of an agency proceeding, and making false statements to federal investigators.[103]

THE DANIEL PATRICK MOYNIHAN U.S. COURTHOUSE

Having moved to the Thurgood Marshall U.S. Courthouse in 1936 when 11 judges served on the Southern District, the district court by 1961 had more than doubled in size and by 1990 had expanded to include 28 district judges. The position of magistrate judge (then called "magistrate") was established in 1968, and in 1978 Congress also created the position of bankruptcy judge, as part of a reorganization of the bankruptcy system.[104] With the addition of all of those positions, plus the welcome continued service of senior district court judges, the lack of space in the Thurgood Marshall U.S. Courthouse—then the only courthouse for the Southern District of New York and the Second Circuit—reached a crisis point.

Daniel Patrick Moynihan, the senior Senator from New York, worked to push Congress, the GSA, and various New York City mayors to build a new courthouse, even arguing that lack of courtroom space was impeding the enforcement of national drug laws. In 1988 the GSA announced plans for the addition of a new U.S. courthouse at 500 Pearl Street and a separate office building (the nearby Ted Weiss Federal Office Building at 290 Broadway), as part of a plan to revitalize the Foley Square area. Groundbreaking for the building took place on March 29, 1991. The enabling legislation specified that the new Foley Square courthouse should be respectful of the old, staying within the frame of reference established by Cass Gilbert in the design of the Thurgood Marshall U.S. Courthouse.[105] Largely completed by the end of 1994, the U.S. Courthouse at 500 Pearl cost $350 million, coming in slightly under budget. The Southern District judges began moving in the next year, although the building was not dedicated until June 3, 1996.[106] Construction took place at a time when unemployment in the construction trades was high. As a result, the project both helped the industry and was accomplished at prices lower than those of the previous decade.[107] The courthouse, which won a GSA design excellence award in 1996, was later named in honor of Daniel Patrick Moynihan under legislation sponsored by Senator Charles E. Schumer. It was officially rededicated on December 4, 2000.

Moynihan had a long and varied career in public service and academia. Born in Tulsa, Oklahoma in 1927, he moved to New York City at an early age, attended public and parochial schools, graduated first in his class from Benjamin Franklin High School in East Harlem, worked as a longshoreman, and then attended City College of New York for a year before joining the Navy in 1944.[108] He received his BA from Tufts University in 1948, an MA in 1949 and later a PhD from Tufts's Fletcher School of Law and Diplomacy, and also studied at the London School of Economics while on a Fulbright Scholarship.

The Pearl Street entrance to the Daniel Patrick Moynihan U.S. Courthouse.

Moynihan worked on the mayoral campaign of Robert F. Wagner, served as a speechwriter for W. Averell Harriman's gubernatorial campaign in 1954, and then rose to become Harriman's chief aide. For the next 20 years, Moynihan alternated between academia and the federal government, working at the Labor Department under the Kennedy and Johnson administrations from 1961 to 1965 and teaching at Syracuse, Wesleyan, and Harvard. The author of 18 books, he first became well known for writing *Beyond the Melting Pot*, about the effect of immigration on American culture,[109] and for his probing but controversial writings about the impact of unemployment, welfare, and illegitimacy rates on African American families. Although a lifelong Democrat, in 1968 he joined the Nixon White House as Assistant to the President for Urban Affairs, served as Ambassador

Above: The Daniel Patrick Moynihan U.S. Courthouse, behind the New York Supreme Court Building, seen from Foley Square.

Following pages: Aerial view showing the relationship of the Moynihan courthouse to the Thurgood Marshall U.S. Courthouse and other surrounding buildings. Daniel Acker/Bloomberg/Getty Images.

THE SOUTHERN DISTRICT OF NEW YORK | 75

The spacious passageway between the Moynihan courthouse Pearl Street Lobby and its Worth Street entrance.

to India from 1973 to 1975, and was appointed by President Ford as Ambassador to the United Nations in 1975. He resigned from that post early the next year, ran successfully for Senate from New York, and was reelected three times with landslide victories, until he retired in 2000. As a Senator, Moynihan teamed with New York's Republican Senator Javits to pass legislation to guarantee $2 billion in New York City obligations at a time when the City faced bankruptcy, worked to ensure that the Social Security system would remain viable into the 21st century, and presciently foresaw the decline of the Soviet Union. Moynihan has been recognized as having had an enormously influential impact on courthouse architecture (see Introduction). In the Guiding Principles of Federal Architecture that underlie the GSA's Design Excellence Program he advocated the principle that federal buildings "must provide visual testimony to the dignity, enterprise, vigor and stability of the American government."[110]

Like the Thurgood Marshall courthouse, the Moynihan courthouse is located in what during the 19th century was the notorious Five Points slum—indeed, at what used to be the Five Points intersection itself. The two-acre lot, which runs southwest–northeast between Pearl and Worth Streets, formerly served as a parking lot for the State Supreme Court. Rather than looking out onto Foley Square proper, the courthouse is tucked behind the New York Supreme Court Building and across Pearl Street from the Thurgood Marshall U.S. Courthouse and the Metropolitan Correctional Center.

The building, like the lot, is roughly T-shaped, with two main sections: a rectangular nine-story base that begins on the northeast (Worth Street) side of the lot and matches the height of the nearby Supreme Court

78 | CHAPTER TWO

The 9th floor Ceremonial Courtroom in the Moynihan courthouse.

building, and the crossbar of the T, a 27-story tower that parallels Pearl Street and echoes and roughly aligns with the taller nearby tower of the Thurgood Marshall courthouse.[111] At 921,000 square feet, the courthouse is two-thirds the size of the Pentagon and was the largest federal courthouse in the country at the time it was built (now surpassed by the Thomas F. Eagleton U.S. Courthouse in St. Louis).

The architects, Kohn Pedersen Fox, explain that the three groups of people who use the building—the public, the judges and courthouse staff, and prisoners—helped drive the building's design: the tower houses the courtrooms and chambers, and the lower building accommodates the court support and administrative functions, including the jury assembly room, offices of the Clerk of Court, and the U.S. Marshal Service, as well as the ceremonial courtroom.[112]

Most of the building is clad in beige Kershaw granite from South Carolina, and for their first five floors, the tower and base share a similar exterior: the tops of the ground floor and the sixth floor are delineated by horizontal bands that echo the cornices on the nearby federal and state courthouses, and four rows of rectangular windows regularly punctuate the space between the horizontal bands except over the two entrances, where the windows are linked in three vertical stripes separated by grooved pilasters. On the next two floors, the windows are linked vertically on the lower wing and on a portion of the tower that projects toward Park Row on the southeast side of the building, with another horizontal band running above that level.

The lower building has a setback to form a terrace on the east side, with two-story-tall windows. The lower building is finished with a final section clad in

Maya Lin's *Sounding Stones* outside the Moynihan courthouse.

Imperial Danby, a white marble from Vermont, with smaller square windows surmounted by a vaulted roof. The main body of the tower is roughly rectangular in shape, with a series of shallow setbacks on its long sides.

The building has two public entrances. The tower is entered by means of a shallow staircase that sweeps up to two brass revolving doors on either side of a center panel. Above the doors are tall panels of glass divided into three sections, decorated with horizontal and vertical bands and rectangles of brass whose placement evokes the design of the tower itself. The frieze above the doors reads, "Daniel Patrick Moynihan United States Court House," and over it two fluted pilasters, with clear windows on either side, lead up to a horizontal stone band four stories above the entrance. Two stories above that is another horizontal band. Each of the horizontal bands is composed of a main section, with one setback above and two below that emphasize the horizontal element and reflect the similar, although much larger, vertical setbacks that define the entrance.

A similar entrance on the Worth Street side of the building is at ground level and has doors on either side with a single revolving door in the center. This entrance, like that on Pearl Street, is also flanked by cylindrical lights encircled in brass bands, mounted atop eight-sided pillars.

The outdoor plaza contains the four large granite blocks of the Maya Lin sculpture *Sounding Stones*, created as part of the Art in Architecture Program. The stones mark the path between the Pearl and Worth Street entrances to the building. Each block was drilled to allow a view of the neighboring blocks and to permit observers to hear the sound of internal fountains while the flowing water remains out of sight.

Inside the Pearl Street entrance, a small lobby opens into a larger lobby area, all of which is faced in white marble. Four large, shallow brass-and-frosted-glass lamps hang inside the entryway, with 12 pie-shaped sections in each radiating out from a smaller hexagon in the center. A 16-foot-high bronze sculpture, *Justice*, by sculptor Raymond Kaskey, commands the back wall of the main lobby—it depicts a blindfolded figure of

Raymond Kaskey's bronze sculpture *Justice* in the main lobby of the Moynihan courthouse. © Raymond Kaskey 1996.

Convicted insider trader Raj Rajaratnam outside the Moynihan Courthouse. Andrew Burton/Getty Images.

Justice balancing on one foot as though she is running, with her outspread arms acting as the beam of a scale as she holds weighing pans in either hand. Long octagonal brass and frosted glass lamps hang on either side of the massive firgure.

A spacious gallery, clad in white marble, runs the length of the lower section of the building and past the jury assembly room, connecting the Pearl Street lobby with the smaller lobby of the Worth Street entrance. Fourteen tall windows, in groups of two, look out on the pedestrian plaza that extends between the Moynihan and New York courthouses. Seven long octagonal lamps, like those in the Pearl Street lobby, are centered in the hallway in line with each pair of windows, and seven vertical lights are embedded in the hallway wall opposite the windows.

The courthouse has 29 district-judge courtrooms, 14 magistrate-judge courtrooms, a large ceremonial courtroom, 42 chambers, a judge's conference room, and space for a U.S. Attorney's office trial preparation suite and U.S. Marshals' offices. *The New York Times* said of the mahogany ceremonial courtroom used for naturalization ceremonies, judicial inductions, multi-defendant trials, and en banc sessions of the Court of Appeals that "Learned Hand might feel at home on the three-tiered bench, framed by elegant millwork and pilasters of Vermont Verde Antique marble." The newspaper added, "Attention was also lavished on the 300-seat jury assembly room, overlooking a garden through ample windows, with a lounge area, generous chairs, cherry paneling and black marble pilasters."[113]

Many high-profile cases have been seen in the courthouse, including the 2009 guilty plea of Bernard Madoff, former non–executive chairman of the NASDAQ stock exchange. Madoff's plea came in response to a criminal complaint charging him with 11 felonies and asserting that his Ponzi investment scheme had defrauded his clients of more than $65 billion. Then–district court (now Second Circuit) Judge Denny Chin sentenced Madoff to the maximum 150 years in prison. The Moynihan courthouse also was the forum for the first piracy case in the U.S. since the 19th century, against Abdiwali Abdiqadir Muse, the lone surviving hijacker from the Somali pirate attack on the cargo ship *Maersk Alabama*. After a five-day standoff, U.S. Navy Seals rescued the captain and killed the other three captors. Muse pled guilty in February 2011 before Chief Judge Loretta A. Preska to the hijacking, kidnapping, and hostage-taking charges and was sentenced to 33 years and 9 months in prison.[114]

In a high-profile securities-fraud case, hedge fund billionaire Raj Rajaratnam received the longest prison sentence imposed up to that time for insider trading—eleven years—from Judge Richard J. Holwell in October 2011. A jury convicted Rajaratnam of securities fraud and conspiracy in May 2011, following a two-month trial in which extensive wiretap evidence was produced of his phone calls with colleagues, including former executives of Intel, IBM, and consulting firm McKinsey & Company, who allegedly provided him with inside information.[115]

Other well-known fraud trials have taken place in the Moynihan courthouse, including *U.S v. Rigas* (Adelphia) in 2004 before Judge Leonard B. Sand; *U.S. v. Ebbers* (WorldCom founder and chief executive Bernard Ebbers) in 2005 before Judge Barbara S. Jones; and *U.S. v. Gupta* in 2012 before Judge Jed S. Rakoff.

The Charles L. Brieant Jr. Federal Building and U.S. Courthouse in White Plains, designed by Skidmore, Owings and Merrill.

THE CHARLES L. BRIEANT JR. FEDERAL BUILDING AND U.S. COURTHOUSE

On October 17, 1983, the U.S. Courthouse in White Plains first opened for business in a leased building at 101 East Post Road, with the Honorable Lee P. Gagliardi presiding.[116] White Plains, with approximately 57,000 residents, is in Westchester County, 25 miles north of the other Southern District courthouses. The impetus for opening a federal courthouse in White Plains was the substantial burden on litigants and lawyers who lived north of New York City having to travel to the southern tip of Manhattan to appear in federal court.[117] The White Plains courthouse serves the six northernmost counties in the Southern District of New York—Westchester, Rockland, Putnam, Orange, Dutchess, and Sullivan—which as of 2013 had an estimated population of 2,138,523.[118]

By all accounts, the courthouse at 101 East Post Road, a converted office building, had substantial deficiencies, although it was determined to be the best option available until a new courthouse could be constructed.[119] The building had insufficient space, and its interior columns and low ceilings made it difficult for judges, attorneys, jurors, and witnesses to see one another. The building also posed security issues. For example, as it had only one elevator it was not unusual for the public, judges, and criminal defendants all to ride together in the same elevator.[120] Moreover, criminal defendants were discharged in the open air in the back of the building.[121] Because of the inadequacies of 101 East Post Road as a courthouse, not long after it opened Chief Judge Charles Brieant of the Southern District and other interested parties began lobbying Congress to appropriate funds for building a proper federal courthouse for White Plains.¹²² In 1991 Congress authorized the funds, through legislation sponsored by then-Senators Daniel Patrick Moynihan and Alfonse D'Amato.¹²³

The GSA held a design competition for the new courthouse, won by the prominent architectural firm Skidmore, Owings & Merrill.¹²⁴ The new courthouse's construction was also substantially assisted by White Plains Mayor Alfred Del Vecchio, who had saved the corner of Lexington Avenue and Quarropas Street from a prior urban-renewal project to be the site of a federal courthouse and convinced the federal government that it should build one there.¹²⁵ The new courthouse is located just a few blocks from the original White Plains federal courthouse on East Post Road, and only a few hundred yards from the site of the Revolutionary War's Battle of White Plains. That battle, which the British won, took place on October 28, 1776, and was part of Britain's 1776 campaign to capture New York City and George Washington's army.¹²⁶

Skidmore, Owings & Merrill developed what some have characterized as a postmodernist ("neo-neo-classical," according to *The New York Times*) exterior design for the courthouse, with white stone on the bottom and top floors sandwiching a middle of dark red Hudson River brick.¹²⁷ Broad steps, flanked by a ramp, lead up to the semicircular projecting entrance, whose cornice is supported by four unfluted columns and topped by a domed roof.

Large arched doorways lead into the building, and huge arched windows on either side of the entrance, set off by columns of two smaller rectangular windows on either side, complete the front. Six arched windows continue on both sides of the edifice. Above the rusticated white stone base is a cornice projecting far beyond the base, followed by three stories faced in brick, with rectangular windows and decorative white stone elements set into the brick between the second and third of those levels. A projecting stone band marks the top of the brick, and the top floors are faced once again in white stone, with long vertical windows crossed by a narrow horizontal band. The center third of the front of the brick and top stone stories and the roof over that section are slightly recessed, visually dividing the building vertically into thirds.

The courthouse's design pays tribute to the Hudson River Valley brick industry, a historically significant regional industry, through its use of Hudson River red brick for much of the building's exterior. Drawing on the massive clay deposits found alongside the Hudson River, hundreds of brickmaking factories existed along the Hudson from the late 1700s through the 1940s.¹²⁸ At the industry's peak, over 130 brickyards operated along the Hudson.¹²⁹ The courthouse's red brick was acquired from the last operating brickyard on the Hudson River, just south of Albany.¹³⁰

The most significant exterior feature, a tribute to the Battle of White Plains, is a series of large bronze medallions encircling the courthouse above the upper-level windows that depict a Westchester County militiaman. Another militiaman appears as an etching in a large window behind the bench in the Ceremonial Courtroom.¹³¹ The jury room formerly showcased a tapestry depicting Sybil Ludington, the 16-year-old

One of a series of large bronze medallions on the exterior of the courthouse above the upper-level windows depicting Westchester County militiamen, in a tribute to the Battle of White Plains.

White Plains maintenance staff superimposed images of the World Trade Center towers and the words "In memory of 3000 lives, RIP," on an American flag following the September 11th terrorist attacks. The spontaneous memorial was signed by all courthouse employees, including judges.

Revolutionary heroine who rode 40 miles through the night in April 1777 to summon the Dutchess County Militia to resist British troops who had captured nearby Danbury, Connecticut.[132]

Ground was broken on the new courthouse in 1992, and it was completed in 1995, on time and within its $35 million budget.[133] The budget was tighter than had been hoped for, as the White Plains courthouse was competing for funds with the new federal courthouse at Foley Square, being built simultaneously.[134] As a result, the new courthouse, while attractive, was not as lavishly decorated as Foley Square.[135] A number of challenges had to be overcome during construction. A stream named Davis Brook ran through the construction site, and the courthouse was designed so that the brook would flow through a conduit under the courthouse steps. At the request of the City of White Plains, the steps were installed so that they could be removed by crane if it became necessary to open up the Davis Brook conduit. In addition, part of the building site was determined to be contaminated with oil, and the building's contingency fund had to pay for the remediation.

On the inside, the building was designed like an old county courthouse, with the entry on the first floor and the ceremonial courtroom on the second floor. On the interior of its top floor, it contains a unique decorative feature prompted by the terrorist attacks of September 11, 2001. Following the attacks, the courthouse's maintenance department spontaneously created a giant painted memorial in the building's upper mechanical space—a huge 20-foot-high American flag with the New York skyline painted on it, inscribed with the words "In memory of 3000 lives, RIP." The entire courthouse supported this spontaneous memorial, and all of the employees, including the judges, signed the flag after the memorial's completion.[136]

The courthouse contains facilities for four district judges, two magistrate judges, and one bankruptcy judge. In addition, it also houses clerks' offices for both the district and bankruptcy courts, the U.S. Attorney's Office, the U.S. Marshals Service, and

A fifth-floor courtroom in the Charles L. Brieant Jr. Federal Building and U.S. Courthouse.

other court-related functions.[137] Despite White Plains' modest size, the courthouse's docket is similar to the docket at Foley Square with respect to both the number of cases per judge and types of cases.[138]

The White Plains federal courthouse was named for Chief Judge Charles Brieant following his death in 2008. Judge Brieant was a prominent federal district court judge and public official from Westchester County.[139] He served on the federal bench for 36 years and was Chief Judge of the Southern District of New York from 1986 to 1993.[140] He was the primary motivator for construction of a new federal courthouse in White Plains, as well as a major force behind the construction of the new Manhattan federal courthouse at 500 Pearl Street.[141]

During its relatively brief existence, the federal courthouse in White Plains has already been the site of a number of significant and interesting cases. In the 1980s, it was involved in the largest civil litigation in United States history up to that time—part of the litigation between Texaco, then headquartered near White Plains, and Texas-based Pennzoil over the right to acquire Getty Oil. Pennzoil claimed that Texaco's bid interfered with its prior contract with Getty. Pennzoil sued Texaco in Texas state court for tortious interference, where it won a jury verdict of $10.3 billion in compensatory and punitive damages. The Texas state court insisted that Texaco post a bond for $10.3 billion plus interest as security pending appeal. Texaco, represented by David Boies, then commenced a federal civil-rights action in the federal court in White Plains asking that the court enjoin Pennzoil from collecting on its judgment until Texaco's appeals were completed.[142] Judge Brieant, who presided over the case, blocked Pennzoil from collecting its damages until the appeals were concluded and lowered the amount of the bond required on appeal to $1 billion.[143] Judge Brieant's decision was affirmed in part by the Second Circuit, but was then reversed by the Supreme

86 | CHAPTER TWO

Court, which issued a significant decision concerning issues of federal jurisdiction and the federal abstention doctrine.[144] When Pennzoil rejected a $2 billion cash settlement offer, Texaco, the nation's second-largest oil company, filed for bankruptcy in the White Plains federal court, saying that it could not afford the bond for its appeal.[145] The parties ultimately settled the dispute for $3 billion.[146]

The Brieant Courthouse was also the site of major employment-discrimination litigation involving Texaco, presided over by Judge Brieant. In 1994 approximately 1,400 African American employees of Texaco sued the company for race discrimination. Two years into the litigation, tapes were disclosed in which Texaco officials were heard disparaging African Americans and plotting to destroy documents.[147] Following the disclosure of the tapes, Texaco agreed to settle the case for $176 million, the largest amount that had been paid to that date to settle a discrimination lawsuit. Notably, the settlement also required Texaco to form a seven-member "equality and tolerance task force" to give the plaintiffs a say in hiring and promotion policy at Texaco.[148]

Above: Following the conclusion of a major race discrimination case against Texaco, two of its executives were tried for, and acquitted of, obstruction of justice in a jury trial before Judge Barrington D. Parker, shown in a drawing by Christine Cornell.

Following pages: The Beaux-Arts Alexander Hamilton U.S. Custom House houses the Southern District Bankruptcy Court in New York City as well as the National Museum of the American Indian-New York.

The White Plains courthouse also has been the site of a number of significant criminal trials. In 1997 the first successful prosecution took place under the Violence Against Women Act, a statute that made it a federal crime to cross state lines to commit an act of domestic violence. In an ironic twist, the first conviction under the statute, which was primarily designed to protect women, was used to convict a wife: Rita Gluzman was convicted of traveling from New Jersey to New York to kill her husband with an ax. She was sentenced to life in prison.[149] Another notable criminal case took place in 2000, when Al Pirro, the husband of then–Westchester District Attorney Jeanine Pirro, was tried and convicted in the Brieant courthouse of tax evasion for improperly claiming that $1.2 million in personal expenses were business costs. Pirro was sentenced to two and a half years in federal prison.[150]

The Brieant courthouse continues to hear a wide range of cases that reflect its region. It has amply fulfilled its purpose of providing a modern setting for the sophisticated litigation of a major urban center in the Southern District of New York that is convenient to litigants.

THE ALEXANDER HAMILTON U.S. CUSTOM HOUSE

Sitting at the tip of lower Manhattan on the site of what from 1626 to 1787 was Fort Amsterdam, the U.S. Bankruptcy Court for the Southern District of New York is housed in the Alexander Hamilton United States Custom House—a Beaux-Arts building designed to be a "palace for commerce" and a "monument to the United States Customs Service, the City of New York, and sea trade." With deep roots in New York City and the United States, the building today houses the Southern District Bankruptcy Court in New York City and also houses the National Museum of the American Indian–New York. It is named a New York City Landmark (1979), listed on the National Register of Historic Places (1972), and designated as a National Historic Landmark (1976).[151]

Alexander Hamilton U.S. Custom House. *Top:* The sculpture *America* at the left of the main entrance. *Bottom:* The sculpture *Symbols of Government* above the main entrance.

Constructed from 1900 to 1907, the U.S. Custom House is located directly across the street from Manhattan's oldest public park, Bowling Green, which was used at various times as a cattle market, a parade ground, and a bowling green. This area of Manhattan was known as "Steamship Row" because of the high concentration of shipping companies that resided in the area—indeed, many of the buildings still bear the names of these companies engraved in their facades. Herman Melville was born nearby and memorialized the area's streets in the opening paragraphs of *Moby Dick*. The U.S. government purchased the site in 1892, and the U.S. Customs Service occupied the current building from 1907 to 1973, when it was relocated to 6 World Trade Center to serve as an anchor tenant in what was a newly built complex.[152]

The U.S. Custom House was designed in 1899 by renowned architect Cass Gilbert, who went on to design such noted civic buildings as the Supreme Court Building, the Thurgood Marshall U.S. Courthouse, the U.S. Chamber of Commerce building, the West Virginia State Capitol, and the Woolworth Building. Gilbert's plans were selected by the U.S. Treasury Department pursuant to a competitive building process among the most prestigious architectural firms of the day.[153] In designing the Custom House, Mr. Gilbert stated, "The ideal for a public building like the Custom House was that it served as an inspiration toward patriotism and good citizenship … a symbol of the civilization, culture, and ideals of our country." [154]

The Custom House was intentionally designed to face Bowling Green, rather than the harbor, as is the usual orientation for customs houses.[155] The most significant exterior decorative features are the four monumental sculptures by Daniel Chester French representing the four continents of international commerce: America, Europe, Asia, and Africa.[156] Mr. French also sculpted the statue of Abraham Lincoln that sits in the Lincoln Memorial in Washington, D.C.

In addition, the building's facade is adorned with 12 sculptures of seafaring powers: Greece, Rome, Phoenicia, Genoa, Venice, Spain, Holland, Portugal, Denmark, Germany (later changed to Belgium due to anti-German sentiments during World War I), France, and England.[157]

Considered one of this nation's finest examples of the Beaux-Arts style, the Custom House features monumentality, accurate symmetry, and elaborate ornamentation. Its design unites classical Greek and Roman architectur-

Fresco paintings (left to right) *Explorer Hudson, SS Washington Passing Ambrose Lightship,* and *Explorer Block,* in the rotunda of the Alexander Hamilton U.S. Custom House.

al elements with then-modern architectural techniques of the 20th century, with generous use of columns, pilasters, cartouches, archways, and grand staircases and entrances. Only seven stories tall and standing 142 feet, its dramatically high ceilings and interior archways nevertheless enclose a volume of space equal to approximately one-quarter of the Empire State Building—a building of 1,453 feet and 102 floors. Sculptures and paintings are integrated into the building's design. The building was renamed in honor of Alexander Hamilton in 1991.[158]

After the U.S. Customs Service moved from the building in 1973, the structure was vacant and minimally maintained. The building was saved from demolition by the creation of the Custom House Institute in 1973 and the passage of the Public Buildings Cooperative Use Act of 1978, which encouraged the federal government to reuse its historically and architecturally significant buildings. In 1979 Congress authorized $26.5 million for the building's restoration and rehabilitation. Beginning in 1983, a 12-year rehabilitation project upgraded and modernized the facility.[159]

On September 14, 1987, the Bankruptcy Court moved from its cramped quarters in Foley Square into the Custom House, while work in the other areas of the building continued. This was not a completely smooth transition, however. During winter holidays in 1989, little more than two years after the court settled into its newly renovated environs, the basement of the building flooded with water that reached all the way up to the

A fireplace in the Alexander Hamilton U.S. Custom House below the painting *New Amsterdam*.

first floor and poured into an adjacent subway station. The building's electrical power and phone lines, all of which were housed in the basement, were rendered inoperable. A navy SEAL in scuba equipment was called in to repair the pipe and stop the water flow. The on-duty judge needed to use a kerosene lamp before the bankruptcy court was temporarily relocated across the street to a nearby building on Whitehall Street. The flood was caused by a vandal who had stolen some brass valves from a main water pipe and left the water flowing.[160]

More recently, on September 11, 2001, the U.S. Custom House, with its sturdy construction and close proximity to the site of the former World Trade Center, provided refuge not only for the bankruptcy court personnel and other federal employees who work in the building, but also for many other people seeking shelter from the destruction and chaos that reigned on the streets of lower Manhattan that day. For Judge Richard L. Bohanon (now retired), who was sitting that day in the New York bankruptcy court by designation from the Bankruptcy Court for the Western District of Oklahoma, this tragic event was an ironic twist of fate—he had witnessed firsthand from his judicial chambers one block away the bombing of the Alfred P. Murrah Fed-

92 | CHAPTER TWO

eral Building in Oklahoma City on April 19, 1995.¹⁶¹ In 2012 the U.S. Custom House was hard-hit again, left without power, steam, Internet, or telephone service for many days following Hurricane Sandy.¹⁶²

The Bankruptcy Court of the Southern District of New York was and continues to be the venue for some of the largest and most important corporate bankruptcy cases in the United States, including the reorganization of General Motors and the bankruptcy estates of Enron, Global Crossing, WorldCom, Lehman Brothers, and Bernard Madoff.¹⁶³ During 2012 it handled more than 14,000 bankruptcy cases distributed among 10 judges. The Southern District handles 20 percent of all bankruptcy cases filed within the Second Circuit. Over 1,500 of these were Chapter 11 cases filed by businesses seeking to reorganize, giving the Southern Bankruptcy Court more reorganizations to handle than any other court in the country.¹⁶⁴

But it is not always hard work at the U.S. Custom House. Its beauty and grandeur have also graced movies such as *Ghostbusters II*, *Working Girl*, *Batman Forever*, *Inside Man*, *Analyze This*, *Autumn in New York*, *The Front*, *Cruising*, *How to Lose a Guy in 10 Days*, and, most recently, the remake of *Arthur*. It is also the official starting point for New York City's biggest ticker-tape parades, and championship teams and prominent dignitaries gather in the rotunda of the Custom House hosts for pre-parade breakfasts. In recent years, parades featuring the New York Yankees, the New York Giants, and Nelson Mandela have begun their marches up the Canyon of Heroes from the doors of the Custom House.

The Lehman Brothers offices in New York City on September 15, 2008, the day it filed for Chapter 11 bankruptcy protection. Associated Press Mark Lennihan.

CHAPTER THREE

THE NORTHERN DISTRICT
OF
NEW YORK

The Northern District of New York covers the largest geographic area of any New York federal district. It includes 32 upstate New York counties, bounded on the north by Canada and the St. Lawrence River, on the east by Lake Champlain and the States of Vermont and Massachusetts, on the South by the State of Pennsylvania and the Southern District of New York, and on the west by the Western District of New York.[1]

The district came into existence by Act of April 9, 1814, which divided the original District of New York into two separate districts, the Northern District of New York and the Southern District of New York.[2] Judge Matthias B. Tallmadge, the more senior of the two judges then serving the District of New York, was assigned to the Northern District.[3] That assignment of the more senior judge to the Northern District has led one chronicler to claim that it should be viewed as the eldest child of its District of New York "Mother Court," challenging the direct lineage asserted by the Southern District.[4]

In 1900 the Northern District's 17 westernmost counties were carved out to become the Western District of New York.[5] With the separation of the Western District, Binghamton and Syracuse terms were added to the Albany, Utica, and Auburn terms of the Northern District, and Syracuse was designated a place for holding the circuit court, which still existed at that time. The Northern District gained three more counties—Columbia, Green, and Ulster—in 1978, when those

Opposite, top to bottom: the James T. Foley U.S. Post Office and Courthouse in Albany, New York; the James M. Hanley Federal Building in Syracuse, New York; the Federal Building and U.S. Courthouse in Binghamton, New York; the Alexander Pirnie Federal Building in Utica, New York.

The Old Post Office and Courthouse in Auburn, New York.

counties were separated from the Southern District of New York.

The federal courthouses currently in use in the Northern District are the James M. Hanley Federal Building in Syracuse, the James T. Foley U.S. Post Office and Courthouse in Albany, the Federal Building and U.S. Courthouse in Binghamton, and the Alexander Pirnie Federal Building in Utica. The modern, geometric Hanley Building was completed in 1976. The Foley courthouse and the Binghamton Federal Building and U.S. Courthouse both were built as part of a wave of New Deal courthouse construction that took place during the 1930s, each replacing earlier buildings from the 1880s. Utica's Alexander Pirnie Federal Building was constructed during the 1920s on the site of an earlier 1880s courthouse building, portions of which were incorporated into the new structure. For nearly 100 years, the Northern District was also served by a courthouse in Auburn, since transferred to Cayuga County. That courthouse was built in 1888–1890 in Richardsonian Romanesque style.

Memorable copyright, patent, and trademark rulings, such as an 1887 decision that "Alexander Graham Bell was and is the original and first inventor of the telephone,"[6] have been heard in the courthouses of the Northern District. The district experienced an explosion of business during the era of Prohibition, as bootleggers were caught transporting liquor across the Canadian border. To deal with the press of this business, one judge held special one- or two-day "booze terms" for malefactors to come in and be sentenced, according to a contemporary news account.[7] During the same era, the government made two attempts in the Northern District to convict the bootlegger Arthur

Flegenheimer, better known as "Dutch Schultz," of tax fraud, one heard in a no-longer-used courthouse in rural Malone, the hometown of Judge Frederick H. Bryant. The district has had its share of war protest cases and, in hard times, of bankruptcy cases. The broad array of other subjects over which its judges have ruled have included First Amendment, civil rights, and prisoner rights issues.

AUBURN, NEW YORK: THE OLD POST OFFICE AND COURTHOUSE

The Old Post Office and Courthouse in Auburn, New York, was designed by the Supervising Architect of the U.S. Treasury Department, Mifflin E. Bell, in distinctive Richardsonian Romanesque style. The courthouse was built between 1888 and 1890, with expansions occurring in 1913–1914 and 1937. The lot on which it was built lies in the civic and commercial core of downtown Auburn. It is a solid, asymmetrical two-and-a-half-story building, roughly rectangular in plan. The lower walls are made of limestone, with red brick beginning at the second level. The roof is shingle-clad slate. Two massive arched entrances flank a cylindrical three-story limestone tower on the southwest corner. On the third level, triangular dormer windows on either side of the tower extend above the roofline almost to the height of the tower, clad in brick and framed in granite. Various sections of the complex roofline are ornamented by elaborate foliate-motif frieze carvings and large modillions—ornamental brackets under cornices. The building also includes a two-and-a-half-story stair tower.

Over its long period of use, the Auburn courthouse saw notable trials. In 1916 an early mail-fraud case was brought against the promoters of a weight-gain product known as "Sargol," first sold in 1908. Widely marketed as a product that could put pounds of good, solid flesh onto a thin weakling, Sargol had rapidly become a hot seller and revenue producer for its Binghamton-based owners. Its advertisements extolled the virtues of being fat and plump; for example, one headed "Let Us Make You Fat" showed two beachgoers who appeared to say of a considerably leaner couple nearby, "Gee! Look at that pair of skinny scarecrows! Why don't they try Sargol!"

Sargol's marketing campaign attracted the scrutiny of the *New York Tribune's* muckraking journalist Samuel Hopkins Adams and, eventually, of the federal government, resulting in the 1916 indictment. The 12-week jury trial was prosecuted by Assistant U.S. Attorney Frank J. Cregg before U.S. District Judge George W. Ray, with defendants represented by former U.S. Attorney George B. Curtiss and New York City attorney Abel I. Smith.

More than 40 witnesses travelled to Auburn from throughout the country to testify that they had taken Sargol and failed to gain weight.[8] Among the medical experts called by the government to testify that taking Sargol would not affect a person's weight was Dr.

The use of advertisements such as this one for the claimed weight-gain product Sargol was the subject of a 12-week jury trial in the Auburn courthouse.

Harvey Wiley, the chemist who had spearheaded passage of the Pure Food and Drug Act of 1906 and served as the first commissioner of the U.S. Food and Drug Administration.[9] The defense countered with its own experts and lay witnesses who claimed to have benefited from Sargol.[10]

Cregg's day-long closing statement for the government, in a courtroom crowded with spectators, urged the jury not to put its "stamp of approval" on Sargol's business. He accused its two owners of "sacrific[ing] their integrity on the altar of greed" and argued that "their moral conscience has been dulled in the whirlpool of iniquity."[11] Cregg's tactics, including shameless vouching for the credibility of his expert witnesses, would not have passed muster under today's more rigid standards for prosecutorial comment. After seven hours of deliberation, the jury delivered a verdict of guilty for the defendant owners. They received stiff fines, and Sargol was banned from the mails.

In 1927 U.S. District Judge Frederick H. Bryant, sitting at Auburn, became the second judge to declare that "fight films"—films depicting boxing matches—could legally be shown in New York or any other state, even though a federal law, the Sims Act of 1912, then banned the interstate transport of such films. The movement to ban fight films had gained steam after the victory of African American boxer Jack Johnson over white boxer James Jeffries in 1910. Judge Bryant ruled that exhibitors receiving fight films from persons other than common carriers could legally show the films, absent evidence that the exhibitor was himself involved in the illegal transport.[12] The Sims Act was repealed in 1940.

In the 40 years following 1927, no federal jury trials were held at the Auburn courthouse. Instead, terms of the Northern District of New York rotated among a circuit of several cities within the district, including Albany, Binghamton, Syracuse, and Utica. Rural Malone, the hometown of Judge Bryant, was also part of the circuit for a time. Auburn resumed hosting jury terms with the appointment to the bench of Judge Edmund Port in 1964.

In the turbulent 1960s and 1970s, the Auburn courthouse played host to proceedings touching on some of the most contentious issues of the day. Bruce Dancis, president of the Cornell chapter of Students for a Democratic Society, tore up his draft card at a rally on Cornell's campus on December 14, 1966, in full view of television cameras and mailed it to his local draft board.[13] In doing so, Dancis became one of the first people in the country to publicly destroy a draft card. His action sparked widespread antidraft protests, with Dancis and other Cornell activists organizing the first large-scale draft-card burning in New York's Central Park in April 1967. Dancis was convicted of mutilating his draft card after a one-day nonjury trial before Judge Edmund Port, who sentenced him to an indefinite term of imprisonment under the federal Youth Corrections Act. The trial was held at Syracuse, with the sentencing in Auburn.[14] On appeal, a Second Circuit panel affirmed the conviction,[15] and Dancis served 18 months in jail.

On November 2, 1970, several inmates at the Auburn Prison seized a microphone and declared "Black Solidarity Day" in the prison courtyard. Such a commemoration had not been authorized, and 14 prisoners were confined to their cells as punishment. This action touched off a larger breakdown in prison order on November 4, as rebelling "inmates armed with pipes and boards seized thirty guards as hostages." The inmates succeeded in taking control of the entire prison, except the administration building, for nearly seven hours, and the disturbance was quelled only with the arrival of hundreds of state troopers.[16] Six Auburn inmates were indicted in January 1971 by a Cayuga County grand jury for their involvement in the riot. Subsequently, the six prisoners filed a federal civil action contending that their continued confinement at Auburn, particularly their segregation from other prisoners and abuse by guards, was unconstitutionally interfering with their ability to prepare their defense to the criminal charges. They requested that the Court order their transfer to a federal penitentiary.

The James T. Foley Post Office and U.S. Courthouse shown in a 1935 photograph, when it was newly opened.

During a trial held in spring 1971 before Judge Port, the prisoners alleged that they had been subject to beatings and abuse from guards in the months following the riot. Youthful student protesters supporting the "Auburn Six" filled the courthouse during the trial. Several prison officials, called as witnesses for the state, denied mistreating the inmates.[17] Judge Port never issued a ruling in the case. By July 1971, the state had transferred each of the Auburn Six to other prisons.[18] Five of the six inmates ended up pleading guilty to reduced charges stemming from the riot.[19]

Judge Port assumed senior status in 1976, serving until his death in 1986. The Auburn courthouse was taken out of service by the federal government in 1984. It was acquired by Cayuga County, New York, and now houses the Cayuga County Supreme Court and the Auburn City Court. The Northern District of New York continued for some time to use these courtrooms by prior agreement with the county, usually for about one week each year during summer. The courthouse was added to the National Registry of Historical Places in 1991 as an excellent example of Richardsonian Romanesque architecture.

ALBANY: JAMES T. FOLEY POST OFFICE AND U.S. COURTHOUSE

The James T. Foley Post Office and U.S. Courthouse has served Albany since 1934. In earlier years the court had sat in the 1880s U.S. Custom House and Post Office designed by Supervising Architects James G. Hill and Mifflin E. Bell, a building now in use by the New York State Department of Education.

The Foley building was designed through the collaborative efforts of two local Albany architectural firms, Gander, Gander & Gander and Norman R. Sturgis, and a New York City–based consulting architect named Electus Litchfield. The five-story building is Art Deco in style, combining modern forms with ornate yet stylized decorative elements. The walls are of light Vermont

One of the two imposing public entrances to the Foley courthouse. An eight-foot high eagle carved from Vermont marble by sculptor Albert T. Stewart sits inset above each entrance to the Foley courthouse just in front of an Art Deco aluminum screen by artist Benjamin Hawkins.

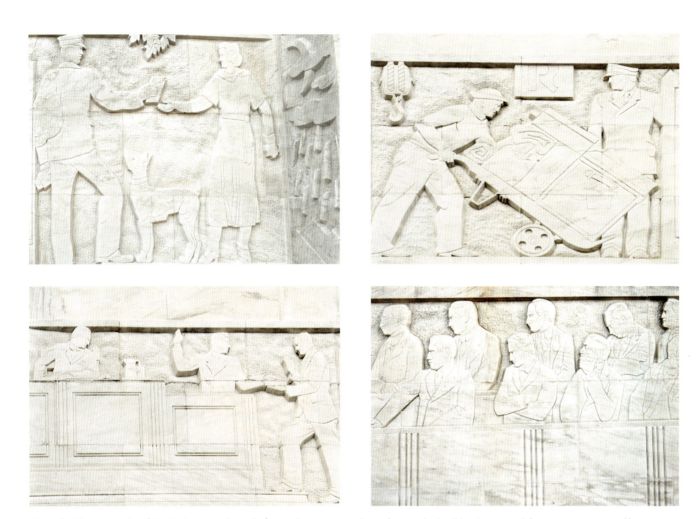

Top left: The west side of the Foley courthouse's frieze shows scenes that relate to the building's original function as a post office, here showing the delivery of mail. *Top right*: The north side of the frieze shows scenes relating to the building's original function as a custom house, here showing baggage being transported. *Bottom*: The south side of the frieze shows scenes that relate to the building's function as a courthouse, such as the one on the left, showing a witness being sworn in, and on the right, showing a jury.

Eureka marble, rising from a granite base with vertical lines of windows emphasizing the height of the building. The main facade has two monumental public entrances, one at each end, and is slightly recessed in the center. When discussing the building, the architects used the term "modern classical" to describe the bones of the building, instructing observers, "Squint your eyes, look in perspective and note the classical proportions."[20]

Wide granite stairs at each end of the courthouse, lead up to the entrances. Sculptures of imposing eagles, more than eight feet high, are inset above each entrance, just in front of Art Deco aluminum screens by artist Benjamin Hawkins. The eagles were carved from a 17-ton Vermont marble block by English-born New York sculptor Albert T. Stewart.[21]

Sculptor Stewart also was commissioned to design a bas-relief frieze band for the building. Perhaps the building's most remarkable exterior feature, the frieze runs high along the north, east, and west facades at the fifth-floor level, attracting the eye upward. To make the frieze scenes visible from the street, Stewart modeled its figures as large as eight feet tall. The scenes celebrate the three traditional federal functions originally served within the Foley building: post office, custom house, and federal court. On the front, or west, facade of the building, the scenes relate to the transport and delivery of mail. The images on the north side relate to the shipping and inspection of goods. Images on the south facade show legal proceedings.

Top: Oil-on-canvas murals by Ethel M. Parsons on the ceiling of the James T. Foley U.S. Courthouse and Post Office's massive lobby depicting the seven continents. *Bottom left*: Parsons' mural originally showed Europe and the flags of its nations as they appeared in 1935, but the post-World War II German flag was later painted over the original 1935 German swastika. *Bottom right*: The mural of North America.

Top: The Art Deco interior of the Foley courthouse. *Bottom left*: The Foley courthouse's interior stairway has marble treads, black marble risers, and aluminum railings with stylized inserts designed by Italian artist Enea Biafora. *Bottom center and right*: Stylized motifs in the courthouse's interior stairway railing such as the scales of justice relate to the building's multiple original functions.

One of two original courtrooms still in use in the James T. Foley U.S. Courthouse and Post Office with its ornamented ceiling, Art Deco light fixtures, and ornamental grillwork depicting a stylized eagle.

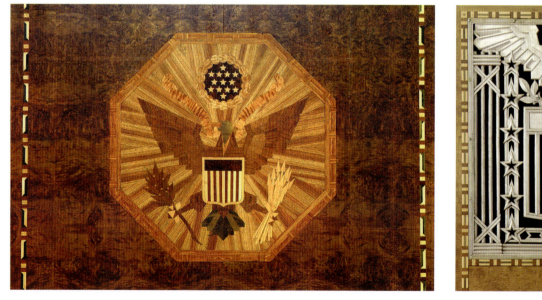

Left: An elaborate wood inlay behind the judge's bench shows an eagle clutching 13 arrows and an olive branch and other elements of the U.S. seal, such as stars and stripes. *Right:* Ornamental grillwork also depicts a stylized eagle.

On the judicial portion of the frieze, a scene of a 12-member jury observing trial proceedings reflects the natural variances in juror attentiveness that many trial lawyers have come to experience. Several jurors appear to be listening carefully, but most of the jurors seem markedly less conscientious and one seems to be sleeping.

Another section of the frieze depicts a trial proceeding where a witness is being sworn in for testimony. The witness appears to appreciate the solemnity of the occasion. The judge, however, sneers down at the witness, appearing peeved. According to local legend, these scenes memorialized frieze sculptor Stewart's perception of friction during the building's design and construction efforts between its Albany architects and the New York City-based Litchfield. The three conscientious jurors are said to bear the likenesses of the Albany architects, while the impatient judge is said to resemble Litchfield.[22]

Another part of the frieze depicts a portion of a clock tower, showing a time of 4:10. The clock bears a close resemblance to the clock tower of Independence Hall, which is depicted on the back of the $100 bill. According to the Bureau of Engraving and Printing of the U.S. Department of the Treasury, that image of the Independence Hall clock (when examined under sufficient magnification) reflects the time of 4:10.[23]

The courthouse's interior is Art Deco in style. The interior walls and floors include six types of marble. Marble mosaic medallions are inset in the north and south lobby floors. Marble pilasters divide the massive main lobby into nine bays, each with a ceiling mural.

Artist Ethel M. Parsons painted the oil-on-canvas murals in 1935 depicting the seven continents, the North Pole, and the United States, with each country indicated by its national flag. Because the maps were intended to portray the world as it was in 1935, the European map displayed the German swastika as a national flag. Many years later, when the maps were restored, the GSA required the postwar German flag to be painted over the swastikas to prevent the map from being offensive to viewers, even though that flag did not exist in 1935. Interspersed with the murals are plaster plaques by Italian artist Enea Biafora portraying famous Americans, such as Abraham Lincoln, Benjamin Franklin, and George Washington.

The interior courthouse stairs have marble treads with black marble risers and cast-aluminum railings, also designed by Biafora, with stylized motifs such as an airplane and the scales of justice that relate to the multiple original functions of the building. The two original courtrooms retain many original features, including marble floors, ornamental grillwork, an inlaid eagle on the wood wall behind the judge's bench, ornamented plaster ceilings, and Art Deco light fixtures. In 1980 the building was listed in the National Register of Historic Places as part of the Downtown Albany Historic District.[24]

In 1988 the courthouse was named after the Honorable James T. Foley. Prior to his appointment to the federal bench by President Truman in 1949, Foley served as law secretary to a New York state supreme court justice. He interrupted his legal career to enlist in the U.S. Navy and served in combat in both the Atlantic and Pacific theaters of World War II.[25] Following his elevation to the bench, he served as U.S. District Judge for 40 years. He was Chief Judge of the Northern District of New York from 1963 to 1980, and he issued noteworthy decisions in the fields of civil and prisoner rights, labor law, and railroad disability law. At the courthouse dedication ceremony on October 27, 1988, Second Circuit Judge Roger Miner said, "Harry S. Truman . . . unleashed two powerful forces [on the world]: the Atomic Bomb and James T. Foley. In designating the building the James T. Foley Courthouse, Congress has recognized the more powerful of the two."[26]

Notable cases adjudicated at the Foley courthouse include a ruling on the applicability of the First Amendment to a 1981 rugby game. That year, while South Africa remained subject to apartheid, the South African Springboks rugby team toured the United States to play a series of matches against American teams. People across the country called for cancellation

The James M. Hanley Federal Building and U.S. Courthouse and Sol LeWitt's painted aluminum sculpture *One, Two, Three* (center far left). The building's white plaza incorporates green space.

of the matches to protest apartheid, believing that cancellation would send a clear message of condemnation to the South African government. In response to the opposition, matches were canceled in New York City and Chicago. When the City of Albany decided to allow the match scheduled at its Bleecker Stadium to proceed as planned, Governor Hugh Carey intervened and canceled the game, on the basis that the match would require massive cost for police and crowd control.[27] However, the American all-star Eastern Rugby Union (slated to play the Springboks) did not agree with the cancellation. They took the position that they were not interested in politics and just wanted to play the game they loved against the world's elite team. The team's president, interviewed on a September 14, 1981 telecast of ABC's *Nightline*, told host Ted Koppel that the Eastern Rugby Union "does not have a foreign policy."[28]

The Eastern Rugby team filed suit in federal court to enjoin the Governor's cancellation edict, thus raising the novel question: did the First Amendment protect the right to play a sporting event? Northern District Judge Howard G. Munson decided that, indeed, a sports team's refusal to acknowledge political implications of a sporting event did deserve First Amendment protection. Thus the Governor's cancellation unconstitutionally deprived the players of "their right to withstand political criticism by pursuing an activity which they choose to view as apolitical."[29] The Second Circuit affirmed, allowing the match to proceed.[30] In response to an emergency application to the Supreme Court, Justice Thurgood Marshall refused to stay the game. It was played in the pouring rain while Hudson Valley resident and noted songwriter Pete Seeger led a crowd of 1,000 gathered outside the stadium in singing protest songs. Inside the stadium, a small crowd of approximately 300 spectators watched the Eastern Union All-Stars lose to the Springboks, 41–0.[31]

More recently, the courthouse was the site of proceedings against former New York State Majority Leader Joseph Bruno on corruption charges. After a week of jury deliberations, Bruno initially was convicted in 2009 of two charges of carrying out a scheme to defraud the State of New York of his honest services by using his office for personal gain, and acquitted of other charges. His conviction was later overturned by the Second Circuit after an intervening Supreme Court ruling that "honest services" convictions require proof of direct bribes or kickbacks, which had not been charged. A re-trial resulted in his acquittal.[32]

In a 2012 voting-rights case, Chief Judge Gary L. Sharpe ruled that to protect voting rights, the New York primary had to be held early enough that absentee ballots from overseas could be counted. His opinion began, "Nothing is more critical to a vibrant democratic society than citizen participation in government through the act of voting. It is unconscionable to send men and women overseas to preserve our democracy while simultaneously disenfranchising them while they are gone."[33]

SYRACUSE: JAMES M. HANLEY FEDERAL BUILDING

On September 9, 1966, Representative James M. Hanley unveiled plans for a new federal building in Syracuse, New York, which would include space for the district court, besting 179 communities across the nation for the funds. Hanley, a Democratic Congressman in largely Republican upstate New York, had been working to obtain funding for the project since his election in 1964. As reported in the *Syracuse Post-Standard*, both the GSA and the U.S. Bureau of the Budget approved $24 million for construction.[34]

The Hanley building's centrally-located plaza has been favored as a site by demonstrators. John Berry/*The Post-Standard*.

The earlier Syracuse federal building, which also housed a post office and other federal offices in addition to the district court, included only 10,100 square feet for the court, although Syracuse was at the time the largest city in the Northern District and handled its heaviest caseload. The new plans called for almost double the space, to address what the GSA called the "deficient" and inadequate facilities, "unsatisfactory" arrangement of the courtrooms, and "sub-standard" courtrooms."[35]

The Syracuse firm Sargent, Webster, Crenshaw & Folley was chosen to design the new courthouse. Construction was not without difficulty. As the *Syracuse Herald-Journal* reported, the building's completion lagged about 15 months behind schedule as a result of "strikes by subcontractors, a fire in March 1975, and a delay in the installation of the new ceiling." Move-in finally began in May 1976 and was undertaken in stages.[36] At the time of the building's completion, there reportedly were no plans for a name for the complex. It was later named the Hanley Federal Building, in honor of the man who had championed its construction.[37]

Representative Hanley served eight terms in the U.S. House. He was an early supporter of Medicare, the Elementary and Secondary Education Act, the Head Start program, and the "war on poverty."[38]

A courtroom in the Hanley building, now in use as a magistrate judge's courtroom.

The high-rise structure named for him comprises four rectangular blocks of white, reinforced, poured concrete. The blocks, of varying heights, are arranged on a platform. The strong verticals of the high-rise are balanced by the horizontal lines of alternating windows and scored concrete. As one commentator noted, "the play with rectangular forms is repeated in narrow window bands and in the ribbing of the concrete blocks."[39]

The plaza area of the Hanley Federal Building was reconstructed in 2007 as part of the GSA's First Impressions Program, which applies federal Design Excellence Principles to existing federal buildings, particularly their public areas, such as lobbies and plazas.[40] The new plaza has a clean white entry that incorporates green space. The courthouse showcases a sculpture by Sol LeWitt, called *One, Two, Three*, commissioned by GSA as part of the Art in Architecture Program. The minimalist painted-aluminum sculpture combines open rectangles, repeating the building's stark geometric forms.[41] Today, the plaza incorporates the needs of its diverse user groups, respects the historic integrity and design intent of the original building's architecture and landscape architecture, and provides a civic space for daily use and special events.

Since its construction, the Hanley Federal Building has served as a cornerstone of the historic Clinton Square district in downtown Syracuse. Between the early 1980s and 2009, a local charitable organization called the "UpDowntowners" partnered with the GSA to produce a weekly summertime event called "Party in the Plaza," which brought thousands of attendees to evening concerts.[42] More recently, a community garden was planted in the building's lawn as part of a national effort by the Department of Agriculture to support First Lady Michelle Obama's emphasis on gardening and healthy lifestyles.[43]

Chambers in the Hanley building of the Hon. Frederick J. Scullin Jr., Senior U.S. District Court Judge.

As a symbol of government and a downtown focal point, the courthouse plaza also has seen its share of community protests. In recent times, the Hanley Federal Building Plaza has been a venue for demonstrations by groups as diverse as the Tea Party, Planned Parenthood, and Occupy Wall Street.[44]

In 2005, the courthouse was the site of the controversial trial of Dr. Rafil A. Dhafir, an Iraqi-born American physician charged with violating the Iraqi Sanctions Regulations by transferring funds and resources to persons in Iraq. The charges arose from a charity called Help the Needy, which provided food, medicine, and other support to Iraqi citizens, and which, the indictment claimed, was not licensed to provide such humanitarian relief. While the charges attracted protests, the conviction was upheld by the Second Circuit, although it remanded the case to the district court for resentencing.[45]

The courthouse has been the site of major patent and trademark litigation. In 2008 Judge Randall Ray Rader, sitting by designation from the Federal Circuit, presided over a trial in which the jury found that Hewlett-Packard had infringed patents held by Cornell University by incorporating their method for out-of-order instruction processing, a way of increasing computer speed by allowing simultaneous processing of certain instructions. The $184 million awarded to Cornell University was later reduced to $53.5 million in an influential ruling on the proper method for determining patent infringement damages.[46]

In hard economic times, the court has seen bankruptcy filings by entities ranging from the Oswego Speedway to the Syracuse Symphony Orchestra. On a brighter note, the courthouse has been the site of naturalization proceedings for a large number of prospective United States citizens.

The Federal Building and U.S. Courthouse in Binghamton as it originally appeared in 1935.

BINGHAMTON FEDERAL BUILDING AND U.S. COURTHOUSE

Binghamton's Federal Building and U.S. Courthouse was built between 1934 and 1935 during the increase in courthouse construction that took place during the Great Depression. The court had previously sat in the U.S. Post Office and Courthouse, a towered structure built in 1891 under Supervising Architect Will A. Freret.[47]

Property for a new building was acquired in 1916, but World War I and other events kept the building project dormant for many years. The building's construction was originally authorized under the Public Buildings Act of 1926, which allocated $165 million for new federal buildings across the country. The Keyes-Elliott Act of 1930 permitted private architectural firms to compete for certain federal projects. Local Binghamton architecture firm Conrad & Cummings took advantage of this opportunity and won the project in 1934, just before the amendment lapsed and government architects resumed responsibility for federal buildings. The contract for construction of the courthouse was awarded to the Chicago firm Coath & Goss in July 1934. It completed the building in 1935, for $448,200.

The Federal Building and U.S. Courthouse is classical in style, with a strong Art Deco influence. The design epitomizes the credo of Louis A. Simon, superintendent of the Treasury Department's Architectural Division from 1905 to 1933 and its Supervising Architect from 1933 to 1939: "Moderne Traditionalized,

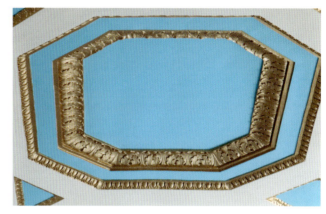

Top left: An Art Deco-style American eagle appears in a panel above each entrance to the Binghamton Federal Building and U.S. Courthouse. *Bottom left:* Green window frames installed during a renovation restore the window frames' original color, which had faded to gray. *Top right:* Original Art Deco bronze, copper and glass pendulum light fixtures, still in use in the courthouse lobby. *Center right:* The courthouse's blue ceiling decoration. *Bottom right:* Green-veined white American Pavanazzo marble is used in the courthouse lobby.

Left: The second floor courtroom in Binghamton's Federal Building and U.S. Courthouse. *Top:* One of the original Art-Deco light fixtures in the second floor courtroom. *Above:* The second floor courtroom's decorative cast-iron ceiling grille.

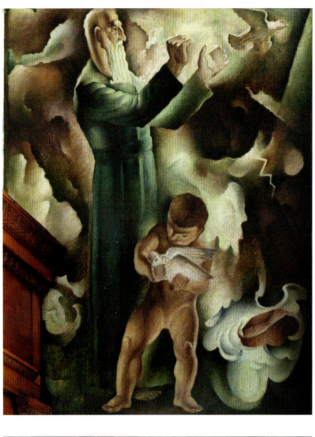 

Figures from four of the eight murals by Kenneth Leland Washburn on the Binghamton courthouse's upper walls.

the Traditional Modernized." The steel-framed building's principal cladding materials are Indiana limestone above a granite base. The U-shaped four-story structure comprises 105,000 square feet. An austere and temple-like facade consists of a seven-bay-wide, three-story colonnade surmounted by a continuous Greek key frieze. The centered entranceway grouping is recessed behind a monumental limestone colonnade. Each of the three entries has a carved marble surround with inset panels of cast-iron semicircular scallops set below larger panels, each depicting an Art Deco–style American eagle.

The building once housed the Social Security Administration office, as well as the U.S. Post Office. Eye-level slots in the "spying gallery" still remain in walls in the basement, where postal inspectors patrolled alleys within the walls and secretly peered out at the mail sorters to ensure that cash or contraband was not taken out of the mail envelopes.

Many changes have been made to the building over the years. In 1967 the U.S. Post Office and Social Security Administration moved out of the building to a new location several blocks away. The building now houses U.S. agencies such as the IRS and FBI, as well as the U.S. Attorney's Office and includes office space for New York's U.S. Senators. In 1986 Thomas J. McAvoy became the first judge to be permanently assigned to the courthouse. At Judge McAvoy's request, soon afterward the building security checkpoint was moved from the second floor to the building lobby.

In 2002, as a result of the leadership of U.S. Congressman Maurice Hinchey, the Federal Building and U.S. Courthouse became one of the first federal buildings to be wind-powered. Alternative energy, provided by wind farms in upstate New York, provides 100 percent of the building's power. Other changes have been made to restore the building to its original form. Outside window frames had been gray for so long that gray was thought to be the original color. A review of early photographs revealed that the frames were originally green, and new green window frames were installed during a recent renovation. After the U.S. Post Office moved out, a brass sign placed on the building's front facade had eliminated "United States Post Office" from the name, so that it read instead: "Federal Building and Courthouse." Several years ago, the brass sign was removed so that the original name etched in stone can be seen, reading once again: "United States Post Office and Courthouse."

While much of the courthouse's interior has changed, the lobby and second-floor courtroom feature their original finishes. The marble in the lobby is American Pavanazzo, a green-veined white variety. The lobby has its original blue ceiling decoration and Art Deco bronze, copper, and glass pendant light fixtures. The lobby upper walls feature eight murals by artist and Cornell University Art Professor Kenneth Leland Washburn. These large-scale murals include scenes of local agriculture, industry, the U.S. Mail Service, and clothed figures releasing doves, unfolding in muted colors below a cloud-filled background with nude figures, including one blowing wind toward sailing ships.

The double-height second-floor courtroom features original entry doors clad in vinyl with brass studs, brass kick plates, and oval windows. A paneled oak wainscot surrounds the space. The judge's bench, gallery benches, and turned-spindle court rail are original. The paneled ceiling features decorative cast-iron grilles and original light fixtures.

As Binghamton is the birthplace of many technology companies, such as IBM, Lockheed Martin, BAE Systems, and Rockwell Collins, this court, too, has seen its share of patent- and technology-related cases. In the political arena, one of its most famous trials involved the "St. Patrick's Day Four," a group of antiwar protesters who in 2003 threw their own blood on an army recruiting center, a soldier, and an American flag. The four, representing themselves pro se, claimed that their actions were legally justified because they acted to stop the United States from invading Iraq. They were each found guilty of three counts of damaging federal property.[48] During the economic downturn following the 2007–2008 financial crisis, the courthouse saw many individual bankruptcy cases, as well.

The courthouse has landmark status and is listed in the National Register of Historic Places as a contributing building to the State Street–Henry Street Historic District. The Binghamton Federal Building and U.S. Courthouse has changed with the times, while still conveying the dignity and the authority of federal government intended by its sponsors when the building was constructed in the midst of the Great Depression.

UTICA: ALEXANDER PIRNIE U.S. COURTHOUSE AND FEDERAL BUILDING

The first session of the Northern District was held in Utica in 1815, in the Old Utica Courthouse on John Street, with Judge Matthias B. Tallmadge presiding.

Utica, New York's earlier Broad Street courthouse, completed in 1882 and partially demolished in 1928. Portions of the courthouse were incorporated into the present-day courthouse, the Alexander Pirnie Federal Building and U.S. Courthouse.

A U.S. Courthouse and Post Office designed by the Supervising Architect of the U.S. Treasury Department, James G. Hill, was completed in 1882 and housed both the district court and, until its abolition, the circuit court.[49] Situated on Broad Street, the courthouse was built in the heart of the City of Utica. It was partially demolished in 1928 and replaced with the present courthouse, which incorporates portions of the earlier building's stone walls and its basement vaults. The present Alexander Pirnie U.S. Courthouse and Federal Building was completed in 1929. It was designed by Louis A. Simon, at the direction of Supervising Architect of the Treasury James A. Wetmore.

The three-story building sits above a slightly raised basement. The basement, first floor, and second floor are roughly square, with the third floor U-shaped. The walls are clad in buff-colored brick, except for the base and center front, which are clad in limestone. The front face on Broad Street is divided into 11 bays marked by two-story Corinthian pilasters supporting an entablature—a horizontal part in classical architecture that rests on the columns and consists of architrave (beam), frieze, and cornice. The entablature extends the full length of the front facade and around both sides. In the center of the frieze are the words "Post Office," "Court House," and "Custom House." Like many federal buildings of the day, it originally included a post office and a custom house, in addition to courtrooms. The post office remained in the building for about fifty years. The two entrances, at the opposite ends of the building, feature fluted Tuscan pilasters and an entablature, each approached by granite steps bounded by limestone-clad sidewalls.

The east-facing, John Street side of the building is divided into 13 bays, covered by a pitched slate roof. The western, Franklin Street side is similar, except that the rear six bays of the third floor extend above the pitched roof to allow for the height of the courtroom. The rear of the building adapts to its U-shaped third floor.

The public lobby extends across the front of the building and is one of its most elaborate spaces. The floor is terrazzo with red and white marble borders. Wide arched openings lead to stairways. Wide corridors extend toward the rear of the building.

The architectural style is sometimes described as "Starved Classicism," a popular style for public buildings of the 1920s and 1930s, characterized by a restrained, unornamented take on Neoclassical Revival. Today, in addition to the federal courts, the building holds offices of several federal agencies. Remnants of the post-office facilities, such as its boxes and windows, can be seen in the building's lobby.

The courthouse is named for Alexander Pirnie, the Republican congressman who represented the area in the House of Representatives from 1959 to 1973, after serving in Europe in World War II. While in the House, Pirnie drew the first capsule of the Vietnam draft lottery on December 1, 1969. Since 1999, U.S. District Judge David N. Hurd has held court at the Utica courthouse. The United States Bankruptcy Court for the

Alexander Pirnie Federal Building and U.S. Courthouse in Utica.

Northern District of New York also sits at Utica, with Bankruptcy Judge Diane Davis currently serving as the resident judge.

During the 1920s, Utica was the site of several notable criminal trials arising under the National Prohibition Act, also known as the Volstead Act. In 1927 two Utica residents, Rosario Gambino and Joseph Lima, were arrested near the Canadian border after New York state troopers searched their vehicle while Gambino was inside. The agents found liquor, which they seized as evidence, and Gambino and Lima were indicted for conspiracy to import and transport alcoholic beverages. In a defense strategy that became more common in a later era, the defendants moved to suppress the liquor as evidence on the ground that government agents searched the vehicle without a warrant or probable cause, in violation of their constitutional rights. Judge Frank Cooper of the Northern District denied suppression and held the evidence admissible.

In *Gambino v. United States*,[50] the Supreme Court reversed the defendants' convictions. The opinion of the Court, delivered by Justice Brandeis, concluded that the search had violated the defendants' Fourth and Fifth Amendment rights. Although the Bill of Rights at that time applied only to the federal government, the Supreme Court held that the state troopers were effectively acting as federal agents because they were searching for evidence only of federal crimes, given that New York State then had no Prohibition laws of its own.

A later case heard in the Alexander Pirnie courthouse led to a Supreme Court decision that was, at the time, a key step forward in consideration of mandatory auto-insurance laws. The case arose under a New York statute that allowed the license of an uninsured driver

THE NORTHERN DISTRICT OF NEW YORK | 117

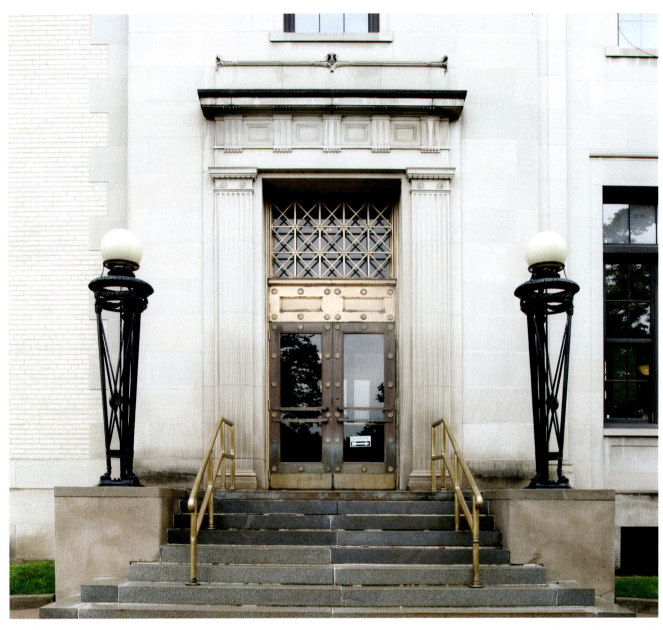

Alexander Pirnie Federal Building and U.S. Courthouse in Utica. The entrance feature fluted Tuscan pilasters and an entablature and are approached by granite steps, flanked by tall torcheres.

found at fault in an accident to be suspended until the driver purchased insurance. The suspension could last for up to three years if a judgment arising from the accident remained unpaid. A motorist, George C. Reitz, challenged the constitutionality of this legislation on the ground that it deprived him of property without due process of law. Reitz also argued that the New York statute conflicted with the federal Bankruptcy Act, by requiring him to pay a judgment for damages arising from the accident in order to restore his driving privileges, although the judgment had been discharged in bankruptcy. A three-judge panel of the district court upheld the statute, opining that drivers with a financial interest in being safe were less likely to drive carelessly.[51] The Supreme Court affirmed the Northern District's ruling, in a subsequently overruled 5–4 decision.[52]

The courthouses of the Northern District, varied in their architecture and settings, continue effectively to serve the district's enormous geographic range and its wide-ranging and diverse cases.

118 | CHAPTER THREE

Top: Reminders of the former post-office facilities can be seen in the Pirnie building's lobby.
Bottom: A wood-paneled courtroom in the Pirnie courthouse.

CHAPTER FOUR

THE EASTERN DISTRICT OF NEW YORK

Two striking contemporary courthouses and a restored Romanesque building dating back to 1892 serve the wide-ranging docket of the Eastern District of New York. In Brooklyn, the district court sits in the Theodore Roosevelt U.S. Courthouse, where a Cesar Pelli–designed building, completed in 2006, smoothly integrates with the 1960s Emanuel Celler Courthouse. Due south, Eastern District bankruptcy proceedings take place in the Conrad B. Duberstein U.S. Bankruptcy Courthouse, the same building that once served as the district court's first permanent home. Restored and expanded in 2005 by R. M. Kliment & Frances Halsband Architects, and now listed on the National Register of Historic Places, the Duberstein building also contains the U.S. Postal Service, the U.S. Attorney's Office, and the U.S. Trustee's Office.

In Central Islip, Long Island, the district court's home is the starkly modern Alfonse M. D'Amato U.S. Courthouse, opened in 2000, designed by architect Richard Meier. Both the two modern courthouses and the redesigned Duberstein courthouse use glass and light-filled interior space to exemplify the transparency of the justice system and its openness to the public. The architecture also reflects and embodies the accessibility and sense of collegiality for which the Eastern District has become known over its 150-year history.

Opposite, top to bottom: Theodore Roosevelt U.S. Courthouse, connected by a central entranceway to the Emanuel Celler U.S. Courthouse; Conrad B. Duberstein U.S. Bankruptcy Court; Alfonse M. D'Amato U.S. Courthouse.

One of the Eastern District's earliest locations, at 189–91 Montague Street.

EARLY HISTORY

The Eastern District began as a separate district in February 1865, when President Lincoln signed into law a bill "to facilitate proceedings in admiralty . . . in the Port of New York."[1] The Act removed Long Island and Staten Island from the then Southern District, creating the new Eastern District of New York.[2] In its earliest years, the Eastern District consisted of a single judge, the Honorable Charles L. Benedict, and had no permanent quarters.[3] Its first court session was held at Brooklyn City Hall, with later sessions held in the County Courthouse, the City Court of Brooklyn, at 168–170 and 189–191 Montague Street, and in two remodeled buildings at 40 Clinton Street, where a courtroom was erected in the back yard.

Brooklyn at the time was still Long Island's "big city," with a population of almost 300,000.[4] It had not yet been consolidated into Greater New York, as it would be in 1898. Its diverse economy included shipyards, some of the country's largest breweries, hat factories, glue factories, and chemical works. Commercial and political life centered around Brooklyn City Hall, later to be called Borough Hall, where the Brooklyn federal courthouses would be built.

After the Brooklyn Bridge, proclaimed the "Eighth Wonder of the World," opened in 1883, providing easy access between Manhattan and Brooklyn, Brooklyn's population increased dramatically.[5] New Yorkers began leaving their crowded island for the aristocratic sections of the larger borough. This growing population meant, among many other things, that Brooklyn needed a new post office to handle its mail. In 1885 planning began for this first federal building the Eastern District would call home.[6]

UNITED STATES POST OFFICE AND COURTHOUSE

On April 22, 1892, the Eastern District moved into the newly opened U.S. Post Office and Courthouse building, located on what is now known as Cadman Plaza East, a site it occupied for the next 72 years.[7] Built from 1885 to 1892, the original building (now restored as the Duberstein Courthouse) reflected the typical Romanesque Revival style of late 19th-century federal buildings.[8]

The Supervising Architect of the Treasury Department, Mifflin E. Bell, designed the original four-story building with strong, simple forms. A belt course encircling the building distinguishes the four levels, each articulated in a slightly different way: round arches of polished granite dominate the first story; rectangular windows surrounded by contrasting trim were used on the second floor; round-arch openings were used on the third; and the fourth story has steeply pitched dormers with round-arch windows under a slate-covered mansard roof topped with ornamental ironwork cresting. Because much of the original appropriation for the building had been spent purchasing the costly site near Brooklyn City Hall, some of the more elaborate architectural details of Bell's original design, such as larger corner towers, were never executed.[9]

The courthouse's original interior included an atrium extending from the second to the fourth floor and a main staircase featuring a decorative cast-iron balustrade with lantern-style newel posts. Mahogany Tennessee marble wainscot was used to line the stairwell walls—the same type of wainscot used on the walls of the original 1892 courtrooms. Large courtrooms wrapped around a skylit central court. On the exterior, the peaked bell tower rising above the roof of the original building has been part of the downtown Brooklyn skyline for over a century.

Expansion began almost immediately after the U.S. Post Office and Courthouse opened, when truck yards were added in 1916. In 1933 a new annex tripled the building's size. The seven-story U-shaped addition was dressed in granite and a granite-like terra-cotta. Inside, the original courthouse's light-filled central court became the sorting room for the postal workers. Although elsewhere in the United States courthouse architects were designing in the federal classicism of the time, the annex was perceptibly Romanesque, like the original building.

As anticipated, admiralty cases made up much of the Eastern District's early caseload. The court heard cases arising out of collisions, strikes, maritime liens, groundings, injuries to longshoremen, and the operation of tugboats, yachts, and oceangoing vessels. After the passage of the 1919 National Prohibition Act, also known as the Volstead Act, ensuing cases included ones involving the seizure of vessels used in importing banned alcohol.[10] Cases concerning the seizure of foreign vessels also passed before the court during war periods.

World War I brought new cases, including issues relating to enforcement of selective-service laws. World

The Duquesne spy ring, whose members are shown here in their mug shots, inspired the book and film "The House on 92nd Street."

THE EASTERN DISTRICT OF NEW YORK | 123

The Eastern District court occupied this building in 1892, whose tower has long been part of the Brooklyn skyline.

War II ushered in an era of dealing with spies and treason. In one such case, known as the Duquesne conspiracy, Herman Lang and 32 other defendants were charged with conspiracy "to act as agents of the German Reich without prior notification to the Secretary of State," transmitting military information to Germany, and unlawful conspiracy to disclose national defense information.[11] Fourteen of the defendants were convicted, with one successfully overturning the most serious charge on appeal because the information he disclosed had already become public.[12] The case inspired the 1945 film *The House on 92nd Street*."[13]

In another case, a U.S. army officer was sentenced to 25 years for the rarely charged crime of treason, after he flew a P-38 from Pomigliano Airfield, north of Naples, Italy, to Milan to defect to the Nazis and cooperate with their propaganda officers.[14]

In 1958 Russian master spy Col. Rudolph I. Abel was found guilty of spying in a case that involved the classic elements of mystery novels—hollowed-out bolts, coins and pencils with coded microfilm messages, and false identity papers.[15] The case was dramatized in the 1959 film *The FBI Story*.[16] Abel, sentenced to 30 years, was exchanged in Berlin in 1963 for Gary T. Powers, the U-2 pilot shot down and held in Russia for spying. Abel's attorney subsequently wrote about the case in the best seller *Strangers on a Bridge*.[17]

Aircraft litigation proliferated in the Eastern District after the opening of LaGuardia Airport in 1939 and later Idlewild Airport (now John F. Kennedy International) in 1948. In one early case, the court reviewed an attempt by the Village of Cedarhurst to prohibit flights above it at less than 1,000 feet.[18] Luckily for aviation, the court held the village's prohibition unconstitutional. If enforced, the prohibition would have closed down Kennedy Airport. More recently, multidistrict litigation arising from the downing of Pan Am Flight 101 at Lockerbie, Scotland, was consolidated in the Eastern District by the Judicial Panel on Multidistrict Litigation.[19]

The Eastern District has one of the busiest naturalization dockets in the nation. On Veterans Day 1954, naturalization proceedings took place all over the country, including one at Ebbets Field in which the court naturalized 6,982 individuals in a single ceremony.[20]

In the years between 1940 and 1960, the population of Queens, Nassau, and Suffolk Counties skyrocketed. Former stretches of farmland turned into suburban communities, while suburban areas became urban-like centers. As the population expanded, so did the diversity and number of cases heard in the Eastern District.

THE EMANUEL CELLER FEDERAL BUILDING AND COURTHOUSE

In 1965 the Eastern District court moved to new quarters in the Emanuel Celler Federal Building and Courthouse. The six-story limestone and granite building was designed by the architectural firm Carson, Lundin & Shaw in spare modernist style with strong vertical elements typical for its time. When it opened the space was greeted with great enthusiasm. With its 11 courtrooms, ample judges' chambers, conference rooms, library, and lawyer's lounge, it was viewed as a "magnificent home for the United States District Court for the Eastern District of New York" and praised as "practical in every detail."[21] Reserve space for expansion was even planned on the sixth floor.

The courthouse was part of a larger federal complex, with a separate Federal Building constructed next door. The courthouse and adjacent federal building were named for Emanuel Celler, a Brooklyn-born Democrat who served in the U.S. House of Representatives from 1923 to 1973.[22] Among Celler's prominent achievements was his introduction of the Civil Rights Act of 1957—the first civil-rights law enacted by the United States since the Civil War.

Fittingly, the court heard important civil-rights cases during its tenure in the Celler courthouse. Perhaps none of the Eastern District civil-rights cases of this era is better known than the lengthy litigation over the Willowbrook State Development Center on Staten Island. The case began in 1972 before Judge Orrin G. Judd and did not conclude until 1987 before Judge John R.

On November 11, 1954 at Ebbets Field, 6,982 individuals became naturalized United States citizens in a single ceremony. © Bettmann/Corbis.

Bartels.[23] Willowbrook, with a capacity of 2,950, once housed 5,200 developmentally impaired individuals in wholly inadequate facilities.[24] When Judge Judd visited the institution, he saw toilets and fountains that did not work, as well as 53 men lying nude and unattended. Shocked by such evidence, the court held that those who live in state institutions are entitled to reasonable protection from harm, and ordered remedial steps.[25] A consent decree approved in 1975 led to subsequent improvements, including a reduction of the center's population and continuing judicial oversight, culminating, finally, in the center's 1987 closure.

Willowbrook was only one of the important civil-rights cases heard in Eastern District courthouses. In 1982, for example, Judge Charles P. Sifton found that the New York City Fire Department discriminated against women in its hiring practices.[26] In 1993, in a decision later reversed by the Second Circuit, Judge Eugene H. Nickerson struck down the Pentagon's "Don't Ask, Don't Tell" policy.[27] He also presided over three trials of police officers stemming from their attack on Haitian immigrant Abner Louima.[28] Louima, a Haitian immigrant, had been arrested at a Brooklyn nightclub and then brutally attacked at a nearby police precinct. The case quickly rose to national prominence as a tale of racial bias and police misconduct. A civil rights case against the City by Louima before Judge Sterling Johnson Jr. was settled in 2001 for $8.75 million.[29] In 1997 Judge David G. Trager presided over another civil rights case, the trial of Lemrick Nelson Jr. and Charles Price, who had been acquitted in state court on charges that they killed Yankel Rosenbaum during the Crown Heights riots. The resulting conviction was later reversed by the Second Circuit because

A brutal attack on Haitian immigrant Abner Louima at a Brooklyn police station spawned civil rights litigation and a series of trials of police officers before Judge Eugene H. Nickerson, one of which is shown here in a drawing by Christine Cornell.

of what it found to be flawed efforts by Judge Trager to create (with the parties' consent) a racially balanced jury reflective of the community. A third trial of Nelson followed after Price pleaded guilty.[30] In the First Amendment area, Judge Carol Bagley Amon enjoined a law requiring the Bureau of Alcohol, Tobacco, and Explosives to deny the use of the name "Crazy Horse" on distilled spirits, wine, or malt beverage products.[31]

There has been no shortage of large-scale litigation in the Eastern District. The PATCO cases, presided over by Judge Thomas C. Platt during the Reagan administration, were particularly notable.[32] Air traffic controllers who were members of the PATCO union violated the terms of an earlier injunction by organizing a strike together. The strike resulted in fines, the bankruptcy of the union, and ultimately the historic firing of the striking controllers by President Reagan. In path-breaking Agent Orange cases in the 1980s, Judge Jack B. Weinstein presided over settlements for hundreds of thousands of Vietnam veterans exposed to the pesticide.[33] Attorney Kenneth Feinberg, special master in those cases (and later special master of the 9/11 Victim Compensation Fund), called the Agent Orange settlements "the fundamental pillar, the precedent for all the subsequent compensation schemes" in mass tort cases.[34]

The Eastern District also has an active criminal docket, including large multi-defendant criminal cases, with a particular focus on organized crime. Chief Judge Amon has heard several high-profile organized crime cases, including the trials of members of the Gambino crime family[35] and the trial of David Thai, leader of the "Born to Kill" gang.[36] Judge I. Leo Glasser presided over the trial of an early terrorism case involving a multi-year bombing plot, and a trial of John Gotti,[37] who was

A six-story entranceway to the Theodore Roosevelt U.S. Courthouse creates a gently curving connection between the new and older courthouse buildings. *Beacon* sculptures by Lisa Scheer flank the entrance.

prosecuted by then-Assistant U.S. Attorney, now Eastern District Judge John Gleeson. Judge Sterling Johnson Jr. oversaw the case of Dandeny Munoz-Mosquera, the chief assassin for the Medellin Cartel of Colombia, who was prosecuted by then-Assistant U.S. Attorney, now Eastern District Magistrate Judge Cheryl L. Pollak.[38]

While the Celler courthouse had seemed more than ample when it opened in the 1960s, with time the Eastern District began to outgrow it, and other difficulties, including security concerns, began to emerge. The Celler complex had no secured corridors; members of the public could virtually walk into judges' chambers. In a district that handled such high-profile criminal cases, weak security risked the safety of court personnel and the public alike. Meanwhile, a wave of bombings by the Puerto Rican Armed Forces of National Liberation ("FALN") hit New York, including, on December 31, 1982, one at Cadman Plaza that tore into the courthouse.[39]

THE EASTERN DISTRICT IN TODAY'S COURTHOUSES

By the mid-1990s, a decision was made to build a new courthouse. It would prove a lengthy project. Initial proposals to construct the building over the Long Island Rail Road terminal were rejected because the courthouse would be too far from the administrative center of Brooklyn. A plan to build the courthouse over the original U.S. Post Office and Courthouse Building was rejected after objections were made to its proposed height and the potential disfigurement of that historic building. Finally, a blueprint was produced to build the new courthouse next door to the Celler Courthouse on the site of the Federal Building, which would be razed.

THEODORE ROOSEVELT U.S. COURTHOUSE

Architect Cesar Pelli designed the Eastern District's current Brooklyn courthouse under the GSA's Courthouse Management Group. Pelli was known for designing some of the world's most recognizable high-rises, such as the Petronas Twin Towers in Kuala Lumpur (for a time the world's tallest buildings) and the World Financial Center complex in downtown Manhattan. In 1991 the American Institute of Architects listed Pelli among the 10 most influential American architects then living.[40]

Working the new building into the preexisting structure raised interesting design challenges. Exterior materials were chosen to meld the old and new courthouses into a unified structure that would fit with the other buildings in Brooklyn's civic center. For example, the plinth of the new courthouse—a four-story French Chamesson limestone base—references the grayer Indiana limestone and granite of the earlier courthouse, providing structural continuity.[41]

When, at one point, the possibility of replacing the limestone base was proposed, Pelli announced that if the French limestone was removed, he would remove his name, as well.[42] The new 15-story courthouse was connected to the existing six-story Cellar courthouse next door by a six-story entry hall. Tall rectangular windows combine with the limestone base to complement the vertical lines of the earlier courthouse. The entranceway creates a gently curving connection when viewed from outside. When viewed from the interior, the courthouse entranceway is a vaulting, light-filled space. Judge Glasser served on the space and facilities committee that wrote the original guidelines for the new building.

The committee made innovative decisions about space usage, such as arranging the judges' chambers in a collegial fashion on a chambers floor between the court floors, separated from the judges' courtrooms. The committee also created a separate arraignment court to be shared by the magistrate judges on criminal duty. This design feature reflects the extensive criminal docket of the Eastern District, as well as the roles and responsibilities of these magistrate judges, who now occupy much of the upper-level space in the courthouse.[43]

Construction of the courthouse proved unusually difficult because of a combination of community resistance, acts of terrorism, and other factors. Before it was completed, work on the courthouse lasted more than a decade. About a month after the design process began, on April 19, 1995, a bomb-laden truck destroyed the Alfred P. Murrah Federal Building in Oklahoma City. Tighter security requirements nationwide affected the new courthouse's design. Legislation introduced after the bombing classified federal buildings into five levels of security; at the judiciary's request, federal courthouses were newly ranked at the higher Level IV (buildings with a high volume of public contact) instead of Level III (buildings with routine activities and a moderate level of public contact).[44] Among other enhancements, the new security guidelines for federal buildings required windows with laminated glass and structural frames that could withstand explosions.[45] Because most of the deaths in the Oklahoma City bombing were caused by the building's progressive collapse and not by the blast itself, it became important to include progressive-collapse protection in the new courthouse's infrastructure.[46]

Almost from the beginning, the new building project encountered local community opposition. In 1997, after the GSA completed two years of studies and public hearings, a group called the Downtown Brooklyn Alliance for Courthouse Alternatives brought suit in the Southern District of New York to halt the project. The group, which included residents in a nearby apartment complex, argued that the large tower integral to the new

The Theodore Roosevelt U.S Courthouse in winter showing the narrower aspect the building presents from the side.

One of the two fourteen foot high bronze sculptures by Lisa Scheer, created as part of the Art in Architecture program, that flank the entrance to Theodore Roosevelt U.S. Courthouse, illuminated at night.

building's design would block views and sunlight, draw more cars to congested downtown Brooklyn, and worsen air pollution.[47] Judge Robert P. Patterson Jr. ruled against the resident group, finding that they had failed to prove that the project violated environmental laws.[48] Nonetheless, the building's design was modified to create a more tapered, curved building.[49]

Above the base, the tower is designed with setbacks and gently curved tiers along the north and south faces. The finished building also includes tall, narrow limestone panels alternating with enameled glass that emphasize the building's verticality. Streamlined aluminum finials on the upper tiers evoke New York's older skyscrapers. Providing a dramatic "gateway building" into Brooklyn, the new federal courthouse appears narrow from Brooklyn Heights, but wider when seen from the Brooklyn Bridge.

As part of the Art in Architecture Program, two bronze sculptures by Lisa Scheer mark the courthouse entrance. The 14-foot-high abstract cast bronze sculptures stand on 10-foot concrete pylons. They evoke flames rising upward, perhaps echoing the torch of the Statute of Liberty. The sculptures are identical but rotated 180 degrees from each other so that they never look the same from a single vantage point. Scheer designed the lighting of the sculptures so that the flames would be particularly dramatic when illuminated at night.[50]

In 2000 Senator Daniel Patrick Moynihan attended the ribbon-cutting ceremony, marking the commencement of construction. By September 11, 2001, the 15th story of the structural frame had been completed. But after the terrorist attacks of September 11 on the World Trade Center towers, construction was halted to allow the crew to assist in clearing Ground Zero.[51] Once

The Ceremonial Courtroom, located in the Emanuel Celler U.S. Courthouse attached to the Theodore Roosevelt U.S. Courthouse.

again, security requirements for courthouses were increased nationwide.

The construction managers, with Pelli, provided a further redesign of the courthouse to comply with these new requirements. During the long construction period, Eastern District judges were ever more cramped in their existing quarters, in some cases sharing courtrooms. As early as 1996, the GSA had ranked Brooklyn and Long Island as having the most overcrowded courts in the United States.[52] The new courthouse finally opened for occupancy in January 2006. After years of delays, District Executive Jim Ward oversaw the move between the old and new courthouses in a single efficient weekend. Judge Sifton, Chief Judge at the time, successfully scheduled a jury trial to begin the Monday after the move.[53]

The new building added 16 courtrooms[54] with better sightlines among judge, jury, and witnesses; improved technology; facilities to accommodate the Americans with Disabilities Act; and more space between the defendants and the public to accommodate large multidefendant trials.[55] Natural light fills the hallways, lobbies, jury deliberation rooms, and some courtrooms, embodying the concept of government transparency. The public areas of the courthouse are gracious and comfortable. The perimeter courtroom lobbies offer views of the East River, lower Manhattan, New York Harbor, and Brooklyn through floor-to-ceiling windows.

The Brooklyn courthouses sit next to Cadman Park, which is named for Rev. Doctor Samuel Parkes Cadman, a renowned minister of the Brooklyn Congregational Church. The land for the park was reclaimed by condemnation in 1935. The proximity of this seasonally changing green space within an otherwise dense

A fisheye view of the Theodore Roosevelt U.S. Courthouse lobby viewed from the center of the third floor.

The main entrance to the Theodore Roosevelt U.S. Courthouse viewed from its second floor lobby.

The Charles P. Sifton Gallery during the exhibit *After Hours*, featuring the work of court officials.

urban setting helps provide the courthouse and its community a distinct, perhaps unique, character.

The court shares its space with the public, providing venues for mock trials, law school events, ABA-sponsored moot court competitions, and more. A ground-floor gallery displays exhibitions by artists who are from the Eastern District or have a connection to the federal judicial system. The gallery is named the Charles P. Sifton Gallery in honor of the Chief Judge who was instrumental both in its creation and in shepherding the courthouse construction project through much of its tortuous history.

At a small ceremony in 2008, led by Senator Charles E. Schumer, the new courthouse was named for Theodore Roosevelt, described by Senator Schumer as a "man of the law."[56] "This naming reinvigorates our knowledge of him and our link with history and its importance to us," Senator Schumer said.

Ironically, the Roosevelt courthouse, whose construction was partly precipitated by acts of terrorism and was affected by terrorists' acts, has since been the site of several terrorism trials. These include Judge Dora L. Irizarry's trial of Abdul Kadir and Russell Defreitas for planning to bomb Kennedy Airport,[57] and Judge Nina Gershon's trial of a defendant charged with conspiring to blow up the Herald Square subway station.[58] Cases with political overtones included Judge David G. Trager's dismissal of a Canadian citizen's challenge against the U.S. government, founded on allegations of engagement in extraordinary rendition.[59] Civil-rights cases also have continued to play an important role on the court's docket, including Judge Nicholas G. Garaufis's series of decisions between 2009 and 2011 finding that the New York City Fire Department administered hiring tests that were discriminatory against black and Hispanic candidates.[60]

Following pages: The restored Romanesque style Conrad B. Duberstein U.S. Bankruptcy Court viewed against the contemporary Theodore Roosevelt U.S. Courthouse across Tillary Street.

The light filled atrium of the restored Conrad B. Duberstein U. S. Bankruptcy Courthouse.

CONRAD B. DUBERSTEIN U.S. BANKRUPTCY COURTHOUSE

After the Eastern District moved out of the U.S. Post Office and Courthouse building, the structure remained in use as a post office. Over time, however, the building fell into disrepair, accelerated when the U.S. Postal Service transferred its sorting facilities to Long Island in the 1980s. The GSA eventually acquired the complex and considered its demolition or its sale to developers. Such plans were opposed by community groups and by Senator Moynihan, and in 1996 the decision was made to restore the building.

The GSA chose R. M. Kliment & Frances Halsband Architects to restore the atrium and reconfigure other spaces without altering the landmarked exterior facade. Today the building houses the U.S. Bankruptcy Court, the U.S. Attorney's Office, the U.S. Trustee's office, and a retail postal facility. The renovation included the addition of new space, the reorientation of the entrance to face Cadman Plaza, and restoration of the existing structure. The New York City Landmarks Preservation Commission mandated that no addition to the existing building could be visible from the ground, so a second-floor mezzanine and a new four-story glass structure were added within the light court of the earlier building, defining a new courtyard. A staircase of steel with marble treads was added within the new structure.

New public entrances on Cadman Plaza were emphasized by granite steps that fit the scale of the plaza. Inside the Bankruptcy Court, which occupies the oldest part of the building, the design team restored the building's central atrium, two courtrooms, and two judges' chambers, complete with their original paint colors and finishes. The restoration included uncovering a skylight

Corridors along the Duberstein courthouse's central atrium lead to courtrooms, which have been restored to their original paint colors and finishes.

closed off to comply with World War II blackout requirements. The resulting light-filled interior space is stunning from many angles. The renovated building received a 1998 Design Award citation from the GSA and is now listed on the National Register of Historic Places.[61]

In 2008 the building was named for Conrad B. Duberstein. A decorated World War II veteran, Duberstein was in private practice until 1981, when at age 65 he began service on the bankruptcy court. Duberstein sat as a bankruptcy judge in the Eastern District from 1981 until his death in 2005. He authored over 170 published opinions, sat on thousands of Chapter 7, 11, and 13 cases,[62] and served as the Chief Bankruptcy Judge from 1984 to 2005. Widely regarded as the dean of the bankruptcy bar as a practitioner, he was not only one of the most highly respected judges in New York, but also one of the most beloved. As one of his many acts of public service, he oversaw the 2005 courthouse renovations. He took great pride and pleasure in helping restore the beautiful building, which was connected to his personal history. His uncle, Samuel C. Duberstein, had been appointed as a bankruptcy referee in 1945, with chambers next to the second-floor courtroom, and Duberstein's own swearing-in had taken place in the building.[63]

A plaque in the lobby of the Duberstein courthouse honors his many achievements, including his "well deserved reputation for intelligence, wit, humility and compassion" and his "unwavering commitment to the fair administration of bankruptcy jurisprudence and the preservation of the dignity of those in financial distress."

ALFONSE M. D'AMATO U.S. COURTHOUSE AND FEDERAL BUILDING

The Alfonse D'Amato U.S. Courthouse and Federal Building provides a forum for cases emanating from Nassau and Suffolk Counties.[64] The courthouse was designed by architect Richard Meier and constructed between 1996 and 2000 on 29 acres of parkland provided to the U.S. Government by Suffolk County.

The building was named in honor of former three-term U.S. Senator and Long Island native Alfonse M. D'Amato.[65] One of the largest federal courthouses in the country, the 12-story, 1,250-foot-long structure consolidates within its walls the facilities and personnel of the Eastern District previously housed in multiple courthouses and buildings located in Uniondale, Hauppauge, and Westbury in Nassau and Suffolk Counties.[66] The courthouse is the first building commissioned under the GSA's Design Excellence Program. Approached through a broad, podium-like plaza, the building's gently curved south-facing exterior consists primarily of large expanses of a glass curtain wall fronted by a series of long, thin horizontal strips of white-enameled metal. The remainder of the building is clad in square white panels, as is the 11-story cone-shaped rotunda, which projects into the outside plaza and serves as the courthouse's public entrance.

After a low entryway, the ceremonial vestibule to the courthouse soars dramatically upward for 190 feet to a rooftop skylight through which sunlight bathes the rotunda's curved circular interior. The atrium is surrounded by nine levels of publicly accessible balconies and walkways, which offer panoramic views of Long Island's Great South Bay, Fire Island, and the Atlantic Ocean through the glass curtain wall. The Long Island judges of the Eastern District made a conscious decision during the courthouse's design to keep this view available to the public.[67] A pair of vibrantly executed art works by Frank Stella, titled *Hooloomooloo IV* and *Joatinga*, commissioned under the Art in Architecture Program, provide focal points of color in the vast white chamber.

Intended from the first by the judges of the Eastern District and the building's architect to be more than an impressive architectural space, the atrium has become something of a "village commons" for the Central Islip community, hosting concerts, art exhibits, craft shows displaying the works of local artisans, public meetings, and even high school theatrical productions.

Just off the atrium is a large ceremonial courtroom. Among its uses are naturalization proceedings in which each presiding judge adds his or her own personal touch, such as playing patriotic music or giving out special pencils to children in attendance. A similar

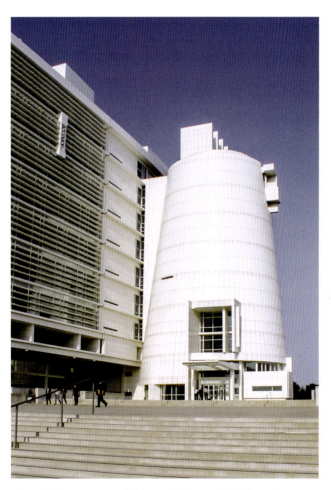

Above: The entrance to Alphonse D'Amato U.S. Courthouse and Federal Building.

Previous pages: The Richard Meier-designed Alfonse D'Amato U.S. Courthouse and Federal Building, constructed between 1996 and 2000 on 29 acres of parkland donated by Suffolk County.

Balconies and walkways in the upper levels of the courthouse make its panoramic views available to the public.

"personal" approach is shared by the district judges and magistrate judges of the courthouse, who eat breakfast and lunch together most working days, some of them having done so for many years.

Other courtrooms are situated off a wall of solid gray granite running east–west through the building. Devoid of marble or classical ornament, the courtrooms are intimately scaled and finished with warm cherry and birch wood paneling. None of their furnishings, including the witness box, are permanently fixed to the floor, but instead may be moved at the judge's direction to permit proper sightlines and simultaneous visual contact among the judge, witness, litigants, and jury.

Under the GSA's Thirty Year Plan, vacant upper floors of the courthouse will be utilized to create as many as 24 additional courtrooms, accommodating the anticipated growth in Long Island's population through the year 2030. Other features of this "modern courthouse in the country" include a gymnasium, a part-time post office, and a nurse's station. An adjacent building, built by GSA to complement the Meier-designed courthouse, houses a childcare facility that can be used by court personnel. Proceeds from the craft shows held in the courthouse help to fund operation of the childcare center.

The courthouse also plays a role in legal education. Several of its judges serve as adjunct professors at Touro Law School, which moved directly adjacent to the courthouse in 2007. Touro students observe oral arguments, jury selections, and trials through the school's Court Observation Program. Inside the Touro Law School building, they can receive electronic updates of court proceedings as they occur. Primary- and secondary-school students also participate in mock trials at the courthouse, over which the courthouse's judges preside.

Vibrant art works by Frank Stella titled *Hooloomooloo IV*—shown here—and *Joatinga* provide focal points of color in the vast white space of the courthouse vestibule, which soars 190 feet toward a rooftop skylight.

Top: *Hooloomooloo IV,* detail of the right side of the painting. *Bottom: Joatinga* uses lacquers over etched aluminum surfaces to create a collage of metallic beams and triangles. The work is part of Stella's Brazil series, taking its name from that Rio de Janiero district.

Corridors of solid gray granite running east-west through the building lead to courtrooms.

In addition to being designed as its own community, the courthouse serves as an anchor for the Central Islip area, which has undergone an economic and cultural renaissance—a goal of GSA's Design Excellence Program. Perhaps due to the business the courthouse has brought into the area, a major shopping center was built just blocks away.

Though young in years, the courthouse has already witnessed cases of significant local interest and national significance. Judges grappled with the issue of whether the Shinnecock Indian Nation constitutes an Indian tribe under common law, with implications for casino gambling on Long Island, and heard litigation relating to the merger of Long Island's two largest hospitals, North Shore Hospital and Long Island Jewish Hospital.

On the national stage, lawsuits against Pan American Airlines and the government of Libya, arising from the 1988 bombing of Pan Am Flight 103 over Lockerbie, Scotland,[68] resulted in congressional amendments to the Foreign Sovereign Immunities Act, strengthening security screening of luggage worldwide, and changes to the Warsaw Convention on liability for passenger losses.

On the criminal docket, there have been repeated prosecutions of the Pagans "outlaw motorcycle gang." A team of Eastern District prosecutors, law-enforcement agents, medical professionals, and forensic scientists also conducted a multiyear investigation into the chilling activities of Michael Swango, a medical doctor who experimented upon, assaulted, and murdered patients with a variety of poisons, prescription drugs, and homemade toxins.[69] Swango's killing spree extended across the United States and into several African nations and Saudi Arabia. In September 2000, Swango pleaded guilty to fatally poisoning three patients at the Northport VA hospital and assaulting a fourth patient with poison. Judge Jacob Mishler sentenced Swango to three consecutive life terms to be served at the "Supermax" prison facility in Florence, Colorado.[70]

More recently, in 2011 a jury convicted a Columbian drug trafficker, Carlos Arturo Patiño Restrepo, of three counts of conspiracy to violate U.S. drug laws for having orchestrated multi-ton cocaine shipments into the United States throughout the 1990s until his arrest in 2007.[71] Patiño had been under arrest in Columbia on suspicion of murdering rivals and possible informants.

The courthouse's design aesthetic—its rejection of formalism and monumental structure—reflects the significantly reconceived role and image of public buildings in 21st-century America. Architect Richard Meier, guided by the judges of the Eastern District, created a fitting building for the administration of justice, as well as a cultural, educational, and community gathering place for the people of Long Island.

The D'Amato Ceremonial Courtroom finished with warm cherry and birch wood paneling.

CHAPTER FIVE

THE WESTERN DISTRICT
OF
NEW YORK

The Western District of New York comprises the 17 westernmost counties of New York State, which were carved out from the original Northern District by Act of Congress in May 1900.[1] Pennsylvania lies to the south, Lake Erie to the west, and Lake Ontario and Canada to the north. The district includes the cities of Buffalo and Rochester, as well as Niagara Falls, the Genesee River, the Finger Lakes, and Chautauqua Lake. Congress provided that court sessions were to be held in Buffalo and Rochester, and, if necessary, in Canandaigua, Elmira, Jamestown, and Lockport.

In the earliest days of the district, cases continued to be heard in U.S. Post Office or combined U.S. Post Office and Courthouse buildings in Rochester, Buffalo, Elmira, Jamestown, and Lockport, just as they had been before the Western District was created.[2] In Canandaigua, cases originally were heard in leased space in the Ontario County Courthouse, an 1859 Greek Revival building designed by architect Henry Searle. Susan B. Anthony's historic federal trial and conviction for voting took place in this courthouse in 1873, while Canandaigua was still situated within the Northern District of New York. After 1912, Canandaigua cases were heard in the U.S. Post Office and Courthouse building.

Today the district court sits in Rochester in the Kenneth B. Keating U.S. Courthouse, where the district court moved from its earlier home in the 19th-century Rochester Post Office and Courthouse Building. The earlier building now

Opposite, top to bottom: the Kenneth B. Keating Federal Building; the Robert H. Jackson U.S. Courthouse.

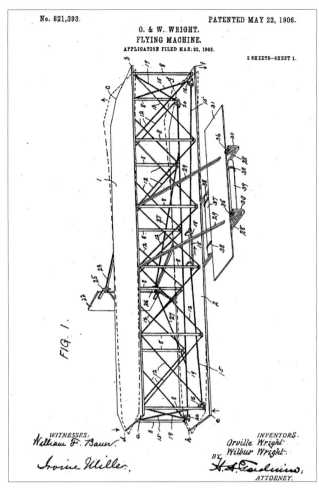

An illustration from the patent for a flying machine that was granted to Orville and Wilbur Wright and upheld in 1914 by Judge John R. Hazel, whose decision was affirmed by the Second Circuit Court of Appeals.

functions as Rochester's City Hall. In Buffalo, the district court sits in the Robert H. Jackson U.S. Courthouse, the Second Circuit's newest courthouse, a glass-clad contemporary 10-story building opened in 2011 that replaced the Michael J. Dillon U.S. Courthouse, where the court sat from 1936 to 2011.

EARLY HISTORY

By 1890, the cities within the Western District had become the center of enormous industrial and commercial growth. This thriving commercial activity and the litigation that accompanied it helped spur the creation of a separate Western District of New York. Between 1890 and 1900, about 400 new factories had been built in Buffalo alone. The City was also the center for barge and rail–lake traffic in grain, ore, and livestock. In Rochester, George Eastman was busy helping turn the art of photography into a worldwide phenomenon.

The first judge for the Western District was John R. Hazel, who was appointed on June 8, 1900, and served until 1931. For more than 27 years, he was the district's sole judge. During the 1920s, William J. "Wild Bill" Donovan was U.S. Attorney in the district, before serving as Assistant Attorney General in the wake of the Teapot Dome scandal. He later was a founder of the U.S. Office of Strategic Services (OSS), the forerunner of the CIA.

Early on, Judge Hazel became a respected expert in patent law, resolving many disputes over inventions. In 1914 he upheld the validity of Orville and Wilbur Wright's patent for a flying machine. The Second Circuit declared itself in full accord with the lower court's reasoning that "the patentees may fairly be considered pioneers in the practical art of flying with heavier-than-air machines."[3] Other decisions by Judge Hazel concerned the validity and infringement of patents relating to the Eastman Kodak Company and the Ford Motor Company.

During Prohibition in the 1920s, the Western District Court was so besieged by cases involving speakeasies and alcohol manufacturing that Judge Hazel sometimes held "bargain days," when he would announce at the beginning of the court session a preset fine amount for anyone willing to plead guilty to bootlegging.

Shortly after his appointment, Judge Hazel was called upon to perform the extraordinary task of administering the oath of office to Theodore Roosevelt after President McKinley was assassinated in 1901 at the Pan-American Exposition in Buffalo. By chance, Judge Hazel was an active Roosevelt supporter, so much so that Roosevelt in his autobiography credited him as instrumental in his nomination for Governor of New York in 1886. Roosevelt took the oath of office in the private home of Ansley Wilcox, today the Theodore Roosevelt National Historic Site / Wilcox Mansion Museum.

Judge Hazel administering the oath of office to Theodore Roosevelt after President McKinley's assassination in 1901 in Buffalo, New York.

Judge Simon L. Adler joined the bench in 1927, serving until 1934, when he was replaced by Judge Harlan W. Rippey, who served until 1936. Judge John Knight was appointed in 1931 and served until 1955. In 1937 Judge Harold P. Burke joined the bench to replace Judge Rippey. Judge Burke continued to serve until his death in 1981 at the age of 84. At his death, Judge Burke held the distinction of being the nation's longest-serving district judge, having served for 44 years.

ROCHESTER
U.S. POST OFFICE AND COURTHOUSE BUILDING

Between 1900 and 1972, Western District cases in Rochester were heard in its U.S. Post Office and Courthouse building designed by architects Harvey and Charles Ellis. Authorized by Congress in 1882, the building was ready for occupancy in 1891. It was the City of Rochester's first federal building, created as a combination federal post office and courthouse during a wave of construction after the Civil War and before the McKinley presidency. Prior to that time, federal functions had been performed in rented space. The building also has housed at different times customs and internal revenue services, a draft-registry center, a weather bureau, and offices for the Social Security Administration, the Federal Housing Authority, and other federal agencies.[4]

Designed in the Richardsonian Romanesque style, the massive building was redesigned and increased in size during the course of its construction when Congress raised its cost limit from $300,000 to $500,000.[5] In typical Romanesque style, the building includes a prominent windowed clock tower, which survived the midconstruction redesign. The tower has small dormer

The U.S. Post Office and Courthouse that served as the district courthouse in Rochester between 1900 and 1972.

The elegant three-story atrium of the U.S. Post Office and Courthouse in Rochester.

windows and a double-hipped roof. The exterior is sheathed in 18-inch-thick Portland brownstone sandstone from the Connecticut River Valley. Dressed stone arches, detailed band courses, and other finishing features enliven the facade.

The plans for the larger building included an interior cortile or atrium, an elegant three-story space with cast-iron work and multicolored marble columns. The atrium has been viewed as one of the building's most successful features, characterized by the local Landmark Society as one of the most beautiful in the country. The building's third-floor courtroom is remarkable for its use of wood trim.

This courtroom was the site of many of Judge Hazel's early cases, such as bootlegging prosecutions and early patent cases. In the 1970s a notable trial of antiwar protestors took place there. The "Flower City Conspiracy" was the self-prescribed name of eight protestors who were tried and convicted after ransacking offices of the FBI, U.S. Attorney, and Selective Service System. In September 1970 the eight were found in the Federal Building amid file drawers that had been broken into and draft registration papers that had been torn and tossed about. In a case that received national attention, they were charged and convicted with six crimes, including interfering with the administration of the Selective Service Act, injuring property in the office of the FBI, and removing records from the U.S. Attorney's office. Seven of the defendants represented themselves, and they attempted to use the trial to publicize their antiwar views. The conviction eventually was overturned as a result of ex parte communications between the judge and jury.[6]

In the late 1960s the federal government began to consider a move to a new courthouse as part of an urban-renewal plan for downtown Rochester. The existing

The Rochester U.S. Post Office and Courthouse's third floor courtroom.

The Kenneth B. Keating Federal Building.

building had significantly deteriorated over the years, and there was considerable public controversy over whether it should be preserved or razed.[7] Ultimately, the argument for preservation prevailed, and the building was sold to the City of Rochester for $1. After considerable rehabilitation, expansion, and renovation, it returned to use as Rochester's City Hall. It was listed on the National Register of Historic Places in 1972 and as a local landmark in 1973.

KENNETH B. KEATING FEDERAL BUILDING

In 1972 the new Rochester Federal Building was dedicated. Standing within sight of the earlier building, it consists of two linked structures, both modern and simple in design, one rising two stories, the other six, connected by a low central entranceway. The two-story building was created for the federal court. The larger six-story building houses executive branch offices of the FBI, ATF, and Secret Service, as well as legislative offices. The detached design of the two was intended to emphasize the separation between the branches of government.

In 1979 the complex was renamed, becoming the Kenneth B. Keating Federal Building in honor of longtime Rochester public servant Kenneth B. Keating. Keating served as a Congressman from 1947 to 1959 and as a U.S. Senator from 1959 to 1965. He served thereafter on the New York State Court of Appeals, from 1965 to 1969. He went on to be Ambassador to India from 1969 to 1972 and Ambassador to Israel from 1973 until his death in 1975.[8]

The sculpture *Equilateral Six* by Duane Hatchett outside the Keating Federal Building.

A striking yellow abstract sculpture by artist Duane Hatchett, titled *Equilateral Six,* was added as part of the federal Art in Architecture Program and stands in front of the courthouse. The courtrooms themselves lack the architectural details of the earlier courthouse and by comparison are austere—typical for federal buildings of the era.

In 2000 the Keating Courthouse saw the resolution before Judge Michael A. Telesca of cases arising from a 1971 takeover of the Attica Correctional Facility in Attica, New York. The four- day takeover of Attica ended with 39 dead, after Governor Nelson Rockefeller ordered the retaking of the prison by state police. The protracted and complex litigation that followed included claims against 62 inmates and one state trooper. Inmates and families of those killed in the melee brought suit in Buffalo against the State of New York for civil-rights violations by law-enforcement officials during and after the retaking of the prison.

In 2000, after 27 years of litigation in both Buffalo and Rochester, a settlement of $12 million was reached with Attica prisoners and their families. A separate $12 million settlement was reached with the families of prison workers. The cases have been viewed as playing an important role in the history of prisoners'-rights litigation.[9]

The Keating courthouse also was home to complex litigation involving the Kodak Company, before its filing for protection under Chapter 11 of U.S. bankruptcy laws in 2012. For example, in 1994 Kodak successfully moved to be relieved, because of changed circumstances, from earlier-imposed antitrust restrictions that had limited its ability to market film under a private label and with photo-processing costs included. In another case against Sun Microsystems, Kodak claimed that Sun's Java programming language violated three of its patents. The trial, presided over by Judge Telesca, saw thousands of exhibits accessed electronically while jurors sat with monitors in front of them. A jury verdict in favor of Kodak was later resolved by settlement. More recently, Kodak sued Apple and HTC claiming that the smartphone makers had used Kodak technology for image transmission without permission. These two suits, along other patent-infringement suits Kodak initiated against several other companies, were dropped when Kodak agreed to sell more than 1,000 of its patents in 2012.[10]

BUFFALO

Between 1900 and 1903, cases in Buffalo continued to be heard in the Romanesque U.S. Custom House where the Northern District had sat. The building, designed by the Supervising Architect of the Treasury Department, Ammi B. Young, and built in 1856, was razed in 1965. Between 1903 and 1936, Buffalo cases were heard in the U.S. Post Office Building completed in 1901 under Supervising Architect Jeremiah O'Rourke. That building is now owned by Erie County Community College. For the almost 80 years between 1936 and 2011, the Western District heard cases in an Art Moderne building that came to be named the Michael J. Dillon U.S. Courthouse. Since 2011, the district court has sat in the Robert H. Jackson U.S. Courthouse.

THE MICHAEL J. DILLON U.S. COURTHOUSE

By the late 1920s, it was clear that federal government–related business resulting from Buffalo's continued growth needed more space. A new Buffalo courthouse to be located on Niagara Square was authorized in 1932 under the Emergency Construction and Relief Act. In 1933, as a result of a New Deal effort to involve local architectural firms in courthouse construction,

A courtroom in the Keating Building.

THE WESTERN DISTRICT OF NEW YORK | 157

Twenty-seven years of litigation in both Rochester and Buffalo followed the 1971 takeover of the Attica Correctional Facility in Attica, New York.

the prominent Buffalo architectural firms of Edward B. Green & Sons and Bley & Lyman were chosen as architects.

The cornerstone for the building was laid in 1936 by then-retired Judge Hazel. The courthouse was dedicated by President Franklin Roosevelt, whose speech stressed the role of new courthouse construction in easing the economic woes of the Depression. Roosevelt called the building part of "a very great program throughout the nation" that "has already started the wheels of trade and commerce turning again."[11]

Originally called the United States Post Office and Courthouse, the building was renamed the Michael J. Dillon U.S. Courthouse in 1986 to honor an area IRS agent who was killed in 1983 while attempting to collect a tax deficiency, the first IRS agent to be killed in the line of duty. The courthouse served the Western District until the opening of the Robert H Jackson U.S. Courthouse in 2011.

The now unused Dillon courthouse occupies an entire pentagon-shaped city block on Niagara Square, Buffalo's civic center. The building has been viewed as a striking example of Depression-era design, particularly because of its unusual shape and combination of classical form with low-relief carved ornamentation. It is listed on the National Register of Historic Places as a contributing element to the Joseph Ellicott Historic District. It has a granite base, yellow-gray sandstone walls, and spare carved detailing concentrated at the first-floor level. Each elevation is divided into bays of vertical windows. Fluted forms that resemble classical colonnades run up the exterior between these vertical strips of windows. The words "United States Court House" are carved in stone above its main entrance just below a monumental carved eagle. A cast-bronze medallion is centered above the middle door.

Many interior changes took place in the Dillon Courthouse over the last years of its use, but some original details were maintained, including a highly ornamented main lobby with fretwork molding decorated with polychrome floral panels and drum-shaped light fixtures in aluminum frames featuring a star motif, and a main-lobby floor decorated with stars set in circles of colored terrazzo. Some walls and columns are still clad in their original travertine.

Four original courtrooms, including the bankruptcy courtroom and two ceremonial courtrooms, featured cork floors, with a dark green marble border and base. The walls included wood-panel wainscoting of American cherry and veneer and, in the bankruptcy court, American black walnut. The bankruptcy court's plaster ceiling was ornamented with a cornice and six medallions. In the ceremonial courtrooms, an ornamental plaster band around the ceiling was composed of alternating squares with stars and flowers.

Of the cases heard in the Dillon Courthouse, perhaps none had more impact than the litigation arising out of Love Canal. The attention given to Love Canal is credited with bringing to public consciousness the problem of toxic chemical wastes as a nationwide issue, as well as playing a part in the passage of the Comprehensive Environmental Response Compensation and Liability Act (CERCLA), commonly referred to as "Superfund."[12] The mile-long Love Canal was what remained of William T. Love's failed 1890s dream of establishing a new connection to the Niagara River. The

The Michael J. Dillon U.S. Courthouse in Buffalo.

abandoned site filled with water and was used by local children as a place to swim in summer. By the 1920s, the site had been turned into a municipal dump for the City of Niagara, and between 1942 and 1952 it served as a dumping site for the company that became known as Hooker Chemical Company. Hooker drained the canal, lined its walls with thick clay, and buried over 21,000 tons of chemicals, many of them toxic.

In 1953 the Niagara school board acquired the site for a school building. A 17-line release in the $1 contract of sale recited that the premises had been filled with chemical waste products and sought to absolve Hooker Chemical of all potential liability. This clause later was the subject of much litigation. Children began attending the school in 1955. That same year, a 25-foot area crumbled, exposing chemical drums. When large puddles formed in this newly caved-in area after rainstorms, children played there happily. In 1957 the City of Niagara began construction of low-income and single-family residences on land adjacent to the landfill site. Construction of sewer beds for the new residences breached the walls of the canal, increasing the buried chemicals' ability to migrate.

By 1977, residents reported puddles of colored liquid in yards and basements. By the summer of 1978, local reporters and a local residents' association began what became a prolonged campaign to seek redress. Love Canal became a national media event. President Jimmy Carter visited the site and afterward declared a federal health emergency. President Carter called for the allocation of federal funds to assist in cleanup efforts, the first time federal emergency funds were used other than for a national disaster. New York Governor Hugh Carey also declared a state of emergency. Eventually, the school was razed and the government relocated more than 800 families.

A half-buried hazardous waste containment tank next to abandoned homes at Love Canal.

By 1979, over 800 cases had been filed against Hooker Chemical, the City of Niagara, the County of Niagara, and the Board of Education, seeking a total of $11 billion. The federal government also sued Hooker Chemical for $124 million. Judge John T. Curtin presided over this massive litigation. Most of the cases were resolved by settlements, including, in 1984, a $20 million settlement to 1,328 Love Canal residents. In 1994 Judge Curtin ruled that Hooker Chemical had been negligent in its waste disposal but that it had not been reckless in its contract of sale.[13] In 1995 Occidental Petroleum, a successor to Hooker Chemical, agreed to a payment of $129 million to cover the cost of the federal government's waste cleanup, resolving the 16-year-old lawsuit against it.

The Love Canal cases were a formative experience for many Buffalo-area lawyers, who had a chance to hone legal skills in a high-stakes arena. Because so many important issues were heard during the case, often for the first time, it was something of a trial by fire for the participants.[14] The disaster spawned books and films. While the toxic chemicals dioxin and benzene were found at the site, controversy continues to this day over the extent to which birth defects and other health issues were in fact attributable to the chemicals disposed of at Love Canal. But there is general agreement that the Superfund legislation and regulations that emerged after Love Canal have contributed to the nation's environmental safety.

The Western District's proximity to various waterways predictably engendered litigation. District Court Judge Burke, a sailor who liked boats, enjoyed dealing with the court's many admiralty cases. In the *Kinsman Transit* case, Judge Burke confronted a matter worthy of a law-school test arising from a series of events on the Buffalo River. In the winter of 1959, a sudden thaw had begun to melt ice on the swiftly flowing waterway, which winds through Buffalo into Lake Erie. A steamship owned by Kinsman Transit, arguably insecurely moored, broke loose under the press of ice and debris and smashed into another boat, the *Tewksbury*, sending both vessels downstream toward the city-owned Michigan lift-bridge. Judge Burke found that although warnings were sent to lift the bridge, no one received them in time because the bridge operator was taking a break at a local tavern. Before the bridge could be lifted, the ships struck it, causing its supports to fall. The resulting pileup dammed the river, caused flooding and waterfront damage for several miles, and disrupted transportation on the river and the busy port for several months. Judge Burke heard the protracted litigation that followed.

Ultimately, the Second Circuit held, in an opinion by Judge Friendly, that although the extent of the damage may have been unexpected, it resulted from forces, such as ice, ships, and river currents, whose foreseeable existence demanded the exercise of due care.[15] It happened that the Vice President and Treasurer for Kinsman overseeing the ill-fated ship's arrival in Buffalo prior to mooring was none other than 28-year-old George Steinbrenner, who later would become the principal owner of the New York Yankees and who, according to Judge Friendly, was at the time "without maritime studies or experience."[16]

In the 1970s Judge Curtin presided over an influential Buffalo school desegregation case. During the 1960s and 1970s, school busing to achieve racial integration was controversial. In Buffalo, the Board of Education refused to comply with a previous 1972 desegregation order, arguing that its school segregation had come about naturally as a result of population shifts. Buffalo civil-rights activists filed suit against the Board of Education in federal court. In 1976 Judge Curtin ruled that the defendants had violated the plaintiffs' 14th Amendment rights to equal protection.[17] In the meantime, perhaps realizing that the ruling would go against them, the Buffalo Board of Education had been

An entrance to the Michael J. Dillon U.S. Courthouse including one of the courthouse's highly ornamental light fixtures.

working on a new desegregation plan called the Buffalo Plan. Under Judge Curtin's guidance, the plan was slightly altered and implemented to become Buffalo's Magnet School System. Specialty schools were designed to draw students across neighborhood boundaries without forced busing. The Buffalo Plan as implemented was widely admired and attracted attention from school planners from around the country.

During the Vietnam era, the Dillon courthouse saw its share of antiwar protest cases. In one, a group of student antiwar protestors in Buffalo were arrested on charges including draft evasion and assaulting a police officer after occupying and being forcibly cleared from a Unitarian church. In the two trials that followed, the protestors used confrontational tactics including

THE WESTERN DISTRICT OF NEW YORK | 161

One of the historic courtrooms in the Michael J. Dillon U.S. Courthouse.

power salutes and a refusal to follow court orders. Contempt citations followed as crowds outside carried signs seeking to "Free the Buffalo Nine." The case, which ultimately resulted in a mixed verdict, drew considerable media attention and became the subject of a symposium featuring the writer Susan Sontag.[18]

A modern-era terrorism case was heard in the courthouse in 2006. Six men, sometimes referred to as the "Lackawanna Six" or "Buffalo Six," pled guilty before Judge William M. Skretny to having provided material support to a foreign terrorist organization after traveling to Yemen to hear Osama bin Laden speak a few months before the September 11 terrorist attacks. It was the first time U.S. citizens were charged under a 1996 statute forbidding material support to foreign terrorist organizations. The prosecution in the Dillon courthouse proved to be a security challenge because the courthouse lacked such security safeguards as separate access for judges and prosecutors. Special security forces were detailed to the courthouse during the proceedings.[19]

The District Court for the Western District ceased using the Dillon courthouse in 2011, when it moved to the Robert H. Jackson U.S. Courthouse.

THE ROBERT H. JACKSON U.S. COURTHOUSE

On November 28, 2011, a sleek, glass-clad, elliptically shaped computer-age federal courthouse opened in Buffalo. Designed by architects Kohn Pederson Fox, it now houses the District Court for the Western District and has offices for U.S. Attorneys, marshals, and the probation service. The new courthouse is named in honor of Chautauqua County native and former Associate Justice of the Supreme Court Robert Jackson. Jackson also was the Chief Prosecutor in the Nuremberg war crimes trials.

The Jackson Courthouse was many years in the making. Originally, when it appeared that the court's business in Buffalo had outgrown the available space in the Dillon Courthouse, an annex to the Dillon Courthouse was contemplated. But increased security

Entrance to the Robert H. Jackson U.S. Courthouse by New York City architects Kohn Pederson Fox

regulations for all new courthouse construction made that plan impossible, and planning for a new courthouse began. The project ran into numerous snags, including a federal moratorium on courthouse construction, GSA funding cuts, and competition from many other cities that vied for new buildings. But the Buffalo courthouse received support from New York's congressional delegation, which fought for its funding. Once begun, the building project benefited from an enormous investment of time and effort by Chief Judge Skretny and former Chief Judge Richard J. Arcara.

The courthouse's primary architect was Bill Pederson, a founding partner and design partner of Kohn Pederson Fox and an experienced courthouse architect. According to Pederson, the Buffalo courthouse used an elliptical design to help meet the challenges of GSA budget requirements without sacrificing design elements, while still meeting modern technology requirements and the stringent post–September 11 courthouse-security requirements. The elliptical shape has less exterior wall surface than a rectangular building and therefore reduces one of the most expensive ingredients of the structure.[20] And rather than glass for exterior walls, the building used precast concrete panels, which were then coated with translucent glass panels, giving a light-reflective visual effect. The concrete panels help meet the very specific federal standards of resistance to potential explosives.

Ground for the building was broken in 2007. It was topped off in 2009. Both Judges Skretny and Arcara signed the beam, as did some local ironworkers and others. In covering the topping-off ceremony, the Buffalo journal *Business First* reported that both judges had worked in the steel industry in their youth (Judge

Arcara had tied rods for the Iron Workers union, and Judge Skretny had spent a summer working at Republic Steel), and memories of those early days were evoked as the last steel beam was placed atop the courthouse.[18]

Several design elements are intended to make the courthouse welcoming to the public. They include an atrium facing Niagara Square and leading into the main courthouse building. In the first-floor lobby, a glass-covered pavilion has the text of the U.S. Constitution etched in glass and placed so that the words cast shadows as people enter the courthouse. Project oversight included making sure each word of the Constitution was carefully vetted.

On the other side of the pavilion lobby, monumental floor-to-ceiling glass panels are installed, each one a different color. The glass panels were created by artist

Above: Elliptical northern elevation.

Opposite: The southern elevation of the Jackson courthouse faces the McKinley Monument in Niagara Square.

Following pages: The glass-covered pavilion of the first floor lobby at night showing the Mangold panels.

The words of the U.S. Constitution are etched in glass on floor-to-ceiling panels of glass near the entrance to the courthouse.

One of the digital-age courtrooms in the Jackson courthouse, finished with wood.

and Buffalo native Robert Mangold as part of the Art in Architecture Program.

The courthouse includes a series of offices for the district clerk's office staff, the U.S. Attorney's Office, grand juries, and the probation department, as well as a laboratory. Its courtrooms are designed for technology, with digital-age voice, data, and electric wiring running under the floors, while their wood panels preserve a sense of warmth.

According to local news reports, the $137 million building, the most expensive in the city's history, has been greeted with admiration since its opening. Those who work in the building have called it spectacular.

Judge Skretny has said that he sees the new courthouse as a link between Buffalo's past and future. "In a real sense, it's not just the building structure that's so exciting, but what it represents," he told the *Buffalo Spree*. "It's the statement that we are prepared to meet the challenges of administering justice in modern times, without disrespecting the reverence for principled administration according to the rule of law without bias of status, age, creed, race, national origin, or gender."[22]

As has occurred in communities elsewhere in the Second Circuit, the construction in Buffalo of this beautiful new courthouse has been hailed as a sign of growth, renewal and positive change.

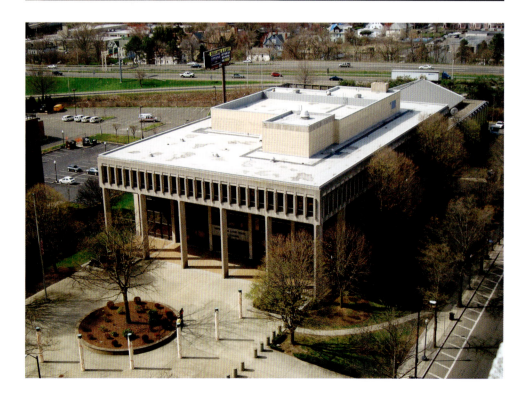

CHAPTER SIX

THE DISTRICT OF CONNECTICUT

The United States District Court for the District of Connecticut is one of the original 13 districts established by the Judiciary Act of 1789. It holds court today in New Haven, Hartford, and Bridgeport. In New Haven, the district court occupies the Richard C. Lee U.S. Courthouse, a Classical Revival building completed in 1919, redolent with character, and now the oldest courthouse in the district. In Hartford, it is located in the unadorned yellow brick and granite Abraham A. Ribicoff Federal Building and U.S. Courthouse. In Bridgeport, the court sits in the modernist 1967 Brien McMahon Federal Building and U.S. Courthouse, the most recently built of the district's federal courthouses.

The colorful history of the district, however, extends back far earlier than these relatively modern courthouses. The district's first judge, Richard Law, was appointed on September 24, 1789. Judges following Law included Pierpont Edwards, son of Jonathan Edwards, the fiery Calvinist theologian of the Great Awakening. Until 1927, only a single judgeship would be authorized for the district.[1]

Connecticut is the site of the nation's first law school, which opened in Litchfield under the auspices of Tapping Reeve, a brother-in-law of Aaron Burr. Reeve had tutored Burr in law and then apparently decided to teach more widely. Graduates of the Litchfield Law School went on to found Yale Law School. Second Circuit Judge José A. Cabranes, lecturing in 1983 as part of a series on the

Opposite, top to bottom: the Richard C. Lee U.S. Courthouse in New Haven; the Abraham A. Ribicoff Federal Building and U.S. Courthouse in Hartford; the Brien McMahon Federal Building and U.S. Courthouse in Bridgeport.

The east facade of the Old State House in Hartford.

history of the Second Circuit's courts, noted that Connecticut lawyers were "an unusually scholarly lot" and that its judges have figured prominently on the Second Circuit Court of Appeals. The early members of the trial bar were not only learned, according to Judge Cabranes, they were also required to be entertaining. Tools of the trade for lawyers included charm, looks, and stamina. In sober New Haven, the city that gave America "blue laws," contemplating the wisdom of the law was an approved pastime, and almost any trial could draw a throng of spectators.[2]

In the early days, federal court sessions were held alternately in Hartford and New Haven in courtrooms lent by the state and located in the state capitol buildings. Both cities were capitals of the state until 1873, when Hartford was established as the sole seat of government. The federal court did not sit in a federally owned building until 1861 in New Haven and 1882 in Hartford.

EARLY HISTORY
HARTFORD

The Old State House where the court sat in Hartford was built in 1796 in dignified Federal style, high on a hill overlooking the Connecticut River. Generally attributed to the well-known New England architect Charles Bullfinch, it is believed to be his first public building; it remains in use today as a museum.

Its first story, which rises 20 feet, is made of Portland, Connecticut brownstone. The second and third stories are patterned brick. The cornice is of wood. The principal entrance is located on the east facade. It has a center porch made of brownstone and three open arches, with the middle arch taller and wider than the other two. A flight of stairs leads to the entrance. All of the first-story windows are surrounded by arches capped with fan-shaped brownstone blocks. A double brownstone horizontal band called a string course separates the first from the second story; a single brownstone string course above the second story windows separates the second story from the third. A second-story portico raises the entire height of the second and third stories with three Doric columns on the southeast and northeast corners and two other columns evenly spaced across the front. Two additional columns adjacent to the wall support the back of the portico. The building's west facade, which faces Main Street, is similar to the east facade but has no portico.

The courtroom used by the federal court occupied the north wing of the first floor. It was 45 feet in diameter, with Doric columns 10 feet from the wall supporting the floor of the representative's chamber, located directly above. While little available description of the interior exists, the judge apparently presided from a semicircular dais set against the north wall.

The building was declared a National Historic Landmark in 1960 and functions as a museum today. It has been substantially renovated and modified many times since it was built, but the exterior still appears largely as it did in 1796 except for a balustrade added to the roof in the early 19th century for the protection of fireman, and a cupola added in 1827. The cupola houses a bell and John Stanwood's statue of Justice.

NEW HAVEN

In New Haven, one of the earliest Connecticut courtrooms used by the federal courts was the New Haven State House, which first came into use in 1830.[3] A home for both the judiciary and the legislature, it was the successor to two prior statehouses, the first having been built in 1717. Each New Haven State House has been located on the New Haven Green, also known as "the marketplace," a lawn area since colonial times featuring many of the town's significant structures.[4]

The Connecticut General Assembly passed a resolution in May 1827 declaring that a new state house should be built in New Haven.[5] At a meeting in New Haven on July 5, 1827, assembly representatives Dennis Kimberly and Charles A. Ingersoll commissioned a

The Old State House on the New Haven Green in 1889, as it was being torn down.

state house to include "a suitable court room, jury room and two lobbies for the accommodation of the courts and of the Bar."[6]

Construction began in 1828.[7] The building was made of marble purchased and shipped from Sing Sing prison in Ossining, New York,[8] and stood about halfway between the Center Church and the west line of the green.[9] Some of the timber and other materials from prior state houses were used in its construction.[10] The planned cost of the project was estimated at $42,000, excluding many subsequent upgrades and additions that occurred during the two years of construction.[11]

There was much discontent in New Haven over the construction because the east side of the building site covered part of an ancient burial ground that extended west through the town toward College Street, where relatives of many residents were buried.[12] Two subcontractors of the building project, Isaac and Charles Thompson, came across several bones, many of which were later reinterred. The workers took great care with the remains so as not to offend the sensibilities of New Haveners.[13] Nevertheless, more than one workman feared that the spirits of those buried were haunting the building in response to the disturbance of their earthly remains.[14]

The State House was designed by Ithiel Town, a prominent Connecticut architect and civil engineer.[15] Town and his firm, Town & Davis, also designed the Center Church and Trinity Church, both located on the green,[16] and the first New York City U.S. Custom House at 55 Wall Street, now Federal Hall.

Town intended the State House to have a "Grecian character," modeling it after the Doric Temple in Athens, constructed in honor of the warrior Theseus in 467 B.C.E.[17] Six columns supported the portico at both the north and south ends of the building, each seven feet in diameter and 40 feet high. Stretching 182 feet from one buttress to another on either side of the edifice, the main building was 130 feet long from pilaster to pilaster and 90 feet in width. The front steps extended an additional 15 feet beyond the buttresses. The building featured 12 large windows on each side.[18] A courtroom was included on the first floor.

Arthur D. Osborne, clerk of the Supreme and Superior Courts of Connecticut, noted that "the arrangement of [the] court room, which proved to be excellent, was chiefly devised by Hon. Alfred Blackman," a judge who had been prominent in New Haven civic life.[19]

The General Assembly held its meetings in the New Haven State House during every other year, alternating with Hartford at a time when the two cities were the co-capitals of Connecticut. The building's distinguished visitors included Noah Webster, General Lafayette, James T. Polk, James Buchanan, and Andrew Jackson.[20] The New Haven State House served as a de facto city center for New Haven.[21] Town meetings were held on the ground floor, right above a jail contained in the cellar. One of the more functional aspects of the State House was a pound, located under the front steps, for stray cattle caught wandering through the center of town. The State House was also the site of a famous Yale activity—the start of a procession honoring the burial of Euclid, a tradition involving costumes and ceremony.

Eventually, Hartford became the sole capital of Connecticut. The courts ceased to use the New Haven State House for their proceedings in 1861. In 1889, after eight years of discussion and debate over what to do with the building, the City of New Haven decided to demolish the State House.[22] By this time, the building had fallen "into decay,"[23] with a number of stones having fallen from outside the east wall.[24] Despite attempts by New Haven citizens to save the fabled public building, on November 26, 1889, the State House was torn down.[25] The demolition was itself an event in the life of New Haven, with more than 3,000 spectators turning out to say goodbye to the building.[26] More than 7,500 carts' worth of material were removed from the site, with much of the brick and stone subsequently being incorporated into the walls of new buildings elsewhere in the City.[27]

The ship *La Amistad* also called simply *Amistad*.

The Amistad Case

Perhaps the most renowned federal case tried in the District of Connecticut in the early days, one that would play a part in the abolitionist movement, arose from events aboard the Spanish schooner *La Amistad* (or *Amistad*). Proceedings unfolded in the courtrooms of both the Old Statehouse in Hartford and the Statehouse in New Haven before the case was ultimately decided in the United States Supreme Court.

In the summer of 1839, the *Amistad* sailed from Havana, Cuba, to Principe, a Cuban coastal town.[28] The ship was transporting a group of prisoners who had been captured in Africa and brought to Havana[29] although an 1817 treaty between Spain and Britain had sought to end the slave trade into the Spanish colonies, and local law therefore prohibited importation of slaves after 1820.[30] Those sailing the *Amistad* included Pedro Montez and Jose Ruiz, Spanish subjects who intended to sell the prisoners as slaves, as well as other crew.[31] On the fifth night at sea, as a storm distracted the captain and his crew, a Mendi African man named Cinque managed to pick the lock on his shackles with a loose nail he had found and freed himself and his fellow prisoners.[32] Cinque and his compatriots rushed a cargo hold that stored a shipment of knives intended for cutting sugarcane, seized the weapons, and staged a rebellion, killing the captain of the schooner, Ramon Ferrer, and the ship's cook, who is claimed to have told the Africans that the Spanish sailors were planning to cook and eat them.[33] The former prisoners let the two remaining Spanish captors, Montes and Ruiz, live, in hopes that they could steer the ship back to Africa.[34]

The former captives instructed their surviving captors to sail them east, back to their homes in West Africa.[35] Montez and Ruiz complied during the daytime, but after nightfall they steadily steered the boat west toward the United States, hoping to land somewhere in the southern portion of the country.[36] Instead, after six weeks of travel, the ship came to the eastern tip of Long Island,[37] where the *Amistad* was found at anchor off Culloden Point by the United States brig *Washington,* which was performing a coastal survey under the

"The Mutiny" by Hale Woodruff, depicting the uprising on board the *Amistad*, is the first in a series of murals by Woodruff commissioned by Talledega College. Collection of Talladega College, Talladega, Alabama. © Talladega College. Photo: Peter Harholdt.

command of Lt. Thomas R. Gedney. Several of the Africans, who had gone ashore seeking provisions, were forcibly returned to the ship. At the request of Ruiz and Montes, Lieutenant Gedney took over the *Amistad* and had it towed to New London, Connecticut.[38] Connecticut was, at the time, a slave state.[39]

The capture led to a series of complex and momentous legal proceedings. They began three days after the *Amistad*'s arrival in New London, with an initial court of inquiry held aboard the *Washington* and conducted by the district judge for Connecticut at the time, Andrew T. Judson.[40] Judson was Connecticut's fourth District Judge and, unlike his predecessors, did not hail from New Haven or from an eminent family. He was a Democrat, a Baptist, and a native of Ashford, in the northeastern part of the state.[41]

The U.S. Attorney for the District of Connecticut, William S. Holabird, filed a complaint for alleged crimes on the high seas within the maritime jurisdiction of the United States based on the mutiny and on the death of Ferrer and the ship's cook. Gedney and his crew indicated that they would file a libel, or claim, for a salvage award for their recovery of the *Amistad*, seeking a portion of the value of the ship and the cargo on board. The ship's cargo was estimated to be worth $40,000; the Africans were claimed to be slaves, with a value of $25,000. Judson heard from witnesses, including Montez and Ruiz, who offered their versions of the revolt.

On the day of the hearing, Judge Judson issued a warrant for the arrest of the adult Africans who were the subject of the indictment. Pursuant to the warrant, the Africans were transported to the New Haven jail to await the next meeting of the grand jury, which was to take place in September 1839 in Hartford. Judge Judson reserved all civil issues of property ownership to be heard at the same time before the circuit court, whose next sitting was also scheduled for September 1839 in Hartford.

In New Haven the Africans were jailed in "several rooms above a tavern across the street from the green."[42] The case created such a stir that the prisoners reportedly had up to 5,000 visitors a day, who were charged 12 and a half cents to view them.[43] The New Haven jailers were not strict with the prisoners, taking the children (who were being detained only as witnesses) on wagon rides about New Haven.[44] The adults were allowed out for exercise on the New Haven Green.[45] The case attracted the attention not only of the public and the press, but also of prominent abolitionists, including Lewis Tappan and Joshua Leavitt, a Yale-educated attorney and publisher of the abolitionist newspaper *The Emancipator*. Tappan enlisted the services of Roger Baldwin, a Yale-educated lawyer from New Haven and a future Governor and Senator from Connecticut, to represent the Africans.[46]

Meanwhile, the *Amistad* case was becoming an international incident.[47] Spain insisted that the United States had no jurisdiction over a Spanish ship and its passengers, and demanded that both the ship and the Africans be returned to Ruiz and Montez, invoking the authority of a 1795 treaty between Spain and the United States providing that ships and merchandise rescued out of the hands of robbers or pirates on the high seas "shall be brought into some port . . . and restored entire to their true proprietors".[48] President Martin Van Buren, soon to be up for reelection, did not want an international incident with Spain but also wished to avoid circumventing the American legal process.[49]

By the time of the September circuit-court hearing, libels for salvage had been filed by Ruiz and Montez asserting that the Africans were slaves, lawfully purchased in Havana, and were therefore lawfully their property. Libels for salvage also had been filed by Thomas R. Gedney and his fellow officer Richard W. Meade, seeking a "reasonable salvage" from the vessel on behalf of themselves and other crew members of the *Washington*, on the grounds that Ruiz and Montez had sought their aid and protection to save the *Amistad*, which would have been lost to them but for the aid they supplied. Under admiralty law at the time, persons who secured ships that were sinking or out of control were entitled to a portion of the value of the salvaged ship. Two other individuals, Henry Green and Palatial Fordham, also filed libels for salvage, alleging that they had "secured a portion of the negroes who had come on shore." Other residents of Cuba also sought return of part of the *Amistad* property.

In a pleading filed on September 19, 1839, U.S. Attorney Halberd informed the court of the position taken by Spain through its Minister and argued that, if that position proved to be well founded, the court should make such order as would allow the United States to comply with its treaty obligations. In the alternative, he argued that if it should prove that the persons described as slaves "are negroes and persons of color who had been transported from Africa, in violation of the laws of the United States," the court should make whatever order was necessary to allow them to be returned to Africa.[50] Baldwin argued on behalf of the captured Africans that they were not legally slaves and were thus free men and not property and that "[N]o power on earth has the right to reduce [the Africans] to slavery." The United States, he argued, should not be a "slave-catcher for foreign slave-holders."

United States Supreme Court Justice Smith Thompson presided over the proceedings in the circuit court, sitting as a circuit justice. His rulings avoided confronting the case directly on the merits. He held that since the events described occurred in international waters without the presence of any American citizens, the court lacked jurisdiction to hear the criminal case.[51] He deferred the property issues until they could be heard at the next sitting of the district court, scheduled for November in Hartford. Judge Thompson denied a habeas petition for release of the Africans, ordering instead that the *Amistad* captives remain detained in New Haven under a warrant of seizure until the civil issues were resolved. Warrants of seizure were used in libels for salvage to require that the property subject to claim be held by the court. It was left for the district court to determine whether the Africans were legally slaves and, as such, were to be considered property to be turned over to Montez and Ruiz (and subject to valuation as part of a salvage claim) or whether they were free men.

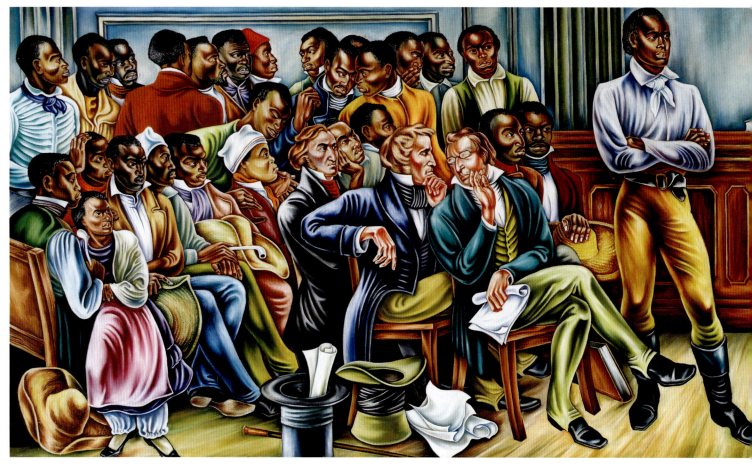

"Trial of the Slaves" by Hale Woodruff, depicting the *Amistad* trial, is the second in a series of murals by Woodruff. Cinque stands defiant in court in the foreground with Roger Baldwin whispering behind him. Woodruff included his own self-portrait behind them.

As trial approached, Josiah W. Gibbs, a linguistics professor from Yale, was enlisted to meet with the Africans. With the assistance of others including James Covey, he succeeded in translating their language. With the language barrier broken, the Africans spoke of the horrible conduct and conditions they had endured, traveling via the "Middle Passage" amid deplorable treatment by their kidnappers and the Spanish sailors alike.[52] Gibbs also was able to testify about how their language bore on their African origins.

The civil trial began in Hartford on November 19, 1839. Baldwin first agued the cases should be dismissed for lack of jurisdiction, on the grounds that Gedney had wrongfully attempted to reduce the Africans to slavery by removing them from the territorial waters of New York, a free state. After a day of conflicting testimony about the exact location of the *Amistad* at the time of seizure, District Judge Judson adjourned to the court's next term, to begin in January in New Haven. Judson sought additional evidence on the location of the *Amistad* at the time of its seizure to determine whether it was within New York territorial waters or on the "high seas."[53]

The trial continued in New Haven on January 8, 1840. On January 13, 1840, after the conclusion of testimony, Judge Judson announced his decision that the Africans were born free, that their "pretend" sale to Ruiz and Montez conveyed no rights to them, and that their capture violated international law.[54] The opinion also concluded that the Africans had been treated with great cruelty and oppression while on board the *Amistad* and that "incited by the love of liberty natural to all men," they had a right to take command of the vessel on the high seas. Judge Judson ordered that the *Amistad* captives be "delivered to President Van Buren for transport

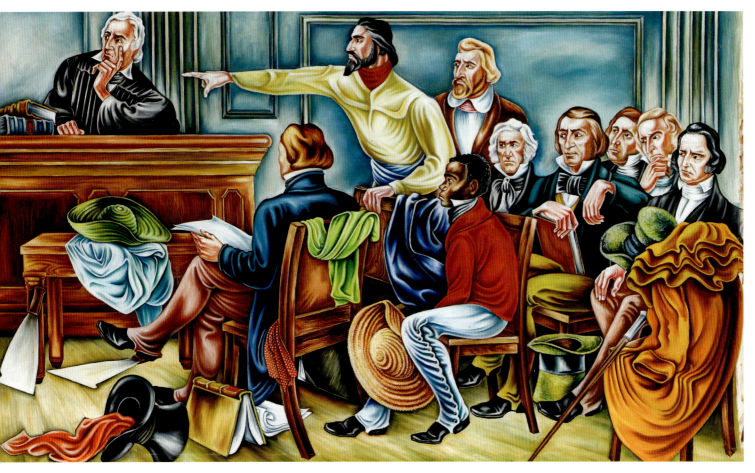

To the right, Pedro Montez stands and points at Cinque with Jose Ruiz behind him. James Covey, interpreter for the Africans, sits at the center. Collection of Talladega College, Talladega, Alabama. © Talladega College. Photo: Peter Harholdt.

back to Africa." In so ruling, he apparently accepted the plea in the alternative that had been advanced by the U.S. Attorney, although the Supreme Court would later view that plea as having been withdrawn by the filing of an amended pleading in November 1839 that did not contain this alternative request.[55] He also ruled on the various salvage claims, allowing Lieutenant Gedney and the crew of the *Washington* to receive one-third of the value of the *Amistad* itself and its cargo (but not its captives) as salvage.[56]

Under instructions from the Van Buren administration, the U.S. attorney appealed Judson's decision to the circuit court in order to press the claims of the Spanish government. The Spanish owners of the cargo on board appealed the salvage award. The lawyers for the Africans urged the circuit court to dismiss the appeal on the grounds that the United States had no right to advance the claims of a foreign government. The circuit court affirmed the district court with a pro forma decree.

The United States again appealed, this time to the Supreme Court.[57] Tappan sought out former President, now Congressman John Quincy Adams and convinced him to join Baldwin in arguing on behalf of the Africans at the nation's highest court.[58] Adams traveled to New Haven to meet with his clients, telling them, "God willing, we will make you free."[59]

Argument in the case began on February 22, 1841.[60] Attorney General Henry Gilpin implored the court on behalf of the government to defer to the wishes of Spain as a matter of respect for another nation, while Baldwin and Adams insisted that it contravened the law for the President to act as a foreign country's enforcer.[61] Adams—whose arguments on February 24 lasted more

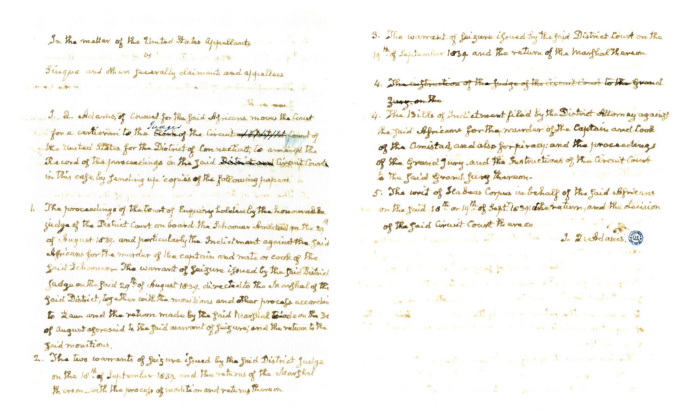

John Q. Adams' request for papers relating to the lower court trials of the Amistad Africans, January 23, 1841, prior to his Supreme Court argument on their behalf in United States v. Libellants and Claimants of the Schooner Amistad.

than 4 hours—cited the Declaration of Independence, proclaiming that "the moment you come to the Declaration of Independence, that every man has a right to life and liberty, an inalienable right, this case is decided. I ask nothing more in behalf of these unfortunate men than this Declaration."[62]

On March 9, 1841, the Court ruled, in an opinion by Mr. Justice Story from which there was only one dissent, that the *Amistad* captives were free men who had been illegally brought to Cuba, and that accordingly they should be set free and returned to their homeland.[63] The Africans, who were free but largely penniless, and their supporters attempted to raise money for the voyage home. The Africans put on frequent shows around New Haven, telling their story and performing acrobatic feats to obtain the funds necessary for their trip. Finally, in November 1841, the former *Amistad* captives returned to West Africa on the ship *Gentleman*.

The *Amistad* story continues to be studied and retold in books and films, such as the film *Amistad* directed by Steven Spielberg, sometimes with fictional details.

THE FEDERAL COURTS OCCUPY FEDERAL BUILDINGS

By the mid-19th century, the federal government had begun to turn away from its early policy of using rented space and to build federal buildings and courthouses. The District of Connecticut saw the fruits of this change, first in New Haven, then in Hartford, and finally in the additional court location of Bridgeport.

NEW HAVEN

U.S. Custom House and Post Office

The U.S. Custom House and Post Office was the first federal building completed in New Haven. The three-story building was designed in the late 1850s by the Supervising Architect of the Treasury Department,

United States of America, ss:

THE PRESIDENT OF THE UNITED STATES OF AMERICA,

To the HONORABLE the JUDGES of the *Circuit Court of the United States for the District of Connecticut*

greeting:

WHEREAS, lately, in the *Circuit Court of the United States for the District of Connecticut* before you, or some of you, in a cause, between *The United States, Jose Antonio Tellincas and others Appelants from a decree of the District Court of the United States for the District of Connecticut, and Jose Cinques & others, severally Claimants and Appellees, wherein the said Circuit Court affirmed the decree of the said District Court except as respects the claims of Jose Antonio Tellincas and the House of Aspa and Laca—*

as by the inspection of the transcript of the record of the said *Circuit Court* which was brought into the Supreme Court of the United States, by virtue of ~~a writ of error,~~ *an appeal* agreeably to the act of Congress in such case made and provided, fully and at large appears.

United States v. Libellants and Claimants of the Schooner Amistad, Statement of the Supreme Court to Circuit Court, March 9, 1841.

The U.S. Custom House and Post Office, New Haven, Connecticut.

Ammi B. Young, in an Italianate palazzo style typical of mid-19th-century post office buildings. With their rounded arches and symmetrical facades, such buildings were in marked contrast to neoclassical designs. The Connecticut District Court sat in this building from its opening in 1860 until 1917.

Richard C. Lee U.S. Courthouse

Now the oldest courthouse in the District of Connecticut, the Richard C. Lee U.S. Courthouse was built in 1913–1919. Its cornerstone was laid by former President William Howard Taft on June 4, 1914. A Classical Revival building containing fine woodwork and stonework, the courthouse had its most dramatic hour 50 years later, when it narrowly avoided being demolished as part of a mid-1960s New Haven redevelopment project. That the building survives today is testimony to the power of judge-inspired civic activism and timely lobbying.

President Taft declared at the cornerstone laying in 1914, "We are building today a building which will evidence the majesty and usefulness of the United States Government and will add significance and importance to this wonderful municipal center."[64] Behind his words was an ironic twist, one of two that have since become part of courthouse lore. Two years previously, during the extended post-1912 election lame-duck session, a public-works appropriation bill was making its way through Congress, and President Taft had initially signaled his opposition to an appropriation for a new federal building in New Haven. However, the departing President was planning to leave Washington to teach constitutional law at the Yale Law School. An appropriation was ultimately included for a post office and courthouse building in New Haven, because, courthouse lore has it, President Taft was reluctant to veto a bill for a major building project in his newly adopted city.

The courthouse was designed by James Gamble Rogers, the architect for a number of Yale University's buildings just across New Haven Green. The building was constructed under the Tarsney Act, which allowed the Treasury Department to hire private architects for government buildings. Over the two decades of its life, the Act had proved controversial because of the allegedly excessive cost of using private, nongovernmental architects. Indeed, the courthouse was the last building constructed under the Act. Rogers's design—for a Greek-inspired building that encompassed both a U.S. post office and a judicial courthouse with offices and two courtrooms—won out against five other plans.

The courthouse was part of a design plan authored by landscape architect Frederick Law Olmsted Jr. (son of the designer of Central Park) and architect Cass Gilbert, both leading designers of the age. Their design was inspired by the City Beautiful movement, which sought, through monumental architecture, to enliven cities and enlighten citizens. While this vision was never fully realized, the courthouse stands as a stunning example of what these city planners sought to accomplish.

Located on the east side of New Haven Green, the courthouse's most notable feature is its entrance porch extending across ten Corinthian columns clad in whitish-gray Tennessee marble. The porch is low to the ground, and the extended length of columns effectively ties the courthouse to the street, harmonizing it with

The Richard C. Lee U.S. Courthouse in New Haven.

the other government buildings surrounding the green. Between the porch and the triangular pediment above is a frieze carrying a verse from Proverbs 9:1 that was the subject of the Reverend John Davenport's 1639 sermon when the members of the Connecticut colony decided to form their government: "Wisdom hath builded her house; she hath hewn out her seven pillars." Other inscriptions on the building commemorate the members of the colony's first governing body (known as the General Court) and illustrious New Haven citizens.

When the courthouse was built, it gained attention in the architectural press, particularly in a lengthy 1919 article in *Architectural Forum*. The magazine piece complimented the building as "nicely calculated" to harmonize with its setting on the New Haven Green opposite two colonial-style churches and as capturing the spirit of government buildings of the age. "Its elegance and repose," the magazine opined, "due to careful proportioning and to extreme restraint in the scheme of architectural embellishment, endow it with a distinction adequate to its purpose and clearly express the dignity and grandeur appropriate to a public building."[65]

In the interior, one enters what was originally the customer hall for the post office, a space with marble floors and pilasters. The post office's working area has been remodeled into two substantial courtrooms, decorated in a neoclassical mode.

The highlights of the building are on the second floor, where the entrance lobby for the original main courtroom is a magnificent 90 x 20–foot marble room with 20 marble columns topped by bronze scrolled Ionic capitals.

With its windows overlooking the green, the light and ornate lobby forms a bright counterpoint to the

THE DISTRICT OF CONNECTICUT | 183

darker wooden walls of the courtroom next door. The main courtroom itself is sumptuously paneled in magnificently worked brownish-gray oak. Visitors sometimes find that this room—simultaneously intimate and grand—takes their breath away. Its high ceiling and small balconies combined with the rich woodwork of the pilasters, decorated cornice, and ceiling beams give it grandeur; yet the close proximity to one another of the counsel tables, witness stand, jury box, and judge's dais conveys intimacy. The 1919 *Architectural Forum* article aptly described the room as "dignified, sumptuous of perfect acoustic qualities." To many who view it, this courtroom is among the finest found anywhere.

Notwithstanding its beauty, the courthouse was slated for destruction in 1965 as part of an ambitious urban-redevelopment project. The New Haven Redevelopment Agency unveiled plans by the architect I. M. Pei to demolish all the buildings on the courthouse's side of the green (including the courthouse and City

Top: The main courtroom in the Lee courthouse. *Bottom*: The word "Justice" is prominent above the judge's bench in the main courtroom.

Lee courthouse. *Top*: Bronze details on the exterior. *Bottom*: Bronze detailing above elevator doors,

Following pages: The second floor lobby of the Lee courthouse, a 90 x 20-foot room with 20 marble columns.

THE DISTRICT OF CONNECTICUT | 185

The Lee courthouse, while undergoing the extensive renovations that took place during the early 1980s.

Hall) and replace them with a 29-story office building and other modern buildings to be used for government offices. The district court was to be moved a block away, to a new federal office building it would share with several other federal agencies. The GSA approved the plans and received funding authorization.

On June 27, 1966, the GSA presented the plans to the district's judges. The reaction was immediately unfavorable, and an extraordinary battle led by Chief Judge William H. Timbers ensued between the judiciary, who wanted the building to remain a dedicated single-purpose courthouse, and the GSA, which wanted to raze the building. Critics of the plan objected that the court would be treated as if it were just another government agency or, as Judge Timbers viewed it, "as some sub-agency of an executive department." To the District of Connecticut's judges, a separate courthouse was essential, a reflection of our nation's tradition of having the judiciary established as a separate and coordinate branch of the government.[66]

The courthouse's splendor galvanized public opinion. In keeping with a then-growing preservationist appreciation of America's architectural heritage—an awareness revitalized following the destruction of New York City's old Pennsylvania Station in 1963–1964—the New Haven Preservation Trust took up the case. So did New Haven native Vincent J. Scully Jr., a professor in Yale University's Art Department and one of the country's leading architectural critics. On October 19, 1966, Scully addressed an overflow crowd at Yale Law School, attacking the GSA proposal and declaring that "the new project is like an act of undeniable vandalism so gross that one cannot believe it was proposed without irony." A month later, the New Haven Preservation Trust symbolically placed a landmark plaque on the courthouse, with Judge Timbers speaking at the ceremony: "The New Haven Landmark plaque which we place on our Courthouse today is, I think, a fitting mark of recognition of the beauty and strength of this notable building," he told those assembled. "It is also, I venture to suggest, an appropriate recognition of one of the most basic, precious principles of our heritage as American citizens: a free and independent federal judiciary. On behalf of all the federal judges of this State, I give you our solemn pledge that a free and independent judiciary we will remain—in this United States Courthouse on this land of the United States!" [67]

In December 1966, I. M. Pei withdrew from the project and the New Haven Redevelopment Agency abandoned plans for the skyscraper. The GSA, however, continued planning to demolish the courthouse and move the court to the new location around the corner. Only after lobbying by Senator Thomas Dodd, Senator Abraham A. Ribicoff, and Congressman Robert N. Giaimo did the GSA adopt a plan to instead renovate the building for exclusive court use and, at the same time, to erect a separate federal office building behind it. The House of Representatives approved the renovation plan in November 1967, making available $3.17 million.

While the building had been saved, and congressional approval given for its renovation, it took an astonishing 18 years before the judges were operating in a renovated building. In significant part, this resulted from the Postal Reorganization Act of 1971 abolishing the postal service as a cabinet-level department and turning it into the U.S. Postal Service, a corporation-like independent agency. As part of the Act, the postal service obtained title to the courthouse building. GSA could not renovate the building until the postal service evacuated the structure and moved to a new facility. It was not until 1979 that the new facility was available, with the postal service selling the courthouse to the GSA for $2.5 million.

The postal service had allowed the building to deteriorate during the 1970s. Over time, conditions became dire, with plaster falling off interior walls, entrances being boarded up, and daylight becoming visible through holes in the roof. The New Haven Fire Marshal declared the building a serious potential fire hazard in need of immediate attention.

Again, the judges of the court had to lobby Washington. In 1980 Judges José A. Cabranes and Warren W. Eginton met with senatorial staff to let them know of the conditions, and that same year the GSA created revised renovation plans and requested additional funding. At the hearing of the House Subcommittee on Public Buildings on July 24, 1980, written and oral statements and testimony supporting the renovation were provided from such figures as Connecticut Governor Ella Grasso, New Haven Mayor Biagio DiLieto, Dean César Pelli of the Yale School of Architecture, attorneys, bar associations, and Judges Cabranes and Robert C. Zampano. In December 1980, a $6.8 million funding appropriation was approved and signed by President Carter. For three years during construction, from September 1982 until June 1985, the court's judges relocated to cramped quarters nearby.

Since 1985, the Richard C. Lee U.S. Courthouse has remained dedicated to the work of the federal judiciary. Together with the office building next door, it now houses four district court judges, one magistrate judge, and their staffs. A senior-status judge has his chambers in an office building next door.

In 1999 the building was renamed the Richard C. Lee U.S. Courthouse. Richard C. Lee was New Haven's mayor from 1954 to 1970. Mr. Lee, a Democrat, had leveraged hundreds of millions of dollars from the state and federal governments to redevelop New Haven.[68] Although some had lauded these redevelopment plans for New Haven at the time, the plans, ironically, almost cost the City the courthouse now named for him.

The district court in New Haven has seen more than its share of controversial cases. In 1978 the courthouse was at the forefront of a dispute involving the convergence of patent and antitrust laws in *SCM Corp. v. Xerox Corp.*[69] SCM, a maker of coated-paper copier machines, brought suit under the Sherman and Clayton Acts against Xerox, the "world leader in plain paper

THE DISTRICT OF CONNECTICUT | 189

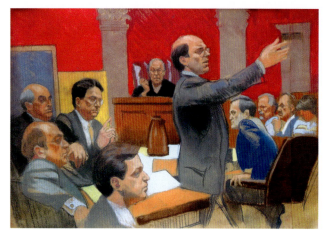

Top: New Haven firefighters outside the Lee courthouse. Associated Press Jessica Hill. *Bottom:* The trial before Judge Whitman Knapp of Bronx Democratic Leader Stanley Friedman and others, shown in a drawing by Christine Cornell..

copiers," alleging that Xerox had excluded SCM from entering the market of plain-paper copiers and caused SCM upward of $500 million in damages. The crux of SCM's complaint was that Xerox had monopolized the market by refusing to license patents to its competitors, including SCM. The ensuing trial, during which evidence was presented over 215 days, and which required 38 days of jury deliberation, took 14 months to complete. The trial transcript totaled 46,802 pages. The jury returned a mixed verdict, finding that Xerox had, in some instances, violated antitrust law and inhibited SCM's entry into the market.

After the jury's finding of liability, Judge Jon O. Newman determined what money judgment, if any, should be entered. He held that while Xerox's refusal to license to SCM might suggest anticompetitive conduct, some accommodation was necessary in order to promote the progress of science and the useful arts and that, despite the jury's findings, Xerox's conduct in refusing to license the patents was not a basis for a monetary damages award.[70] The Second Circuit affirmed the decision and the Supreme Court denied certiorari.[71]

Most recently, the New Haven court issued a major civil-rights decision,[72] stemming from a lawsuit brought against the City of New Haven by 20 New Haven firefighters. The plaintiffs (19 of whom were white) alleged that the City had discriminated against them when it invalidated the results of a civil-service exam on which no black firefighter had scored high enough to be considered for a promotion. The City had feared the test results would be challenged as having an adverse impact on minorities. District Court Judge Janet Bond Arterton granted summary judgment in defendants' favor, and a Second Circuit panel (including then-Judge Sonia Sotomayor) affirmed the district court's decision in a summary order. The same panel, after an en banc hearing was requested, later issued a unanimous per curiam opinion, in which it described the district's court decision as "thorough, thoughtful and reasoned," while also noting the lack of any "good alternatives." However, in a 5–4 decision, the Supreme Court reversed, holding that the City of New Haven's invalidation of the test was a violation of Title VII.[73] The Court cited the absence of a "strong basis in evidence" for the City's position that it faced liability because of the test's adverse impact. Shortly after the decision, the City of New Haven promoted 14 of the 20 firefighters and paid $2 million in damages to the plaintiffs, as well as substantial attorneys' fees.

The courthouse also played host in 1986 to a major public corruption trial before Judge Whitman Knapp. Bronx Democratic Leader Stanley Friedman and four others were tried on racketeering charges involving bribery and corruption in the New York City Parking Violations Bureau. The case was transferred to

New Haven at the defendants' request and tried with a Hartford jury pool because the grand jury investigation had generated massive and potentially prejudicial publicity in New York.[74] Southern District U.S. Attorney Rudolph W. Giuliani conducted the examination of Friedman, and seeking to establish profiteering, asked at one point: "You got paid $10,000 to make two calls on behalf of the taxi drivers association?" "That was one call, Mr. Giuliani," Friedman responded. He was convicted and served four years in prison.

HARTFORD

In 1882 the U.S. Post Office and Customhouse opened in Hartford. The three-story building was designed by U.S. Supervising Architect Alfred B. Mullet in grand Second Empire style. It was distinguished by tall proportions, an offset tower, a high mansard roof with dormers, and rich decoration. It was used by the district court from 1882 until 1933. By the 1920s, Hartford residents had begun a campaign for a new postal building to replace the overcrowded Second Empire structure.

William R. Cotter Federal Building

In 1928 the government selected a site for the new building, a trapezoidal block in downtown Hartford bounded by High and South Church Streets and Foot Guard and Hoadley Places. Two years later, it chose the local architectural firm of Malmfeldt, Adams & Prentice to design the building, taking advantage of the 1930 Keyes-Elliot amendment to the 1926 Public Buildings Act, which permitted private architectural firms to compete for certain federal projects. Construction began in 1931, and the cornerstone was laid on April 14, 1932.

The three-story building included the functions of a post office, courthouse, and office building. It was designed in neoclassical style with traditional classical exterior forms and Art Deco interior decorative elements. Like many other Depression-era federal buildings, it was intended to convey the federal government's dignity and stability.

The building, which rests on a granite foundation, covers its entire trapezoidal block with an irregular footprint. The exterior is faced with Indiana limestone. The facade facing High Street consists of a three-story central block flanked by pavilions. The central section is separated into bays by limestone pilasters and topped by a flat cornice with decorative cresting projecting above the bays. Narrow aluminum bands divide the central and side casement windows within each bay on each story, and wide aluminum bands with decorative eagles separate the windows of the first and second stories, while similar undecorated aluminum bands separate those of the second and third stories. A frieze above the facade's third story bears a six-line, two-part inscription alluding to postal duties, divided by low-relief figures on horseback transferring a message in the style of the Pony Express. Projecting pavilions with modified Corinthian columns frame the two main entrances, one at each end of the building as it faces High Street. At each end of the building's cornice, massive aluminum eagles sit with their wings uplifted against the skyline, looking toward the entrance steps. The entrances themselves are surrounded by Wisconsin black marble.

Inside, a principal corridor connects two main lobbies on the first floor. The floors are of black terrazzo

The Mullett-designed U.S. Post Office and Customhouse in Hartford, Connecticut used by the district court from 1882 until 1933.

The William R. Cotter Federal Building, used by the district court from 1933 until 1962.

inlaid with decorative patterns, including, at each end of the corridor, a brass-and-terrazzo panel with an envelope motif. The courthouse's first floor ceiling is decorated with medallions that depict George Washington, Thomas Jefferson, Benjamin Franklin, and Abraham Lincoln. Stylized spherical aluminum light fixtures are set along the length of the ceiling within recessed panels with small metallic stars encircling the lights.

Stairs from the first-floor lobbies have black soapstone treads with a decorative aluminum railing. Several original three-panel aluminum doors remain, decorated with stars. A light court, on the second and third stories, admits natural light into the interior.

Widely admired when it was built, the structure was listed in the National Register of Historic Places in 1982. In the same year it was renamed the William R. Cotter Federal Building in honor of Connecticut Congressman Cotter. Cotter served as Democratic member of the United States House of Representatives from 1971 until his death in 1981. A native of Hartford, he had previously served as Connecticut's Insurance Com-

missioner and Deputy Insurance Commissioner, and he had been a member of the Hartford Common Council and an aide to Governor Abraham Ribicoff. The district court vacated the building in 1962 for its new quarters in the Abraham A. Ribicoff Federal Building.

Abraham A. Ribicoff Federal Building and U.S. Courthouse

The United States District Court for the District of Connecticut now sits in Hartford in the Abraham A. Ribicoff Federal Building and U.S. Courthouse. The eight-story, 190,000-square-foot building, originally named the U.S. Courthouse and Federal Building or, more simply, the Hartford Federal Building, was completed in 1963 as part of an effort to house all of the federal government's Hartford activities in one location.[75] Located on Main Street and bounded by Sheldon and Prospect Streets, it borders the eastern edge of the Buckingham Square Historic District. This district, listed on the National Register of Historic Places in 1977, originally included some 60 buildings and has

One of the two main entrances to the Cotter building. An eagle with uplifted wings sits at each end of the cornice.

THE DISTRICT OF CONNECTICUT | 193

 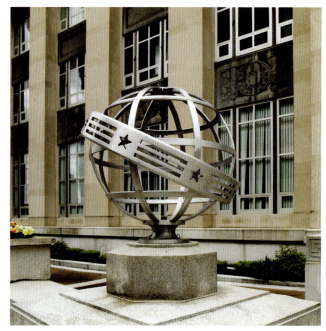

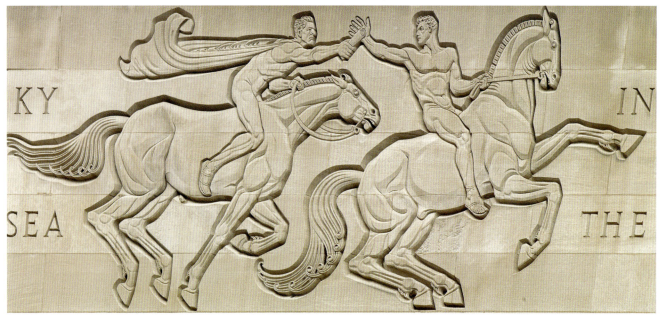

Top left: A closer view of one of the two eagles at the Cotter building shows the careful details of its upraised wings and fierce expression. *Top right*: An armillary sphere, said to represent celestial order, was placed at each courthouse entrance. On the facade, wide aluminum bands with decorative eagles separate the windows of the Cotter courthouse's first and second stories. *Bottom*: Figures on horseback transfer a message in the style of the Pony Express at the center of the courthouse facade.

been described as a 19th century urban ensemble whose commercial buildings and townhouses are "important examples of the Italianate, High Victorian and Richardsonian styles," that preserve "a moment of the city's 19th century urban development."[76] The Ribicoff Federal Building, by contrast, is unadorned in style, an eight-floor, low-rise building with a granite foundation, regular glass windows, and tannish-yellow brick walls and marble trim covering reinforced concrete.[77] Its two-story entrance is defined by contemporary marble columns. Designed by the firm Ebbets, Frid and Prentice of Hartford, and Douglas Orr of New Haven,[78] the building was intended to match the appearance of the nearby public library.[79v]

William R. Cotter Federal Building. *Top*: The first floor corridor, showing its ceiling, light fixtures, and terrazzo floor.
Middle: Original three-panel aluminum door, decorated with stars.
Bottom: The original interior stairway.

Following pages: The Abraham D. Ribicoff Federal Building and U.S. Courthouse in Hartford.

A courtroom in the Ribicoff courthouse.

The building took more than two years to complete at a cost of approximately $6.7 million. Its construction required the demolition of 11 brick and wood-frame neighborhood buildings.[80] It was one of the first structures in Hartford to include accommodations for wheelchairs. In approving funds for the building, the House Appropriations Committee strongly urged the GSA to "leave out all unnecessary features and trimmings" and "that no architect be permitted to build a local monument to himself."[81] Reflecting the concerns of the times, the building included a fallout shelter, although one had not been included in the original planning.[82] The U.S. Senate approved an extra $180,000 for the shelter,[83] a grim reminder that in 1961 a fallout shelter was not considered an unnecessary feature.

The Ribicoff Federal Building contains 11 federal courtrooms, which flank its central courtyard. A branch office of the U.S. Citizenship and Immigration Service occupies a 26,000-square-foot facility on the ground floor. When it opened in 1963, the building also contained numerous other governmental agencies, including a branch office of the IRS with a public exhibit on moonshine in Connecticut, complete with a "small still recently seized in the Hartford area."[84]

The building was named in honor of Connecticut native and public servant Abraham A. Ribicoff on September 15, 1981, the result of a bill introduced by Connecticut Senator Lowell P. Weicker. Ribicoff, born in New Britain, Connecticut, to a Polish immigrant family,[85] attended New York University for a year before receiving his law degree from the University of Chicago in 1933.[86] From 1938 to 1942 he served in the Connecticut Legislature, and from 1941 to 1943 and 1945 to 1947 as a judge in the Hartford Police Court, before being elected to Congress from the First District in 1949. After serving in the 81st and 82nd Congresses,

Ribicoff made an unsuccessful bid for U.S. Senate in 1952, losing to Prescott Bush. He practiced law for two years before unseating John Davis Lodge, the incumbent Governor of Connecticut, by just over 3,000 votes, to become the state's first Jewish governor. He served as Governor of Connecticut from 1955 to 1961. Ribicoff was afterward nominated by his friend President John F. Kennedy to become the Secretary of the Department of Health, Education and Welfare. He had reportedly turned down the post of Attorney General, suggesting that President Kennedy nominate his brother Robert instead.[87] In 1962 Ribicoff was elected to the U.S. Senate, where he served three terms. As a senator he was well known for his work in the areas of finance, international trade, education, environmental regulation, and auto safety. After leaving the Senate, Ribicoff served as special counsel to Kaye Scholer in New York.[88] In his retirement he came to deplore the growing meanness in politics, reflecting that "politics is not what it used to be."[89]

In 1992 a $3.5-million ground-floor annex was completed behind the original building. The annex includes updated courtrooms designed to replace the original "drab, cavernous rooms where spectators often had to strain to hear testimony."[90] A metal sculpture titled *Citizen* by Timothy Woodman is part of the Ribicoff Annex. In 2007 the building underwent significant renovations, including replacement of its 40,000-square-foot roof, which had been damaged during a seismic event. Portions of the building's exterior walls were repaired and replaced with material designed to match the original construction. The annex also underwent revitalization. This work including the replacement of 18,000 square feet of roofing material on nine different roof elevations, to address leakage, and the cleaning and restoration of 22,000 square feet of the exterior granite veneer.[91]

The Ribicoff building's courtrooms have been home to many well-publicized and important cases. A 1983 robbery of $7.1 million from a Wells Fargo depot in West Hartford captivated the State of Connecticut and led to one of the "lengthiest and most complex criminal cases in Federal court history."[92] On September 12, 1983, Victor Manuel Gerena, a Wells Fargo guard, held two co-workers at gunpoint and drove off with 1,100 pounds of cash in what was at that time the second-largest cash heist in U.S. history.[93] In 2011 Gerena became the longest-listed fugitive on the FBI's Ten Most Wanted Fugitive's List. The robbery, code-named "White Eagle," was planned by Los Macheteros—"the machete wielders"—a clandestine Puerto Rican organization seeking the island's independence from the United States. At the trial, prosecutors claimed that the money was stolen to fund Los Macheteros' activities; defendants claimed that the money was stolen to help the people of Puerto Rico. Some $20,000, it was revealed at trial, was used to buy toys to give away to poor children in Hartford. After years of investigation (and more than 1,100 tapes of wiretapped conversations and 150,000 seized documents), 16 defendants were charged with a variety of crimes, including robbery, conspiracy, transportation of stolen money, and weapons violations. The first hearings on the case, Judge T. Emmet Clarie presiding, were held in 1985, with snipers and bomb-sniffing dogs ringing the courtroom. After three years of pretrial hearings and over 2,000 motions, five defendants were tried over a six-period from 1988 to 1989. Four of the five were convicted and sentenced to terms ranging from five to 65 years.

The trial of nine other defendants was delayed as the Supreme Court considered the admissibility of some tape recordings the FBI had delayed in having sealed during the course of the investigation. In *United States v. Ojeda Rios*,[94] the Court determined that the government needed to explain their failure under U.S. wiretapping law to timely apply a seal.[95] After protracted legal wrangling, the remaining defendants reached a variety of plea agreements with the government. In 2008 Los Macheteros conspirator Avelino Gonzalez Claudio was arrested by the FBI in Puerto Rico, where he had been living under an assumed name.[96] Claudio, who was accused of helping Gerena get the stolen cash out of the United

The four-story Brien McMahon Federal Building and U.S. Courthouse in Bridgeport.

States, pleaded guilty in 2010 to foreign transportation of stolen money and conspiracy to rob federally insured banks.[97] Judge Alfred V. Covello sentenced Claudio to seven years in prison and ordered that he repay the stolen money.[98] In 2011 Avelino Claudio's brother, Noberto Gonzalez-Claudio, was arrested in Puerto Rico. He later was sentenced to five years in prison.[99]

In 1991 the prosecution of the Patriarca crime family became the focal point of another noted case in the Ribicoff Federal Building. Nine defendants stood trial on charges ranging from racketeering and murder to RICO violations in one of the most sweeping attacks ever launched on an organized-crime family. The defendants stood accused of being members of the Patriarca crime family, a Mafia organization that had controlled the New England underworld since the 1940s. Another dozen Patriarca defendants would stand trial in Boston on similar charges. Judge Alan H. Nevas presided over the Hartford trial, which focused in part on the death of William Grasso, a Patriarca family underboss whose body was found in the Connecticut River in 1989 with a gunshot wound to the head. It was revealed at trial that Grasso was killed by other members of the Patriarca family in a territorial dispute between the family's Providence and Boston factions. During the three-month trial, the prosecution introduced clips of some of the 1,500 hours of wiretap recordings collected during the investigation. The wiretaps captured the defendants discussing various illegal activities, including Grasso's murder, illegal gambling, and loansharking.

For the first time in a Mafia prosecution, the government presented recorded evidence of a Mafia induction ceremony, during which members of the Patriarca family pledged their lifelong allegiance to the mob. After

15 days of deliberations, the jury returned guilty verdicts against all defendants. At sentencing, defendant Gaetano Milano broke down, renounced the Mafia, and admitted killing Grasso. That confession spared Milano a sentence of life without parole. The other defendants were given sentences ranging from just under 10 years to life in prison. In 2008 Judge Alan H. Nevas reduced Milano's sentence by seven years after Milano brought a habeas action alleging that his conviction was tainted by FBI corruption.

A white-collar criminal case captured headlines in 2004, when Walter Forbes and Kirk Shelton stood trial in Hartford on charges of securities fraud, mail and wire fraud, conspiracy, and lying to the Securities and Exchange Commission in connection with their leadership of Cendant Corporation during a $300 million accounting scandal. Before Enron, WorldCom, or Tyco, Cendant Corporation, a provider of business and consumer services, had been accused of overstating earnings to maximize the company's stock price. When in 1998 the irregularities came to light, Cendant shares lost $14 billion in market value in a single day. In 2000 Cendant settled a class-action shareholder suit for $2.85 billion. Judge Alvin W. Thompson presided over the trial of Forbes, the former Chairman, and Shelton, the former Vice Chairman of Cendant.

After seven months of testimony and 33 days of deliberations, Shelton was convicted on all 12 counts. The jury was unable to reach a verdict on the charges against Forbes. Shelton was sentenced to 10 years in prison and ordered to pay $3.27 billion in restitution to Cendant. Forbes was retried in 2005 on a reduced four counts, but a jury was once again unable to reach a verdict. Forbes was tried for a third time in Bridgeport in 2006 and convicted of conspiracy to commit securities fraud and making false statements to the SEC. Forbes was sentenced to 12 years in prison and also ordered to pay $3.27 billion in restitution.

Important issues of constitutional law have also taken center stage in the Ribicoff courthouse. In 1965 the Connecticut Legislature enacted legislation requiring newcomers to the state to live in Connecticut for one year before they could become eligible to receive permanent welfare assistance.[100] The law applied only when a new resident came "without visible means of support for the immediate future and applie[d] for aid to dependent children."[101] Therefore, newcomers were eligible for assistance only if they had employment prospects or sufficient savings. At the time, Connecticut was one of 40 states with some residency requirement to collect welfare benefits. In 1966, 19-year-old Vivian Thompson, pregnant with her second child, moved to Hartford from Massachusetts. Her application for assistance was denied by the Connecticut Commissioner of Welfare because she had not met the one-year residency requirement. Thompson brought suit against the Commissioner in the United States District Court in Hartford, alleging that the residency requirement deterred indigent people from settling in Connecticut, violated the rights to free travel and choice of residence, and forced involuntary departures. The case was heard in 1967 by a panel of Judge J. Joseph Smith, Judge M. Joseph Blumenfeld, and Judge T. Emmet Clarie.[102]

A horseshoe pit open to all at the Brien McMahon Federal Building and U.S. Courthouse.

Untitled, 1985 metal sculpture by Patsy Norvell in front of the McMahon courthouse.

In a 2–1 ruling, Judges Smith and Blumenfeld held that the Connecticut statute was unconstitutional, finding that the one-year residency requirement violated the constitutional right of interstate travel. The court reasoned that the right of travel "embodies not only the right to pass through a state but also the right to establish residence therein."[103] The statute had the effect of chilling that right.[104] The majority stated that the Connecticut statute violated the equal protection clause by denying assistance only to those needing relief while freely giving assistance to more well-off newcomers.[105] Judge Clarie dissented, finding the statute reasonably related to protecting the state's fiscal responsibilities and not within the ambit of the recognized constitutional right to travel.[106]

Connecticut appealed the ruling to the Supreme Court, and the case was joined with similar cases from Pennsylvania and the District of Columbia.[107] Archibald Cox argued on behalf of the various individuals who were denied assistance, and in 1969 the Supreme Court upheld the district court's decision. Justice Brennan, writing for the six-Justice majority, concluded that the Connecticut statute violated the equal protection clause by imposing a classification that impinged on the constitutional right of welfare applicants to travel from state to state.[108]

BRIDGEPORT
Brien McMahon Federal Building and U.S. Courthouse

The four-story Brien McMahon Federal Building and U.S. Courthouse, built in 1967 on a 3.34-acre site, is a four-story steel-frame structure clad with limestone panels. Before moving to this courthouse, the district court sat in Bridgeport in the Underwood Commerce Building facility, where Judges William Timbers and T. Emmet Clarie formerly heard cases in space leased by the federal government.

The present building is modernist in style, with echoes of the classical elements of columns, portico, and cornice. On its main facade, six tall, column-like exterior supports extend upward to an overhanging top story forming a sheltered entranceway. Frequent vertical lines mark the top story, defining that level's windows. At each of the floors below, reflective glass panels alternate with muted brown panels. These panels mirror the landscape surrounding the courthouse, which includes outdoor tables and a horseshoe pit. It is, in all likelihood, the only federal courthouse in the Second Circuit with its very own horseshoe pit, used by judges and their support staff for lively competition.

While the building's design is spare, any deficit in its architectural splendor is overshadowed by the large personalities who have shaped the court's history. The building is named after Brien McMahon, who accomplished much in his 49 years. McMahon's classmates at Fordham University were prescient when they nicknamed him "The Senator." After graduating from Yale Law School, practicing law in Connecticut, becoming a state court judge, and serving as Assistant U.S. Attorney, the dashing McMahon was elected to the U.S. Senate. As the Senior Senator from Connecticut, he was Chairman of the Joint Congressional Committee on Atomic Energy and a leader in the world peace movement. As U.S. Assistant Attorney General overseeing the Criminal Division, he was involved in the prosecution of John Dillinger's lawyer, Louis Piquette, for harboring a criminal, and in the trials of gangsters

One of the McMahon courtrooms.

Decorative wood courtroom doors to one of the McMahon courtrooms.

associated with Baby Face Nelson. McMahon argued 20 cases before the United States Supreme Court, winning them all.

The federal courthouse in Bridgeport has seen its share of colorful personalities. Judge William H. Timbers served as a district judge from 1960 to 1971, becoming its Chief Judge in 1964 before serving on the Second Circuit. Described by a colleague as tenacious and stubborn, Judge Timbers demonstrated those traits when asked to officiate at a wedding in New Jersey. He prevailed upon Supreme Court Justice Warren Burger to appoint him as a district court judge in New Jersey for 24 hours, starting at midnight the day of the wedding. Accompanied by his two Norwegian elk hounds (who sat with him not only in chambers, but on the bench), Judge Timbers traveled to New Jersey the night before the wedding and stayed at a hotel. The dogs, apparently displeased with their accommodations, started barking and refused to stop, to the annoyance of other hotel guests. When management arrived shortly before midnight to inform Judge Timbers that he must quiet his dogs or the police would be called, he ignored them. When the police did arrive, even closer to midnight, Judge Timbers ignored them, as well. At the stroke of midnight, he opened the door, handing them, in his temporary status as a New Jersey federal court judge, a *ne exeat* order prohibiting them from arresting him. No further 24-hour appointments were given by Justice Burger to Judge Timbers.[109]

Judge T. F. Gilroy Daly ruled on many complex and high-profile cases, including ones involving discrimination in municipal hiring, state police interrogation methods, and public corruption. Appointed to the bench in 1977, Judge Daly served as Chief Judge from 1983 to 1988. At six feet, six inches tall, he was an imposing presence in the courtroom, despite his penchant for describing himself as "just a country lawyer." In a tribute to Judge Daly, Senator Chris Dodd noted: "He was particularly known for handing down harsh sentences to corrupt public officials … . Being a man of such high moral standards, Judge Daly held a particular disdain for anyone who betrayed the trust of the general public. Judge Daly believed that without the people's trust, government cannot function effectively, and his career was dedicated to maintaining the integrity of the Constitution and protecting the rights of the general public."[110] Earlier in his career, Daly had taken leave from his position as Insurance Commissioner to represent Peter Reilly, who had been convicted of the grisly murder of his mother. Daly's dogged investigation uncovered new evidence of a forced confession, shoddy police work, and prosecutorial misconduct in the form of suppression of evidence. After a six-week hearing, Reilly was released from jail.

District Judge Warren Eginton, appointed to the bench in 1979, also oversaw several memorable cases, including a criminal antitrust lawsuit against AT&T,[111] a Hell's Angels extortion case (requiring Judge Eginton to have U.S. Marshals' security when the convicted defendant escaped from jail), an antitrust case brought by Great Northern Nekoosa against Georgia Pacific, and a criminal case in which defense counsel included Roy Cohn and Bill Kunstler.

The first large drug-conspiracy case in Connecticut, involving the Latin Kings, was tried in the Bridgeport Courthouse before Judge Alan H. Nevas, appointed to the bench in 1985. Judge Nevas also presided over the sex-abuse trial of Waterbury mayor Philip Giordano involving two preteen girls. During that trial, Judge Nevas ordered that the girls be permitted to testify from an adjacent room, so that they would not have to enter the courtroom and see the defendant.

The first capital-murder case tried in Connecticut also came before Judge Nevas, who ultimately set aside the jury's conviction of RICO murder (thereby avoiding the death-penalty stage) after finding that the evidence was unclear whether the murder—for which the defendant was also convicted—was in furtherance of a drug conspiracy.[112]

* * *

Through growth as a center for commerce, education, insurance, and finance, the District of Connecticut has expanded from the rented space it once occupied to three courthouses and from the single judge assigned to the district through 1927 to a total of eight judgeships today. Despite growth, the district's courts have, as practitioners readily attest, retained a personal and pragmatic style.

The sex-abuse trial of Waterbury mayor Philip Giordano before Judge Alan H. Nevas shown in a drawing by Christine Cornell.

CHAPTER SEVEN

THE DISTRICT OF VERMONT

The three courthouses that now serve the District of Vermont—located in Rutland, Burlington, and Brattleboro—elegantly personify the state's unique characteristics: sensible, dignified, and consummately democratic.[1] Comprising only 2 percent of the Second Circuit's population and 15 percent of its land area, the District of Vermont never aspired to compete, at least in volume of cases, with its more litigious neighbors to the south. In this sense, as Chief Judge Albert W. Coffrin observed in 1985, the district "is often viewed with considerable envy by any who may be struggling to keep abreast of a burgeoning docket."[2] Size and population are only two of the factors explaining the lesser volume of litigation in Vermont's courts. The plain fact is, as Judge Coffrin wryly observed, that "rank and file Vermonters simply have not been litigiously inclined to any very great degree."[3] Vermont's rural economy historically provided "primarily for life's basic needs and little more," making its residents "practical and frugal."[4] As a result, most Vermonters "shunned the expense of lawyers" as generally unnecessary and "resorted to litigation . . . only in the most compelling of circumstances."[5] Judge Coffrin's theory was that the character of Vermont's people was shaped by the state's early struggles for independence and a desire to be free from the influences of overbearing neighboring states.[6] These traits created a "citizenry of independent spirit, reserved demeanor and conservative leanings" seeking to forge its destiny without "outside help or judicial intervention."[7]

Opposite, top to bottom: the Rutland U.S Courthouse and Post Office; the Burlington Federal Building; the Brattleboro U.S Post Office and Courthouse.

An early courthouse in Windsor, Vermont that later became a post office.

As Vermont has continued to evolve from its entry into the fledgling Union as the 14th state, its courts have steadfastly preserved their special character, marked by a rootedness in the past, an utter lack of pretension, and an abiding respect for the rights of the individual. Such values were exemplified when, upon taking his judicial oath in 1972, Judge Coffrin used the occasion to acknowledge his personal faith in the "dignity of man," pledging to rededicate himself to the "proposition of equal justice under law."[8] When he retired in 1989, Judge Coffrin was praised for his willingness to take positions and stand up for them and "be responsible, whatever the consequences of it," as well as for "a fairness, a sense of objectivity and yet a flexibility" and "no rigid sound philosophy but rather a concern for concrete problems of practical, everyday justice."[9] It is unsurprising that some of the district's most prominent and impactful litigations (especially in recent years) have revolved around social and policy issues vital to the individual Vermont citizen—cutting-edge cases involving health, the environment, civil liberties, and the delicate balance between the power of government and individual rights.

EARLY HISTORY

The District of Vermont was formed in 1791 when, shortly after ascension to statehood, Vermont's first federal judge, Nathaniel Chipman, was appointed by President George Washington. A Yale graduate, Chipman was said to "possess a great intellect," having pursued "a systematic course of study" throughout his life of Hebrew, the Old and New Testaments, and Latin poetry.[10]

Chipman had been a key figure in Vermont's stormy path to statehood. Conflicting land grants issued by the

Duke of York and the Governor of New Hampshire in the mid-18th century had resulted in a 30-year litigious and sometimes violent dispute between New York and Vermont settlers.[11] During this period, Ethan Allen, Vermont's great folk hero, emerged with his Green Mountain Boys to take up the cause of the Vermont-side settlers.[12] Ignoring the Yorkers' efforts to establish a governmental presence in the area, the settlers instead governed themselves through the appointment of town committees.[13] While the Revolutionary War eased tensions, it did not resolve them. Allen and his followers declared themselves an independent republic in 1777 which oddly enough they named "New Connecticut." But the settlers soon dropped that name, adopting instead the name "Vermont" from "Verd Mont" ("green mountain"), as used by the French explorer Samuel de Champlain in 1609 to describe Vermont's mountains.[14]

Nathanial Chipman was instrumental in assisting in the final resolution of this long-standing territorial dispute. As a private lawyer he instigated a movement (in part through correspondence with Alexander Hamilton) to extinguish the land claims of the New York grantees and helped to negotiate a settlement.[15] Following an arduous process, through which New York surrendered its land claims in exchange for a payment of $30,000, the Republic of Vermont was admitted to the Union.[16] At its outset, the district court was in two locations—in Windsor each May and in Rutland in early October. A courthouse in Windsor was later erected in 1852 and remained in use until 1995. This impressive but modest structure still functions as a post office. Designed by Department of the Treasury Supervising Architect Ammi B. Young, it is a fine example of the Italianate Revival style.

RUTLAND COURTHOUSES

One of the district's first courthouse locations (in addition to Windsor) was Rutland, Vermont, then a regional center for commerce, mining, and agriculture. Exemplifying Vermont's frugal (as well as functional)

This two room wood frame building served as the Rutland County Courthouse (1784–1792) and the meeting place for the Vermont legislature (October 1784 and 1786). It was also the site of the of the first U.S. District Court session in Vermont in May 1791.

THE DISTRICT OF VERMONT | 209

side, the same building also housed the Vermont State Legislature and its County Clerk. The courthouse was physically connected to an adjacent inn and tavern by a wooden plank and covered walkway, which allowed for easier and protected passage for both legislators and litigants. In 1858, after the old courthouse burned down, a new one was designed by Ammi B. Young and located closer to Rutland's railway station and downtown area. Now a public library, the building still contains in its basement the cell used to house prisoners awaiting trial.

The current courthouse in Rutland was completed in 1933. It houses a U.S. Post Office on its ground floor and serves as a location for the United States Bankruptcy Court for the District of Vermont, the U.S. Attorney's Office, and the District Court for the District of Connecticut. The building is distinguished by a fine classical architecture style, by a historic courtroom (the subject of recent renovation designed to restore its splendor), and by a series of six magnificent murals on its first floor. Painted in 1937 by Stephen J. Belarski, under the auspices of TRAP (Treasury Relief Art Project), the murals depict the early history of Vermont, including Benedict Arnold's engagement with British forces on Lake Champlain in the first naval engagement of the Revolutionary War, the freeing of the first slave in Vermont in 1777, and the Green Mountain Boys defending the farm of James Breckinridge in 1769.

Chief District Judge Nathaniel Chipman presided as a federal judge in Vermont for just two years, later serving as United States Senator, Chief Justice of the Vermont Supreme Court and, until his death at 91, Professor of Law at Middlebury College.[17] His "handpicked" successor for Chief District Judge, Samuel Hitchcock, was formerly Vermont's Attorney General and was Ethan Allen's son-in-law.[18] In 1798 Hitchcock presided at the Rutland courthouse (along with Circuit Judge William Patterson) over the notorious Sedition Act trial of Congressman Matthew Lyon. Hitchcock was hardly an impartial arbiter, as he was a loyal Federalist and a supporter of Presidents Washington and Adams, serving as their appointed elector in Vermont. The criminal defendant, Congressman Lyon, was a volatile politician, a "fiery pamphleteer," and an ardent anti-Federalist who had run against Hitchcock for Congress and had opposed Hitchcock's nomination to the bench.[19] Lyon had predicted at the time of the Sedition Law's passage that it was designed for and would be used to "ensnare" members of Congress, particularly himself. Indeed, the federal government soon accused Lyon of "stirring up sedition" by authoring and publishing letters and other written materials that brought President John Adams and Congress "into contempt." Lyon's writings (mild by today's standards) attacked

The current Rutland courthouse, which was named the Robert T. Stafford U.S. Post Office and Courthouse in 1988.

The historic courtroom in the Rutland courthouse.

President Adams for allowing "consideration of the public welfare" to be "swallowed up in a continual grasp for power, in an unbounded thirst for ridiculous pomp, foolish adulation and selfish avarice."[20] Lyon emphatically voiced his dissenting views, objecting to "men of real merit [being] turned out of office, for no other cause but independency of sentiment," with the "sacred name of religion" being employed "as a state engine to make mankind hate and persecute one another."[21]

Lyon's trial came at a time when the House of Representatives was equally balanced and was initiated in the midst of his campaign for reelection, necessitating Lyon's temporary withdrawal from Congress. The trial was seen as a bold step on the part of the Adams administration, and it soon became a matter of national political consequence.[22] In a remarkable letter written to Senator James Mason of Virginia and published throughout the country, Lyon described his prosecution and his eventual imprisonment (in Lyon's words, the "fruit" of this "beloved" Sedition Act).[23] Lyon vividly portrayed in his letter his imprisonment in Vergennes, Vermont: "I was locked up in this room, where I am now; it is about sixteen feet long by twelve feet wide, with a necessary in one corner, which affords a stench about equal to the Philadelphia docks in the month of August."[24] The cell, as Lyon described it, was "a common receptacle of horse thieves, money-makers … or any kind of felon." There was no fireplace in the cell "nor … anything but the iron bars to keep the cold out." Lyon was permitted to have visitors, which

THE DISTRICT OF VERMONT | 211

The first floor of the Rutland courthouse displays six murals by Stephen J. Belarski that depict scenes of Vermont's early history including, from top left, Benedict Arnold's engagement with British forces on Lake Champlain; Vermont's first freeing of a slave; and other scenes of early Vermont history.

Top: The historic Montpelier, Vermont courthouse. *Bottom*: The historic Newport, Vermont courthouse.

The Brattleboro U.S. Post Office and Courthouse.

included his brother-in-law Thomas Chittenden, then Vermont's Governor, for whom Chittenden County, home of Burlington, Vermont's most populous region, is named.[25]

At the trial, Lyon (a nonlawyer) represented himself, rather unsuccessfully. Calling no witnesses, he objected that the jury was "packed" against him and that he had been hurried to trial. Lyon's challenge to the Sedition Act's constitutionality was flatly rejected, and the jury was instructed (rather severely) that the only issue they needed to decide was whether Lyon's writings were intended to make the President and Congress appear "odious and contemptible."[26] After deliberating for one hour, the jury found that Lyon's writings did so, and Lyon was convicted and sentenced to four months' imprisonment and a fine of $1,000—the largest fine ever imposed for violation of the Act.[27] In describing this conviction to Senator Mason, Lyon wrote, "So it has happened, and perhaps I, who has been a football for dame fortune all my life, am best able to bear it."[28] While still in prison, Lyon continued his race for Congress. Vermonters rewarded him with the largest number of votes among the various candidates—necessitating a runoff, which Lyon handily won.[29] A later vote to expel Lyon from Congress due to his conviction was defeated for lack of a two-thirds majority.[30] Lyon served his time in prison, paid his fine (which was a condition for his release), and then returned to Congress, although he later left Vermont and moved to Kentucky.[31] After the repeal of the Sedition Act, efforts were made in Congress to remedy the injustice of Lyon's conviction, and in 1840 a bill was finally passed authorizing repayment of the fine, with interest, to Lyon's estate.[32]

Following the Federalists' defeat in the election of 1800, the lame-duck Congress passed the Judiciary

Act of 1801 appointing various "midnight judges," among them Judge Hitchcock, who ascended to a newly created circuit court position.[33] The vacant district court position in Vermont was then filled by another midnight-judge appointee, Elijah Paine. Paine was a successful farmer, businessman, and lawyer, a Harvard graduate, and a close friend of George Washington.[34] In 1808 Judge Paine presided, together with Supreme Court (and then circuit court) Justice Brockholst Livingston, over the trial for treason of Frederick Hoxie. Hoxie stood accused of violating the Embargo Act of 1807, which prohibited U.S. citizens from trading with Britain and France, countries at the time engaged in predatory attacks on American shipping. At a trial held in Burlington, Hoxie was charged with "waging war against the United States" arising from his seizure and attempt to transport a raft filled with timber across Lake Champlain (near Isle La Motte). Originally destined for Canada, the raft had been detained by the federal customs collector.[35] Armed with a dozen muskets, clubs, and spike poles, Hoxie and a group of 60 men seized the raft without resistance from the customs collector. As the raft passed along the shoreline, federal troops fired upon the raft, and Hoxie's men returned fire. All told, 100 shots were fired, fortunately with no injuries. As related at the trial, Hoxie and his men had been promised $800 if they transported the raft successfully to Canada, but nothing if the venture proved unsuccessful. Hoxie claimed he had been told that the federal collector did not object to the raft being taken to Canada and that he would meet with no opposition. Justice Livingston's charge to the jury made it clear that it was treasonous to wage war against the United States but that a private individual's use of force to achieve personal ends was not itself an act of war, since it was not an attempt to "subvert the government, diminish the Union or destroy ... Congress." Showing little hesitation, the Vermont jury promptly acquitted Hoxie of the treason charge.[36]

In 1862, at the outset of the Civil War, the District of Vermont became the center of another nationally prominent case. District Court Judge David A. Smalley (the first native Vermonter to be appointed as a district court judge) oversaw a proceeding challenging a War Department order aimed at preventing the evasion of military duty and authorizing the arrest of persons found to be discouraging enlistments.[37] An appointee of President Franklin Pierce, Judge Smalley had, prior to his ascension to the bench, been Chairman of the National Democratic Committee and was a close friend of Senator Stephen Douglas.[38] An ardent constitutionalist, Judge Smalley ruled that the War Department order was "despotic, illegal and unconstitutional" and granted release of the prisoner from a federal prison. Judge Smalley later found the U.S. Marshal for the District of Vermont in contempt for not complying with his order and enjoined the Marshal from continuing his duties until the fine Smalley had imposed was paid.[39]

As Vermont grew in population—albeit modestly—and as the state experienced industrial growth in the early 1900s, additional federal courthouse and post office buildings were built in Montpelier (1894) and Newport (1904). The district court used both locations until 1948. But Rutland's courthouse remains a treasure. On October 5, 2012, the Second Circuit Court of Appeals held oral argument at the Rutland courthouse for the first time in the court's 123-year history.[40]

THE BRATTLEBORO COURTHOUSE

In 1917 a courthouse and U.S. Post Office building was completed in Brattleboro, one of many signs that Vermont and this small town of 7,500 were progressing quickly into the 20th century. With growth driven by the emergence of manufacturing plants in the Connecticut River Valley, Brattleboro had already appropriated money for a new railway station, concrete walks, and a town-wide electric-lighting plan. The addition of a federal courthouse on Main Street solidified the role of Brattleboro—Vermont's oldest town—as a modern metropolitan destination. The choice of Brattleboro as the site for a new federal building was reportedly

The recently refurbished historic courtroom on the second floor of the Brattleboro courthouse.

spurred by Colonel Kittredge Haskins, a local politician and judge, who served in both the Vermont State Legislature and in the U.S. Congress and was Brattleboro's postmaster from 1912 to 1915.

Erected at a cost of $150,000, the U.S. Post Office and Courthouse is the Brattleboro historic district's only example of the Second Renaissance Revival style, an Italian design aesthetic popularized after the 1893 World's Fair in Chicago, although the Brattleboro courthouse features brick rather than the usual stone facing associated with that style. The main facade of the courthouse faces east onto Main Street and features three round, arched central doorways, with four adjacent elaborate iron lamps, mounted on scrolled brackets, illuminating the entrance.

Shortly after the courthouse was completed, District Judge Harland Howe presided over its first jury trial, *United States v. Clarence H. Waldron,* one of the earliest cases involving religious opposition to World War II. Clarence Waldron, a Baptist minister in Windsor, Vermont, spoke openly about his opposition to the war and distributed antiwar pamphlets to members of his congregation, relating in allegorical terms why a Christian should not bear arms. Waldron was charged with violating the Espionage Act, which prohibited making false reports or statements with the intent to interfere

Today's U.S Post Office and Courthouse in Burlington, Vermont.

with the operation or success of military or naval forces. Some commentators suggest that it might have been Waldron's attraction to Pentecostal doctrine, as much as his antiwar sentiments, that led to these charges.

The trial began on January 8, 1918, and attracted considerable spectator interest. Waldron could not afford counsel, so Judge Howe appointed local Brattleboro attorney Robert C. Bacon to handle Waldron's case. Bacon did not attempt to argue during the trial that Waldron's comments were protected by the First Amendment but instead tried to persuade the jury that Waldron lacked the intent to "interfere with" the military forces as required by the Act. The jury, even after 36 hours of deliberation, was unable to reach a verdict, and a hung jury was declared. The case was later retried in Burlington, again before Judge Howe, and a jury there found Waldron guilty. Judge Howe sentenced Waldron to 15 years in federal prison, but once World War I ended in 1919, his sentence was commuted by President Wilson.[41]

By all accounts, Judge Howe was a "colorful if not flamboyant character."[42] He is said to have once remarked, regarding trials over which he presided, that he "never committed an unconscious error."[43] Following passage of the Volstead Act (Prohibition) in the early 1920s, his sentencing practices manifested his utter disdain for the Act. In one bootlegging case, in which he obviously disagreed with the jury's guilty verdict, Judge Howe sentenced the defendant to pay a fine of one cent, then told the jury that he never wanted to see them again and directed the Court Clerk to strike their names from the jury rolls.[44]

A colorful Brattleboro story is also told about Judge James L. Oakes, who served for one year as a District

THE DISTRICT OF VERMONT | 217

Judge before his distinguished 36-year career on the Second Circuit. Judge Oakes was frequently seen walking down Main Street in Brattleboro, completely engrossed in a newspaper. Onlookers who expected that he might have been poring over the latest news in *The New York Times* were surprised to discover that the judge was in fact studying the latest race results in the *Daily Racing Form*.[45]

THE BURLINGTON U.S. POST OFFICE AND COURTHOUSE

The current courthouse in Burlington was completed in 1960 at a cost of approximately $2.5 million. Designed by Vermont's first architecture firm (Freeman French Freeman), the courthouse was built primarily with reinforced concrete in unadorned modernist style. Its 135,000 square feet accommodate 11 federal agencies and the federal court. One of the special features of its otherwise emphatically functional design is a distinctive marble-and-glass facade at ground level. The present courthouse contrasts markedly with the 1870 Second Empire–style courthouse (Alfred B. Mullett, Supervising Architect) it replaced. While simple in design, today's Burlington Courthouse sits in a remarkable location on the shores of Lake Champlain. Lake scenes are visible from the courthouse roof, including memorable sunsets over the water.

It took some time for the new Federal Building U.S. Post Office and Courthouse in Burlington to become a reality. Although originally approved by the GSA in 1955, funds were not appropriated for its construction until 1957, following an intense lobbying effort by Vermont's senior Senator, George Aiken. Constructed largely on the site of a former Texaco service station, the land also included a parcel owned by the Roman Catholic Diocese. At a special session of the United States District Court held in Montpelier, Vermont, the diocese (represented by future Federal District Court Judge Bernard Leddy) persuaded a jury to award $90,000 as the value of the land, $25,000 more than the federal government had offered. The financing for the building's construction was through a GSA lease–purchase program (with the John Hancock Life Insurance Company), but the loan was soon repaid in full by the GSA when interest rates made it favorable to do so. In laying the cornerstone for the building in December 1958 before an audience of chilled onlookers in zero-degree temperatures, Senator Aiken recalled that a fellow Senator had mocked the idea of a new Burlington Courthouse, predicting that "it would be cold day by the time Burlington got a new federal building." "And he was right," said Aiken.[46]

Throughout its history, many of the court cases emanating from the District of Vermont have borne its unique stamp. In one, *Achilles v. New England Tree Company*,[47] a farmer (Achilles) and his wife sued the local power company's tree-removal service for trespass and negligence for having used a defoliant (a mixture of No. 2 fuel oil and chemical weed killer) too close to the watering hole used by the farmer's cattle. Calling it a "case of rural justice," the Second Circuit affirmed the jury's damage verdict, notwithstanding the defendant's expert testimony that the weed killer was harmless and could not have caused the death and injury to Achilles' cattle. It was not unlikely, the Second Circuit held, "that the jurors had understood that the men spraying the underbrush might not always mix the ingredients according to orders, and … not improbab[ly] [had allowed] some of the raw ingredients [to find] their way directly into the water." It seemed, the court observed, "just a bit silly to try to convince a jury of hardheaded Vermonters that it is perfectly all right to put a combination of chemical weed killer and No. 2 Fuel Oil into a farmer's water supply … . There are cases where common sense is more reliable than any amount of expert witnesses, and this is one of those cases."

Opposite: Sunset over Lake Champlain, a sight visible from many places in Burlington, including the courthouse roof.

The Second Circuit similarly found reason to affirm the common sense and good judgment of Vermont jurors in a negligence case involving a gun owner who had loaned his new deer rifle to his brother-in-law, neglecting to tell him that his wife kept the gun fully loaded because it made her feel more comfortable in their isolated area of Vermont. The brother-in-law accidentally discharged the gun while showing it to a neighbor, fracturing his arm. In reviewing the case, the Second Circuit noted that presiding District Judge Bernard J. Leddy was an "expert marksman," and that all twelve jurors (as voir dire revealed) owned rifles. Affirming the jury's verdict, the Second Circuit observed: "Twelve Vermont jurors have determined that keeping a loaded gun and lending it to another without telling him it is loaded constitutes negligence. They and Judge Leddy are very likely better acquainted with rifles than we are. They are certainly better able to decide what constitutes careless handling of firearms in Saxton's River, Vermont."[48] An avid hunter and fisherman, Judge Leddy is remembered for invariably recessing court during the two-week deer season in November, to the delight of most court personnel, attorneys, litigants, and jury members.[49]

Another Vermont case finding its way to the Second Circuit posed the question of whether a dairy farmer's three bulls should properly be considered "tools of the trade" under Vermont's exemption statute, and therefore not part of the property of the farmer's bankruptcy estate. Although both the Bankruptcy Judge and District Court Judge Franklin S. Billings Jr. declined to interpret the Vermont statute so broadly, finding the bulls to be the essence of the farmer's business and not mere "tools of the trade," the Second Circuit, in overturning the decisions below, disagreed, stating that Vermont's exemption statute was designed to promote a "fresh start" to allow the debtor to keep property that the Legislature deemed essential to living and working. The Vermont statute, said the Second Circuit, required consideration of the function or use of the property in the debtor's trade, rather than its size or type.[50]

The environment, health and safety, consumer privacy, and the First Amendment have also been sources of frequent litigation in the District of Vermont in recent years. One of the earliest landmark cases before the Supreme Court involving class actions, *Zahn v. International Paper,* grew out of a federal lawsuit filed in the Burlington courthouse. In that case, 200 Lake Champlain property owners sued International Paper for making illegal discharges from its New York plant into Ticonderoga Creek (which flows into Lake Champlain), claiming that the discharges polluted the lake and damaged surrounding properties.[51] Although the case was dismissed, the underlying environmental dispute was ultimately resolved. Since the *Zahn* case, Vermont has frequently also been at the forefront of Clean Water Act litigation, as well as other cutting-edge environmental, public health, and safety issues.

In the early 1990s, the Vermont Legislature enacted a law requiring dairy manufacturers to identify products derived from dairy cows treated with rBST (recombinant bovine somatotropin), a synthetic growth hormone used to increase milk production. Some dairy producers protested, arguing that the statute infringed on their First Amendment right "not to speak." District Court Chief Judge J. Garvan Murtha denied their preliminary injunction request, but the Second Circuit reversed.[52] Ironically, the marketplace ultimately succeeded in doing what Vermont's Legislature had sought to accomplish. After one small dairy manufacturer in Vermont voluntarily labeled its products as being rBST-free, other larger manufacturers, citing consumer demand, began to add a similar disclaimer to their packaging, in order to remain "competitive," at least in Vermont.

Another commercial speech issue involving public health in Vermont came before the Second Circuit when Vermont's Legislature enacted a law requiring manufacturers of mercury-containing light bulbs to so label their products and packaging and to inform consumers that such products needed to be recycled or disposed of as hazardous waste. A trade association challenged the

One of the courtrooms in the Burlington, Vermont courthouse.

Vermont law, alleging that the conduct being regulated went beyond Vermont's borders and infringed on the First Amendment. The Second Circuit upheld the law, holding that its extraterritorial effect neither imposed a disproportionate burden on interstate commerce nor violated the manufacturer's free-speech rights.[53]

Most recently, a divided Second Circuit found a Vermont law prohibiting the sale or use of "doctor-identifiable data" in the marketing of pharmaceuticals to be an impermissible restriction on commercial speech. Data-mining companies challenged the Vermont law, which restricted access to information concerning doctors and other prescribers. District Judge Murtha found the law as applied to the data-mining companies, who were using the information collected by pharmacies to pitch drugs to doctors, to be a constitutionally permissible restriction. The Second Circuit reversed (albeit with a lengthy dissent by Judge Debra Ann Livingston), finding that Vermont's law was a "commercial speech restriction that does not advance a substantial state interest asserted by Vermont, and [was] … not narrowly tailored to serve those interests." The Supreme Court later affirmed.[54]

Judge James L. Oakes, perhaps as much as any other Vermonter, epitomized many of the state's most admirable human qualities. Judge Oakes was a fierce champion of civil liberties, with a "deep commitment to fashioning just results" and an abiding concern for how the law works and affects people. He was proud to be a Vermonter and sought to promote its values. These he described as "fairness to all, passion for the environment, and a progressive tradition which views government as potentially an ally in relieving the burdens of life."[55] As Vermont progresses into the 21st century, its courts and judges continue to uphold these traditions.

Hon. Thurgood Marshall, Associate Justice of the Supreme Court.

JUDGES

MAY 2015

U.S. COURT OF APPEALS FOR THE SECOND CIRCUIT

JUDGES OF THE U.S. COURT OF APPEALS FOR THE SECOND CIRCUIT

Number of judges who have served on the court: 71

Altimari, Frank X. (1985–1998)
Anderson, Robert Palmer (1964–1978)
Cabranes, José Alberto (1994–present)
Calabresi, Guido (1994–present)
Cardamone, Richard J. (1981–present)
Carney, Susan Laura (2011–present)
Chase, Harrie Brigham (1929–1969)
Chin, Denny (2010–present)
Clark, Charles Edward (1939–1963)
Coxe, Alfred Conkling Sr. (1902–1917)
Droney, Christopher Fitzgerald (2011–present)
Feinberg, Wilfred (1966–2014)
Frank, Jerome New (1941–1957)
Friendly, Henry Jacob (1959–1986)
Gurfein, Murray Irwin (1974–1979)
Hall, Peter W. (2004–present)
Hand, Augustus Noble (1927–1954)
Hand, Learned (1924–1961)
Harlan, John Marshall II (1954–1955)
Hays, Paul Raymond (1961–1980)
Hincks, Carroll Clark (1953–1964)
Hough, Charles Merrill (1916–1927)
Jacobs, Dennis (1992–present)
Katzmann, Robert A. (1999–present)
Kaufman, Irving Robert (1961–1992)
Kearse, Amalya Lyle (1979–present)
Knapp, Martin Augustine (1910–1916)
Lacombe, Emile Henry (1891–1916)
Leval, Pierre Nelson (1993–present)
Livingston, Debra Ann (2007–present)
Lohier, Raymond Joseph Jr. (2010–present)
Lumbard, Joseph Edward (1955–1999)
Lynch, Gerard E. (2009–present)
Mack, Julian William (1929–1943)
Mahoney, John Daniel (1986–1996)
Mansfield, Walter Roe (1971–1987)
Manton, Martin Thomas (1918–1939)
Marshall, Thurgood (1961–1965)
Mayer, Julius Marshuetz (1921–1924)
McLaughlin, Joseph Michael (1990–2013)
Medina, Harold Raymond (1951–1980)
Meskill, Thomas Joseph (1975–2007)
Miner, Roger Jeffrey (1985–2012)
Moore, Leonard Page (1957–1982)
Mulligan, William Hughes (1971–1981)
Newman, Jon Ormond (1979–present)
Noyes, Walter Chadwick (1907–1913)
Oakes, James Lowell (1971–2007)
Parker, Barrington Daniels Jr. (2001–present)
Parker, Fred I. (1994–2003)
Patterson, Robert Porter Sr. (1939–1940)
Pierce, Lawrence Warren (1981–1995)
Pooler, Rosemary S. (1998–present)
Pratt, George Cheney (1982–1995)
Raggi, Reena (2002–present)
Rogers, Henry Wade (1913–1926)
Sack, Robert David (1998–present)
Shipman, Nathaniel (1892–1902)
Smith, John Joseph (1960–1980)
Sotomayor, Sonia (1998–2009)

Straub, Chester J. (1998–present)
Swan, Thomas Walter (1926–1975)
Timbers, William Homer (1971–1994)
Townsend, William Kneeland (1902–1907)
Van Graafeiland, Ellsworth Alfred (1974–2004)
Walker, John Mercer Jr. (1989–present)
Wallace, William James (1891–1907)
Ward, Henry Galbraith (1907–1924)
Waterman, Sterry Robinson (1955–1984)
Wesley, Richard C. (2003–present)
Winter, Ralph K. Jr. (1981–present)

DISTRICT COURTS

JUDGES OF THE DISTRICT OF CONNECTICUT

Number of judges who have served on the court: 37
Anderson, Robert Palmer (1954–1964)
Arterton, Janet Bond (1995–present)
Blumenfeld, Mosher Joseph (1961–1988)
Bolden, Victor A. (2015–present)
Bristol, William (1826–1836)
Bryant, Vanessa Lynne (2007–present)
Burns, Ellen Bree (1978–present)
Burrows, Warren Booth (1928–1930)
Cabranes, José Alberto (1979–1994)
Chatigny, Robert N. (1994–present)
Clarie, T. Emmet (1961–1997)
Covello, Alfred V. (1992–present)
Daly, T. F. Gilroy (1977–1996)
Dorsey, Peter Collins (1983–2012)
Droney, Christopher Fitzgerald (1997–2011)
Edwards, Pierpont (1806–1826)
Eginton, Warren William (1979–present)
Hall, Janet C. (1997–present)
Hincks, Carroll Clark (1931–1953)
Ingersoll, Charles Anthony (1853–1860)
Judson, Andrew Thompson (1836–1853)
Kravitz, Mark R. (2003–2012)
Law, Richard (1789–1806)

Nevas, Alan Harris (1985–2009)
Newman, Jon Ormond (1971–1979)
Platt, James Perry (1902–1913)
Shea, Michael Peter (2012–present)
Shipman, Nathaniel (1873–1892)
Shipman, William Davis (1860–1873)
Smith, John Joseph (1941–1960)
Squatrito, Dominic J. (1994–present)
Thomas, Edwin Stark (1913–1939)
Thompson, Alvin W. (1994–present)
Timbers, William Homer (1960–1971)
Townsend, William Kneeland (1892–1902)
Underhill, Stefan R. (1999–present)
Zampano, Robert Carmine (1964–1994)

JUDGES OF THE DISTRICT OF NEW YORK

Number of judges who have served on the court: 6
Duane, James (1789–1794)
Hobart, John Sloss (1798–1805)
Laurance, John (1794–1796)
Tallmadge, Matthias Burnett (1805–1814)
Troup, Robert (1796–1798)
Van Ness, William Peter (1812–1814

JUDGES OF THE EASTERN DISTRICT OF NEW YORK

Number of judges who have served on the court: 60
Abruzzo, Matthew T. (1936–1971)
Altimari, Frank X. (1982–1985)
Amon, Carol Bagley (1990–present)
Azrack, Joan Marie (2014–present)
Bartels, John Ries (1959–1997)
Benedict, Charles Linnaeus (1865–1897)
Bianco, Joseph Frank (2006–present)
Block, Frederic (1994–present)
Bramwell, Henry (1974–2010)
Brodie, Margo Kitsy (2012–present)
Bruchhausen, Walter (1953–1976)

Byers, Mortimer W. (1929–1962)
Campbell, Marcus Beach (1923–1944)
Chatfield, Thomas (1907–1922)
Chen, Pamela Ki Mai (2013–present)
Cogan, Brian Mark (2006–present)
Costantino, Mark Americus (1971–1990)
Dearie, Raymond Joseph (1986–present)
Dooling, John Francis Jr. (1961–1981)
Feuerstein, Sandra J. (2003–present)
Galston, Clarence G. (1929–1964)
Garaufis, Nicholas G. (2000–present)
Garvin, Edwin Louis (1918–1925)
Gershon, Nina (1996–present)
Glasser, Israel Leo (1981–present)
Gleeson, John (1994–present)
Hurley, Denis Reagan (1991–present)
Inch, Robert Alexander (1923–1961)
Irizarry, Dora L. (2004–present)
Johnson, Sterling Jr. (1991–present)
Judd, Orrin Grimmell (1968–1976)
Kennedy, Harold Maurice (1944–1952)
Korman, Edward Robert (1985–present)
Kuntz, William Francis II (2011–present)
Matsumoto, Kiyo A. (2008–present)
Mauskopf, Roslynn Renee (2007–present)
McLaughlin, Joseph Michael (1981–1990)
Mishler, Jacob (1960–2004)
Moscowitz, Grover M. (1925–1947)
Neaher, Edward Raymond (1971–1994)
Nickerson, Eugene Hoffman (1977–2002)
Platt, Thomas Collier Jr. (1974–present)
Pratt, George Cheney (1976–1982)
Raggi, Reena (1987–2002)
Rayfiel, Leo Frederick (1947–1978)
Rosling, George (1961–1973)
Ross, Allyne R. (1994–present)
Seybert, Joanna (1993–present)
Sifton, Charles Proctor (1977–2009)
Spatt, Arthur Donald (1989–present)
Tenney, Asa Wentworth (1897)
Thomas, Edward Beers (1898–1906)

Townes, Sandra L. (2004–present)
Trager, David G. (1993–2011)
Travia, Anthony John (1968–1974)
Veeder, Van Vechten (1911–1917)
Vitaliano, Eric Nicholas (2006–present)
Weinstein, Jack Bertrand (1967–present)
Wexler, Leonard D. (1983–present)
Zavatt, Joseph Carmine (1957–1985)

JUDGES OF THE NORTHERN DISTRICT OF NEW YORK

Number of judges who have served on the court: 27

Brennan, Stephen W. (1942–1968)
Bryant, Frederick Howard (1927–1945)
Cholakis, Con G. (1986–1996)
Conkling, Alfred (1825–1852)
Cooper, Frank (1920–1946)
Coxe, Alfred Conkling Sr. (1882–1902)
D`Agostino, Mae Avila (2011–present)
Foley, James Thomas (1949–1990)
Hall, Nathan Kelsey (1852–1874)
Hurd, David N. (1999–present)
Kahn, Lawrence E. (1996–present)
Kampf, Edward S. (1946–1948)
McAvoy, Thomas James (1986–present)
McCurn, Neal Peters (1979–2014)
Miner, Roger Jeffrey (1981–1985)
Mordue, Norman A. (1998–present)
Munson, Howard G. (1976–2008)
Pooler, Rosemary S. (1994–1998)
Port, Edmund (1964–1986)
Ray, George Washington (1902–1925)
Sannes, Brenda Kay (2014–present)
Scullin, Frederick James Jr. (1992–present)
Sharpe, Gary L. (2004–present)
Skinner, Roger (1819–1825)
Suddaby, Glenn T. (2008–present)
Tallmadge, Matthias Burnett (1814–1819)
Wallace, William James (1874–1882)

JUDGES OF THE SOUTHERN DISTRICT OF NEW YORK

Number of judges who have served on the court: 149

Abrams, Ronnie (2012–present)
Adams, George Bethune (1901–1911)
Baer, Harold Jr. (1994–2014)
Batts, Deborah A. (1994–present)
Bauman, Arnold (1971–1974)
Berman, Richard M. (1998–present)
Betts, Samuel Rossiter (1826–1867)
Bicks, Alexander (1954–1963)
Blatchford, Samuel M. (1867–1878)
Bondy, William (1923–1964)
Bonsal, Dudley Baldwin (1961–1995)
Briccetti, Vincent Louis (2011–present)
Brieant, Charles L. Jr. (1971–2008)
Bright, John (1941–1948)
Broderick, Vernon Speede (2013–present)
Broderick, Vincent Lyons (1976–1995)
Brown, Addison (1881–1901)
Bryan, Frederick van Pelt (1956–1978)
Buchwald, Naomi Reice (1999–present)
Caffey, Francis Gordon (1929–1951)
Cannella, John Matthew (1963–1996)
Caproni, Valerie Elaine (2013–present)
Carter, Andrew Lamar Jr. (2011–present)
Carter, Robert Lee (1972–2012)
Casey, Richard Conway (1997–2007)
Cashin, John M. (1955–1970)
Castel, P. Kevin (2003–present)
Cedarbaum, Miriam Goldman (1986–present)
Chin, Denny (1994–2010)
Choate, William Gardner (1878–1881)
Clancy, John William (1936–1969)
Coleman, Frank Joseph (1927–1934)
Conboy, Kenneth (1987–1993)
Conger, Edward A. (1938–1963)
Conner, William Curtis (1973–2009)
Cooper, Irving Ben (1961–1996)
Cote, Denise (1994–present)
Coxe, Alfred Conkling Jr. (1929–1957)

Croake, Thomas Francis (1961–1978)
Crotty, Paul Austin (2005–present)
Daniels, George B. (2000–present)
Daronco, Richard Joseph (1987–1988)
Dawson, Archie Owen (1954–1964)
Dimock, Edward Jordan (1951–1986)
Duffy, Kevin Thomas (1972–present)
Edelstein, David Norton (1951–2000)
Engelmayer, Paul Adam (2011–present)
Failla, Katherine Polk (2013–present)
Feinberg, Wilfred (1961–1966)
Forrest, Katherine Bolan (2011–present)
Frankel, Marvin E. (1965–1978)
Freeh, Louis J. (1991–1993)
Furman, Jesse Matthew (2012–present)
Gagliardi, Lee Parsons (1971–1998)
Gardephe, Paul G. (2008–present)
Goddard, Henry Warren (1923–1955)
Goettel, Gerard Louis (1976–2011)
Griesa, Thomas Poole (1972–present)
Gurfein, Murray Irwin (1971–1974)
Haight, Charles Sherman Jr. (1976–present)
Hand, Augustus Noble (1914–1927)
Hand, Learned (1909–1924)
Hellerstein, Alvin K. (1998–present)
Herlands, William Bernard (1955–1969)
Holt, George Chandler (1903–1914)
Holwell, Richard J. (2003–2012)
Hough, Charles Merrill (1906–1916)
Hulbert, George Murray (1934–1950)
Jones, Barbara S. (1995–2013)
Kaplan, Lewis A. (1994–present)
Karas, Kenneth M. (2004–present)
Kaufman, Irving Robert (1949–1961)
Kaufman, Samuel Hamilton (1948–1960)
Keenan, John Fontaine (1983–present)
Knapp, [Percy] Whitman (1972–2004)
Knox, John Clark (1918–1966)
Koeltl, John George (1994–present)
Kram, Shirley Wohl (1983–2009)
Lasker, Morris Edward (1968–2009)

Leibell, Vincent L. (1936–1968)
Leisure, Peter Keeton (1984–2013)
Leval, Pierre Nelson (1977–1993)
Levet, Richard Harrington (1956–1976)
Lowe, Mary Johnson (1978–1999)
Lynch, Gerard E. (2000–2009)
MacMahon, Lloyd Francis (1959–1989)
Mandelbaum, Samuel (1936–1946)
Mansfield, Walter Roe (1966–1971)
Manton, Martin Thomas (1916–1918)
Marrero, Victor (1999–present)
Martin, John S. Jr. (1990–2003)
Mayer, Julius Marshuetz (1912–1921)
McGohey, John F. X. (1949–1972)
McKenna, Lawrence M. (1990–present)
McLean, Edward Cochrane (1962–1972)
McMahon, Colleen (1998–present)
Medina, Harold Raymond (1947–1951)
Metzner, Charles Miller (1959–2009)
Motley, Constance Baker (1966–2005)
Mukasey, Michael B. (1987–2006)
Murphy, Thomas Francis (1951–1995)
Nathan, Alison Julie (2011–present)
Noonan, Gregory Francis (1949–1964)
Oetken, James Paul (2011–present)
Owen, Richard (1973–present)
Palmieri, Edmund Louis (1954–1989)
Parker, Barrington Daniels Jr. (1994–2001)
Patterson, Robert Porter Jr. (1988–2015)
Patterson, Robert Porter Sr. (1930–1939)
Pauley, William H. III (1998–present)
Pierce, Lawrence Warren (1971–1981)
Pollack, Milton (1967–2004)
Preska, Loretta A. (1992–present)
Rakoff, Jed Saul (1996–present)
Ramos, Edgardo (2011–present)
Rifkind, Simon Hirsch (1941–1950)
Robinson, Stephen C. (2003–2010)
Roman, Nelson Stephen (2013–present)
Ryan, Sylvester J. (1947–1981)
Sand, Leonard Burke (1978–present)

Scheindlin, Shira A. (1994–present)
Schofield, Lorna Gail (2012–present)
Schwartz, Allen G. (1993–2003)
Seibel, Cathy (2008–present)
Sofaer, Abraham David (1979–1985)
Sotomayor, Sonia (1992–1998)
Sprizzo, John Emilio (1981–2008)
Stanton, Louis Lee (1985–present)
Stein, Sidney H. (1995–present)
Stewart, Charles E. Jr. (1972–1994)
Sugarman, Sidney (1949–1974)
Sullivan, Richard Joseph (2007–present)
Swain, Laura Taylor (2000–present)
Sweet, Robert Workman (1978–present)
Tenney, Charles Henry (1963–1994)
Thacher, Thomas Day (1925–1930)
Torres, Analisa Nadine (2013–present)
Tyler, Harold R. Jr. (1962–1975)
Van Ness, William Peter (1814–1826)
Walker, John Mercer Jr. (1985–1989)
Walsh, Lawrence Edward (1954–1957)
Ward, Robert Joseph (1972–2003)
Weinfeld, Edward (1950–1988)
Werker, Henry Frederick (1974–1984)
Winslow, Francis Asbury (1923–1929)
Wood, Kimba Maureen (1988–present)
Woods, Gregory Howard III (2013–present)
Woolsey, John Munro (1929–1945)
Wyatt, Inzer Bass (1962–1990)

JUDGES OF THE WESTERN DISTRICT OF NEW YORK

Number of judges who have served on the court: 16

Adler, Simon Louis (1927–1934)
Arcara, Richard Joseph (1988–present)
Burke, Harold P. (1937–1981)
Curtin, John Thomas (1967–present)
Elfvin, John Thomas (1974–2009)
Geraci, Frank Paul Jr. (2013–present)
Hazel, John Raymond (1900–1931)

Henderson, John Oliver (1959–1974)
Knight, John (1931–1955)
Larimer, David G. (1987–present)
Morgan, Justin Colfax (1956–1959)
Rippey, Harlan Watson (1934–1936)
Siragusa, Charles J. (1997–present)
Skretny, William M. (1990–present)
Telesca, Michael Anthony (1982–present)
Wolford, Elizabeth Ann (2013–present)

JUDGES OF THE DISTRICT OF VERMONT

Number of judges who have served on the court: 20

Billings, Franklin S. Jr. (1984–2014)
Chipman, Nathaniel (1791–1793)
Coffrin, Albert Wheeler (1972–1993)
Crawford, Geoffrey W. (2014–present)
Gibson, Ernest William Jr. (1949–1969)
Hitchcock, Samuel (1793–1801)
Holden, James Stuart (1971–1996)
Howe, Harland Bradley (1915–1945)
Leamy, James Patrick (1940–1949)
Leddy, Bernard Joseph (1966–1972)
Martin, James Loren (1906–1915)
Murtha, John Garvan (1995–present)
Oakes, James Lowell (1970–1971)
Paine, Elijah (1801–1842)
Parker, Fred I. (1990–1994)
Prentiss, Samuel (1842–1857)
Reiss, Christina Clair (2009–present)
Sessions, William K. III (1995–present)
Smalley, David Allen (1857–1877)
Wheeler, Hoyt Henry (1877–1906)

BANKRUPTCY JUDGES (CURRENT)

DISTRICT OF CONNECTICUT

Julie A. Manning
Ann M. Nevins
Alan H. W. Shiff

EASTERN DISTRICT OF NEW YORK

Carla E. Craig
Robert E. Grossman
Nancy Hershey Lord
Louis A. Scarcella
Elizabeth S. Stong
Alan S. Trust

NORTHERN DISTRICT OF NEW YORK

Margaret Cangilos-Ruiz
Diane Davis
Robert E. Littlefield, Jr.

SOUTHERN DISTRICT OF NEW YORK

Stuart M. Bernstein
Shelley C. Chapman
Robert D. Drain
James L. Garrity Jr.
Robert E. Gerber
Martin Glenn
Sean H. Lane
Cecelia G. Morris
Michael E. Wiles

WESTERN DISTRICT OF NEW YORK

Carl L. Bucki
Michael J. Kaplan
Paul R. Warren

DISTRICT OF VERMONT

Colleen A. Brown

MAGISTRATE JUDGES
(CURRENT)

DISTRICT OF CONNECTICUT

Holly B. Fitzsimmons
William Garfinkel
Joan G. Margolis
Donna F. Martinez
Sarah A. L. Merriam
Thomas P. Smith

EASTERN DISTRICT OF NEW YORK

Lois Bloom
Gary R. Brown
Marilyn D. Go
Steven M. Gold
Robert M. Levy
Arlene R. Lindsay
Steven I. Locke
Roanne L. Mann
James Orenstein
Viktor V. Pohorelsky
Cheryl L. Pollak
Ramon E. Reyes Jr.
Vera M. Scanlon
Anne Y. Shields
Kathleen Tomlinson

NORTHERN DISTRICT OF NEW YORK

Andrew T. Baxter
Therese Wiley Dancks
Gary L. Favro
Christian F. Hummel
David E. Peebles
Randolph F. Treece

SOUTHERN DISTRICT OF NEW YORK

James L. Cott
Paul E. Davison
Michael H. Dolinger
Ronald L. Ellis
Kevin N. Fox
James C. Francis
Debra Freeman
Martin R. Goldberg
Gabriel W. Gorenstein
Frank Maas
Judith C. McCarthy
Sarah Netburn
Andrew J. Peck
Henry Pitman
Lisa Margaret Smith

WESTERN DISTRICT OF NEW YORK

Jonathan W. Feldman
Leslie G. Foschio
Jeremiah J. McCarthy
Marian W. Payson
H. Kenneth Schroeder Jr.
Hugh B. Scott

DISTRICT OF VERMONT

John M. Conroy

ENDNOTES

Citations to "permalinks" at perma.cc are intended to provide permanent access to the cited internet pages. Access to some permalinks is restricted to libraries or subscribers to the cited publication.

FOREWORD

i   Senator Daniel P. Moynihan, Address at the Alumni Dinner of the Harvard Graduate School of Design (Nov. 1, 1967), *in Moynihan Assesses the Role of Architecture*, HARVARD CRIMSON, Nov. 4, 1967, *available at* http://www.thecrimson.com/article/1967/11/4/moynihan-assesses-the-role-of-architecture/ [http://perma.cc/NYF4-AE5K].

INTRODUCTION

1   *See* J. WOODFORD HOWARD JR., COURTS OF APPEALS IN THE FEDERAL JUDICIAL SYSTEM: A STUDY OF THE SECOND, FIFTH, AND DISTRICT OF COLUMBIA CIRCUITS 142 (Princeton University Press 1981) (noting the view expressed in a late-1960s survey of circuit judges that the Second Circuit was the front-runner in prestige based on its business, its bench, and its bar, with the D.C. Circuit coming in second); *id.* at xix (referring to the Second Circuit as "the nation's leading commercial court"); Jeffrey Toobin, *The Talk of the Town: George's Choice*, NEW YORKER, Jan 18, 1993, at 31 ("[T]he Second Circuit is often called the second most important court in the nation.").

2   JEFFREY B. MORRIS, FEDERAL JUSTICE IN THE SECOND CIRCUIT: A HISTORY OF THE UNITED STATES COURTS IN NEW YORK, CONNECTICUT & VERMONT, 1787 TO 1987 at 15 n.** (Second Circuit Historical Committee 1987).

3   Judiciary Act, ch. 20, § 9, 1 Stat. 73, 76-77 (1789).

4   *Id.* at § 4, 1 Stat. at 74-75.

5   Joshua Glick, Comment, *On the Road: The Supreme Court and the History of Circuit Riding*, 24 Cardozo L. Rev. 1753, 1771 (2003); *see* Wythe Holt, *"The Federal Courts Have Enemies in All Who Fear Their Influence on State Objects": The Failure to Abolish Supreme Court Circuit-Riding in the Judiciary Acts of 1792 and 1793*, 36 Buff. L. Rev. 301, 311 (1987).

6   *See generally* Glick, 24 Cardozo L. Rev. at 1-7.

7   *Id.* at 7; *see also* 11 Annals of Cong. 38 (1802).

8   Judiciary Act, ch. 4, § 6, 2 Stat. 89, 90 (1801).

9   Fed. Judicial Ctr., Biographical Directory of Federal Judges, http://www.fjc.gov/history/home.nsf/page/judges.html [http://perma.cc/2VW4-GSJY; http://perma.cc/G8BW-5F32 (Benson); http://perma.cc/TF5N-RXSV (Wolcott); http://perma.cc/ZJ9Y-ACF3 (Hitchcock)]; *see also* MORRIS, *supra* note 2, at 35.

10 Marbury v. Madison, 5 U.S. 137 (1803).

11 Act of March 8, 1802, ch. 8, 2 Stat. 132 (repealing the Judiciary Act of 1801).

12 Judiciary Act, ch. 31, 2 Stat. 156 (1802) (also sometimes known as the "Amendatory Act").

13 Judiciary Act, ch. 22, 16 Stat. 44 (1869); Fed. Judicial Ctr., *Circuit Judges for the Second Circuit, 1869-1911,* http://www.fjc.gov/servlet/nGetInfo?jid=2645&cid=257&ctype=cc&instate=2_1869 to 1911&highlight=null [http://perma.cc/WL48-Q8EM].

14 *See* Jurisdiction and Removal Act, ch. 137, 18 Stat. 470 (1875); Fed. Judicial Ctr., *Landmark Judicial Legislation*, http://www.fjc.gov/history/home.nsf/page/landmark_11.html [http://perma.cc/3NDU-XUQW].

15 Judiciary Act, ch. 517, 26 Stat. 826 (1891).

16 Judicial Code, ch. 231, 36 Stat. 1087 (1911).

17 Act of April 29, 1812, ch. 71, 2 Stat. 719.

18 MORRIS, *supra* note 2, at 44 n.*.

19 Act of April 29, 1812, ch. 71, § 2, 2 Stat. 719.

20 PAUL H. BURAK, HISTORY OF THE UNITED STATES DISTRICT COURT FOR THE SOUTHERN DISTRICT OF NEW YORK 3 (Fed. Bar Ass'n. of N.Y., N.J. and Ct. 1962).

21 Act of April 9, 1814, ch. 49, 3 Stat. 120.

22 Act of Feb. 25, 1865, ch. 54, 13 Stat. 438 (creating the Eastern District of New York); *see* Nassau County, *History of Nassau County*, https://www.nassaucountyny.gov/3344/History-of-Nassau-County [http://perma.cc/EFV6-4QC7]; Act of May 12, 1900, ch. 391, 31 Stat. 175 (creating the Western District of New York).

23 Senator Daniel Patrick Moynihan, Opening Remarks at the Biennial General Services Administration Design Awards (March 25, 1999), *quoted in* GSA Public Buildings Service, Balancing Security And Openness (1999), *available at* http://janeloeffler.com/documents/31-Balancing-Security-and-Openness.pdf [http://perma.cc/B8X9-CAAP].

24 Nat'l Park Serv., U.S. Dep't of the Interior, *Federal Courthouses and Post Offices: Symbols of Pride and Permanence in American Communities, in* Teaching with Historic Places Lesson Plans, http://www.nps.gov/history/nr/twhp/wwwlps/lessons/136GSA/136GSA.htm [http://perma.cc/CDW4-UDY5] [hereinafter *Federal Courthouses and Post Offices*].

25 *Id.*

26 U.S. Gen. Servs. Admin., *Architecture and Government*, http://www.gsa.gov/portal/category/25437 [http://perma.cc/CEK3-6MWL].

27 Many courthouses within the Second Circuit bear names today that are different from those originally given to them. For ease of reference, the text uses current names throughout the Introduction.

28 William Searle, *American Vernacular: The Courthouse as a Building Type, in* Celebrating The Courthouse: A Guide For Architects, Their Clients, And The Public 46 (Steven Flanders ed., W.W. Norton & Co. 2006) [hereinafter Searle].

29 *Id.* at 51.

30 *Id.* at 52-53.

31 U.S. Gen. Servs. Admin., *Richard C. Lee U.S. Courthouse, New Haven, CT*, http://www.gsa.gov/portal/ext/html/site/hb/category/25431/actionParameter/exploreByBuilding/buildingId/901 [http://perma.cc/W8AN-S9G3].

32 Searle, *supra* note 28, at 59; U.S. Gen. Servs. Admin., Buildings of the 1950s/60s/and 70s: Growth/Efficiency/and Modernism, *available at* http://www.gsa.gov/graphics/pbs/GEMbook.pdf [http://perma.cc/5NUR-X289] [hereinafter GSA Modernism].

33 Searle, *supra* note 28, at 59.

34 GSA Modernism, *supra* note 32, at 9.

35 *See* Nathan Glazer, *Epilogue: Daniel Patrick Moynihan and Federal Architecture, in* Celebrating The Courthouse, *supra* note 28.

36 *Id.* at 228.

37 Daniel Brook, *A Blueprint for the Future*, Legal Affairs, Nov./Dec. 2005, *available at* http://legalaffairs.org/issues/November-December-2005/feature_brook_novdec05.msp [http://perma.cc/N5SY-RQSM].

38 U.S. Gen. Servs. Admin., *The Design Excellence Mandate*, ch. 2 *in* Design Excellence: Policies and Procedures, *available at* http://www.gsa.gov/portal/content/103738 [http://perma.cc/G5TD-54N6, http://perma.cc/7ZFD-AB7U].

39 Judicial Conference of the U.S., U.S. Courts Design Guide, *available at* http://www.wbdg.org/ccb/GSAMAN/courts.pdf [http://perma.cc/CB8B-2AMG].

CHAPTER 1

1 *See* Morris, *supra* intro. note 2, at 94 for much of this early 20th century history.

2 Joseph J. Korom, The American Skyscraper, 1850-1940: A Celebration of Height 75-76 (Branden Books 2008); Gabriel Gabrielan, New York City's Financial District in Vintage Postcards 69 (Arcadia Publishing 2000).

3 *The Mullet Post Office Site*, N.Y. Times, April 28, 1912, at 16, *available at* http://query.nytimes.com/mem/archive-free/pdf?res=9B02E5DD103AE633A2575BC2A9629C946396D6CF [http://perma.cc/544Z-DFFD].

4 Morris, *supra* intro. note 2, at 94-95.

5 Irving R. Kaufman, *The Second Circuit: Reputation for Excellence*, 63 A.B.A. J. 200, 201 (1977). Much of the early history of the Second Circuit recounted in this section is based, in part, on this source.

6 Edison Electric Light Co. v. U.S. Electric Lighting Co., 52 F. 300 (2d Cir. 1892).

7 Wright Co. v. Herring-Curtiss Co., 180 F. 110 (2nd. Cir. 1910); Wright Co. v. Paulhan, 180 F. 112 (2nd Cir. 1910); Wright Co. v. Herring-Curtiss Co., 211 F. 654 (2nd Cir. 1914); *see* R. Katznelson and J. Howells, *The Myth of the Early Aviation Patent Hold-Up—How a U.S. Government Monopsony Commandeered Pioneer Airplane Patents*, 24 Industrial

AND CORPORATE CHANGE 1 (2015), *available at* http://icc.oxfordjournals.org/content/early/2014/03/03/icc.dtu003.full.pdf?keytype=ref&ijkey=OGyDjFDzzUGU4G9 [http://perma.cc/X5BX-C2GX].

8 Blue Chip Stamps v. Manor Drug Stores, 421 U.S. 723, 762 (1975) (Blackmun, J., dissenting).

9 GERALD GUNTHER, LEARNED HAND: THE MAN AND THE JUDGE 288-89 (2010).

10 Morse v. United States, 174 F. 539 (2d Cir. 1909); *see* MORRIS, *supra* intro. note 2, at 103.

11 Nat'l Park Serv., U.S. Department of the Interior, National Register of Historic Places: Inventory—Nomination Form, "Significance" section at 2 (Aug. 20, 1987) [hereinafter Thurgood Marshall Nomination Form].

12 1 CHARLES DICKENS, AMERICAN NOTES FOR GENERAL CIRCULATION 211-12 (Chapman & Hall 2d ed. 1842).

13 *Collect Pond Park*, http://www.nycgovparks.org/parks/collect-pond-park/history [http://perma.cc/U6PH-85H7]; *Collect Pond*, FORGOTTEN NEW YORK, http://forgotten-ny.com/2011/10/collect-pond/ [http://perma.cc/Y6BK-BU5J].

14 Thurgood Marshall Nomination Form, *supra* ch. 1 note 11, "Significance" section at 2.

15 *See id.* at 3-4.

16 Much of the information for this discussion comes from the U.S. Gen. Servs. Admin., *Report on the Thurgood Marshall U.S. Courthouse* ("GSA *Thurgood Marshall Report*"), and its accompanying materials, including in particular The Paul Partnership, *Historic Structures Report, Cass Gilbert's Federal Courthouse* (Gen. Servs. Admin., Region Two Project #RNY 83093, 1986) [hereinafter *Historic Structures Report*].

17 Editorial, *Thurgood Marshall Courthouse*, N.Y. SUN, April 15, 2003, *available at* http://www.nysun.com/editorials/thurgood-marshall-courthouse/77602/ [http://perma.cc/Y98L-LWVY]. Judge Winter had served as a law clerk for then-Judge Marshall when he was on the Second Circuit.

18 Plessy v. Ferguson, 163 U.S. 537 (1896).

19 Murray v. Pearson, 169 Md. 478 (1936).

20 Brown v. Bd. of Educ. of Topeka, 347 U.S. 483 (1954); see also Brown v. Bd. of Educ. of Topeka, 349 U.S. 294 (1955) (following reargument on the question of relief).

21 School Segregation Cases—Order of Argument, Record Group 267: Records of the Supreme Court National Archives and Records Administration and National Archives; Teaching with Documents: Order of Argument in the Case, *Brown* v. *Board of Education*, http://www.archives.gov/global-pages/larger-image.html?i=/education/lessons/brown-case-order/images/arguments-l.jpg&c=/education/lessons/brown-case-order/images/arguments.caption.html [http://perma.cc/6XDS-FXXJ].

22 Ake v. Okla., 470 U.S. 68 (1985).

23 San Antonio Sch. Dist. v. Rodriguez, 411 U.S. 1 (1973); Milliken v. Bradley, 418 U.S. 717 (1974); Regents of the Univ. of Cal. v. Bakke, 418 U.S. 717 (1974).

24 New York City Citywide Admin. Servs., *New York State Supreme Court Building*, http://www.nyc.gov/html/dcas/html/about/man_supremecourt.shtml [http://perma.cc/L4GW-F6BL]; New York City Citywide Admin. Servs., *Manhattan Municipal Building*, http://www.nyc.gov/html/dcas/html/about/man_munibldg.shtml [http://perma.cc/2X27-689Q].

25 GSA *Thurgood Marshall Report*, *supra* ch. 1 note 16, at 2.

26 Thurgood Marshall Nomination Form, *supra* ch. 1 note 11.

27 The Thurgood Marshall U.S. Courthouse has been much written about, sometimes in varying ways. For example, sources differ in identifying the number of stories in the tower. Compare, e.g., U.S. Gen. Servs. Admin., *Thurgood Marshall U.S. Courthouse, New York, NY*, http://www.gsa.gov/portal/ext/html/site/hb/category/25431/actionParameter/exploreByBuilding/buildingId/868# [http://perma.cc/7TN4-F39P] [hereinafter GSA *Thurgood Marshall Website*] (variously, in the "Architectural Description" section a "thirty-story square tower" and "31 story," and in the "Construction History & Space Inventory" section, "Stories/Levels: 39"), the Thurgood Marshall Nomination Form, *supra* ch. 1 note 11, "Significance" section at 1 ("31-story") and 6 ("thirty-story tower"), and the Preface to the *Historic Structures Report*, *supra* ch. 1 note 16 ("thirty-eight story skyscraper"). While sometimes noting these different descriptions, this text uses as definitive on these points information drawn from consultations with the Second Circuit Executive's Office.

28 Once again, sources differ on this figure. The GSA *Thurgood Marshall Website*, *supra* ch. 1 note 27, at "History & Space Inventory" lists the building as 761,798 square feet, 313,311 of them occupiable. Other sources typically describe the courthouse as 718,000 or 720,000 square feet. *See, e.g.*, Joseph Goldstein, *Facelift Scheduled for Federal Courthouse*,

N.Y. Sun May 8, 2006; GreenbuildingsNYC, *Monday LEEDoff: Thurgood Marshall U.S. Courthouse, 40 Centre Street*, August 6, 2007, https://web.archive.org/web/20080905082619/http://www.greenbuildingsnyc.com/2007/08/06/monday-leedoff-thurgood-marshall-us-courthouse-40-centre-street/ [http://perma.cc/34JD-Y7LV].

29 GSA *Thurgood Marshall Website*, *supra* ch. 1 note 27, "Significance" section.

30 *See* Christopher Gray, *Building the Halls Where History Would Echo*, N.Y. Times, May 7, 2006; Lewis Mumford, *The Sky Line*, The New Yorker, Oct. 13, 1934.

31 Dennis Jacobs, *Postscript*, in Cass Gilbert, Life and Work 289, 291 (Barbara S. Christen & Steven Flanders, eds., 2001).

32 New York City Landmarks Preservation Comm'n, Guide to New York City Landmarks 33 (4th ed. 2009); GSA *Thurgood Marshall Report*, *supra* ch. 1 note 16, timeline.

33 Thurgood Marshall Nomination Form, *supra* ch. 1 note 11, "Significance" section at 1.

34 *See Historic Structures Report*, *supra* ch. 1 note 16, at 118-22.

35 *Id.* at 238-39.

36 Douglas P. Woodlock, *Drawing Meaning from the Heart of the Courthouse, in* Celebrating the Courthouse, *supra* intro. note 28.

37 Thurgood Marshall Nomination Form, *supra* ch. 1 note 11, "Description" section at 4.

38 *Id.* at 5.

39 *Id.* at 4.

40 Joseph Borkin, The Corrupt Judge at 221-22 (Clarkson N. Potter, Inc. 1962); *see* Morris, *supra* intro. note 2, at 134.

41 Benjamin Weiser, *Hang Him Up? The Bad Judge and His Image*, N.Y. Times, Jan. 27, 2009 at A1.

42 Fed. Judicial Ctr., *History of the Federal Judiciary, U.S. Court of Appeals for the Second Circuit*, http://www.fjc.gov/servlet/nGetInfo?jid=965&cid=22&ctype=ac&instate=02&highlight=null [http://perma.cc/FYJ5-GE4C].

43 Morris, *supra* intro. note 2, at 138.

44 *Id.* at 140.

45 Gunther, *supra* ch. 1 note 9, at 471.

46 NLRB v. Associated Press, 85 F.2d 56 (2d Cir 1936), *aff'd*, 301 U.S. 106 (1937).

47 N. Am. Co. v. SEC, 133 F.2d 148 (2d Cir. 1943), *aff'd*, 327 U.S. 686 (1946).

48 United States v. Aluminum Co. of Am., 148 F.2d 416 (2d Cir. 1945).

49 15 U.S.C. § 29 (1940); United States v. Aluminum Co. of Am., 320 U.S. 708 (1943); 28 U.S.C. § 321 (1940).

50 *Aluminum Co. of Am.*, 320 U.S. 708.

51 United States v. District Ct., 334 U.S. 258, 259-60 (1948).

52 *Aluminum Co. of Am.*, 148 F.2d at 427.

53 John Andrew Mahler, Comment, *Draining the ALCOA "Wishing Well": The Section 2 Conduct Requirement After Kodak and Calcomp*, 48 Fordham L. Rev. 291, 302 (1979).

54 Fischman v. Raytheon Mfg. Co., 188 F.2d 783 (2d Cir. 1951).

55 Morris, *supra* intro. note 2, at 152.

56 United States v. Dennis, 183 F.2d 201 (2d Cir. 1950), *aff'd*, 34 U.S. 494 (1951).

57 Irving R. Kaufman, *supra* ch. 1. note 5, at 203, *quoting The Great Judge*, Life, Nov. 4, 1946.

58 Morris, *supra* intro. note 2, at 135-147; *see* United States v. Johnson, 238 F.2d 565 (2d Cir. 1956), *vacated and remanded*, 352 U.S. 565 (1957).

59 Scenic Hudson Pres. Conference v. Fed. Power Comm'n, 354 F.2d 608 (2d Cir. 1965) (with Hays writing the opinion, joined by Judges Lumbard and Waterman).

60 Sostre v. McGinnis, 442 F.2d 178, 181 (2d Cir. 1971).

61 *Id.* at 198.

62 *See* Davidson v. Scully, 694 F.2d 50 (2d Cir. 1982).

63 Pierre N. Leval, Remarks on Henry Friendly, 16 Green Bag 2d 257, 259 (2013), *quoting* John Minor Wisdom, *Views of a Friendly Observer*, 133 U. Pa. L. Rev. 63 (1984).

64 United States v. N.Y. Times Co., 444 F.2d 544 (2d Cir.), *rev'd*, 403 U.S. 713 (1971).

65 *See generally* MORRIS, *supra* intro. note 2, at 189.

66 United States v. N.Y. Times Co., 328 F. Supp. 324 (S.D.N.Y.), *rev'd* 444 F.2d 544 (2d. Cir.), *rev'd*, 403 U.S. 713 (1971).

67 N.Y. Times Co. v. United States, 403 U.S. 713 (1971).

68 Arnold H. Lubash, *Ex-Clerks to Honor Judge Kaufman*, N.Y. TIMES Nov. 8, 1981, *available at* http://www.nytimes.com/1981/11/08/nyregion/ex-clerks-to-honor-judge-kaufman.html [http://perma.cc/ZFX2-Q8CK].

69 Edwards v. Nat'l Audubon Soc., 556 F.2d 113 (2d Cir. 1977).

70 Berkey Photo, Inc. v. Eastman Kodak Co., 603 F.2d 263 (2d Cir. 1979).

71 Press Release, Columbia Law School, Wilfred Feinberg, Venerable Federal Jurist and Distinguished Law School Alumnus Dies at Age 94, *available at* http://www.law.columbia.edu/media_inquiries/news_events/2014/august2014/judge-wilfred-feinberg-tribute [http://perma.cc/UUM6-CWT4] (quoting his former law clerk, then-Columbia Law Professor and Second Circuit Judge Gary E. Lynch).

72 Brandon v. Bd. of Educ., 635 F.2d 971 (2d Cir. 1980).

73 United States v. Visa U.S.A., Inc., 344 F.3d 229 (2d Cir. 2003).

74 Roger J. Miner, United States Court of Appeals for the Second Circuit, *One Hundred Years of Influence on National Jurisprudence: Second Circuit Court of Appeals Decisions Reviewed by the United States Supreme Court*, *in* UNITED STATES COURTS IN THE SECOND CIRCUIT, A COLLECTION OF HISTORY LECTURES DELIVERED BY JUDGES OF THE SECOND CIRCUIT 148 (Fed. Bar. Found. 1992); *see, e.g.*, WNET, Thirteen v. Aereo, Inc., 712 F.3d 676 (2d Cir. 2012), *rev'd sub nom.* Am. Broadcasting Cos. v. Aereo, Inc., 134 S. Ct. 2498 (2014); Cariou v. Prince, 714 F.3d 694 (2d Cir. 2012); Viacom Int'l, Inc. v. YouTube, Inc., 676 F.3d 19 (2d Cir. 2011); Salinger v. Random House, Inc., 811 F.2d 90 (2d Cir. 1986).

75 *Historic Structures Report*, *supra* ch. 1 note 16, at 100.

76 Joseph Goldstein, *Facelift Scheduled for Federal Courthouse*, N.Y. SUN , May 8, 2006.

77 *See, e.g., GreenbuildingsNYC*, *supra* ch. 1 note 28.

78 Information on the renovation provided through consultation with the Second Circuit Executive's Office.

79 Admin. Office of the U.S. Courts, *Table B-1, U.S. Courts of Appeals—Appeals Commenced, Terminated, and Pending, by Circuit,During the 12-Month Period Ending September 30, 2012*, *available at* http://www.uscourts.gov/uscourts/Statistics/JudicialBusiness/2012/appendices/B01Sep12.pdf [http://perma.cc/9KUN-ABMU].

80 Fed. Judicial Ctr., *History of the Federal Judiciary, U.S. Court of Appeals for the Second Circuit*, http://www.fjc.gov/history/home.nsf/page/courts_coa_circuit_02.html [http://perma.cc/V6ZH-5K5Z].

81 ACLU v. Clapper, No. 14-42-cv, 2015 U.S. App. LEXIS 7531 (2d Cir. Sept. 2, 2014); United States v. Newman, Nos. 13-1837(L), 13-1917(Con), 2015 U.S. App. LEXIS 5788 (2d Cir. Apr. 3, 2015).

82 Dennis Jacobs, *Postscript*, *supra* ch. 1 note 31, at 289-90.

CHAPTER 2

1 COMM. ON THE FED. COURTS, N.Y. COUNTY LAWYERS' ASS'N, THE UNITED STATES DISTRICT COURT FOR THE SOUTHERN DISTRICT OF NEW YORK: A RETROSPECTIVE 2, [hereinafter NYCLA RETROSPECTIVE], and BURAK, *supra* intro. note 20, at 1.

2 *See Erection of the First Merchant's Exchange of New York and its Subsequent History*, *in* MANUAL OF THE CORPORATION OF THE CITY OF NEW YORK 1869, at 784-786 (E. Jones & Co.) [hereinafter CITY MANUAL 1869]. Notably, the picture of the building that is included in the Manual is *not* the same Merchant's Exchange that is described in the adjacent entries but instead is of a building erected in 1827. *See also* MORRIS, *supra* intro. note 2, at 15.

3 CITY MANUAL 1869, *supra* ch. 2 note 2, at 784-786.

4 JOSEPH BUCKLIN BISHOP, A CHRONICLE OF ONE HUNDRED & FIFTY YEARS—THE CHAMBER OF COMMERCE OF THE STATE OF NEW YORK, 1768-1919, at 149 (Charles Scribner's Sons 1918).

5 CHARLES M. HOUGH, THE UNITED STATES DISTRICT COURT FOR THE SOUTHERN DISTRICT OF NEW YORK: ITS GROWTH AND THE MEN WHO HAVE DONE ITS WORK, 1789-1919, at 8 (Maritime Law Ass'n of the U.S. 1934).

6 MORRIS, *supra* intro. note 2, at 15; BURAK, *supra* intro note 20, at 2.

7   Manual of the Corporation of the City of New York for the Year 1849, at 334 (McSpedon & Baker) [hereinafter City Manual 1849].

8   *Id.*

9   *Id.*

10 *See* Jedidiah Morse, The American Universal Geography (Isaiah Thomas & Ebenezer Andrews 1802); Charles B. Bickford & Kenneth R. Bowling, The Documentary History of the First Federal Congress of the United States of America (Johns Hopkins University Press 2004).

11 *See* William Winterbotkam, An Historical, Geographical, Commercial, and Philosophical View of the United States of America (1797); James Grant Wilson, The Memorial History of the City of New York-From its First Settlement to the Year 1892, Vol. III at 46 (New York History Co. 1893); Bickford et al., *supra* ch. 2 note 10, at 27, 30, 47.

12 City Manual 1849, *supra* ch. 2 note 7, at 334.

13 City Manual 1869, *supra* ch. 2 note 2, at 784–786; U. S. Senate, *1787-1800, August 12, 1790, Farewell to New York*, www.senate.gov/artandhistory/history/minute/Farewell_NY.htm.

14 Proceedings Had on November 3, 1939 in the United States District Court for the Southern District of New York on the Hundred and Fiftieth Anniversary of its Organization 16 (Merrymount Press 1939). *See also* Burak, *supra* intro. note 20, at 2.

15 United States v. Lawrence, 3 U.S. 42 (1795).

16 Burak, *supra* intro. note 20, at 2.

17 *Id.*

18 Talbot v. Seeman, 5 U.S. 1 (1801).

19 *Id.*; *see also* Cliff Sloan & David McKean, The Great Decision: Jefferson, Adams, Marshall, and the Battle for the Supreme Court 81-82 (Public Affairs 2009).

20 Daily Advertiser, Feb. 20, 1802; American Citizen and General Advertiser, Feb. 20, 1802; *see Public Tours, The Architecture of the City Hall,* http://www.nyc.gov/html/artcom/html/tours/visit_guide_arch.shtml [http://perma.cc/QZ8Q-4QS5].

21 *Public Tours, supra* ch. 2 note 20. Although this website page says that Mangin's name was left off the "cornerstone," the city's November 2003 press release on the 200th anniversary of the building speculates that the cornerstone was removed at some point and that the foundation stone (which is below ground) omitted Mangin's name. *See* Press Release, Mayor Michael Bloomberg et al., http://tinyurl.com/d632a44 [http://perma.cc/7HAH-PKPX].

22 Press Release, *supra* ch. 2 note 21; *History,* http://oldcathedral.org/history/ [http://perma.cc/5WKX-5RHS].

23 Press Release, *supra* ch. 2 note 21.

24 The description of City Hall is largely taken from the city government's descriptions of the building, found at *Public Tours, supra* ch. 2 note 20 and *About City Hall, Architectural History,* http://www.nyc.gov/html/artcom/html/cityhall/architectural.shtml [http://perma.cc/3Y8Z-UQ9F].

25 *See Public Tours, supra* ch. 2 note 20; Carol A. Grissom, Zinc Sculpture in America, 1850-1950, at 208 n.4 (Rosemont Publishing & Printing Corp. 2009).

26 *About City Hall, supra* ch. 2 note 24; *Public Tours, City Hall Sites and the Common,* http://www.nyc.gov/html/artcom/html/tours/visit_guide_common.shtml [http://perma.cc/5963-25HT].

27 Act of April 29, 1812, ch. 71, 2 Stat. 719.

28 Act of April 9, 1814, ch. 49, 3 Stat. 120.

29 *The Story of a Famous Court,* N.Y. Times, April 2, 1899, at IMS4.

30 Burak, *supra* intro. note 20, at 5.

31 Morris, *supra* intro. note 2, at 37.

32 Swift v. Tyson, 41 U.S. 1, 18-19 (1842).

33 Erie R.R Co. v. Tompkins, 304 U.S. 64 (1938).

34 United States v. The Catharine, 25 F. Cas. 332, 341 (S.D.N.Y. 1840).

35 *Id.* at 340-341.

36 *See* Morris, *supra* intro. note 2, at 45-46; *see also, e.g.,* Goodyear v. Cary, 10 F. Cas. 649 (C.C.S.D.N.Y. 1859); Goodyear v. Congress Rubber Co., 10 F. Cas. 674 (C.C.S.D.N.Y. 1856); Goodyear v. Day, 10 F. Cas. 678 (C.C.S.D.N.Y. 1850); Morton v. N.Y. Eye Infirmary, 17 F. Cas. 879 (C.C.S.D.N.Y. 1862).

37 *See Another Fire! Destruction of the New City Hall. The Court-Rooms and Public Offices Destroyed. Documents Rescued from the Flames. Scenes in the Park.*, N.Y. TIMES, Jan. 20, 1854, at 1.

38 *The U.S. Courts,* N.Y. TIMES, Jan. 24, 1854, at 4.

39 *See Removal of the United States Marshal's Office*, N.Y. TIMES, Feb. 28, 1854, at 2 (reporting on rental of the Stevens House for two years, at $16,500 per year); MANUAL OF THE CORPORATION OF THE CITY OF NEW YORK FOR 1855, at 320 (McSpedon & Baker, New York).

40 CHARLES LOCKWOOD, MANHATTAN MOVES UPTOWN 90-92 (Barnes & Noble Books 1995); WAYNE ANDREWS, ARCHITECTURE IN NEW YORK: A PHOTOGRAPHIC HISTORY 7-8 (Syracuse University Press 1995).

41 LOCKWOOD, *supra* ch. 2 note 40, at 104; EDWIN G. BURROWS & MIKE WALLACE, GOTHAM: A HISTORY OF NEW YORK CITY TO 1898, at 715 (Oxford University Press 2000).

42 JOHN F. TROW, TROW'S NEW YORK CITY DIRECTORY, Appendix, Criminal and United States Courts (1855) (District Court listed at "New Court House on Park").

43 *The Story of a Famous Court, supra* ch. 2 note 29; *but see* Letter to the Editor from Robert D. Benedict, N.Y. TIMES, April 9, 1899, at IMS15.

44 *City Items*, N.Y. TIMES, April 5, 1858, at 1; *December Term of the Law Courts*, N.Y. TIMES, December 6, 1858, at 4; *see also Death of Burton, The Comedian.*, N.Y. TIMES, Feb. 11, 1860, at 4 (reporting that the theater had been leased by the government two years earlier); THOMAS ALLSTON BROWN, A HISTORY OF THE NEW YORK STAGE - FROM THE FIRST PERFORMANCE IN 1732 TO 1901, at 359 (Dodd, Med & Co., 1903) (showing that the building was in use as a theater as late as spring 1857).

45 *City Items,* N.Y. TIMES, April 5, 1858, at 1.

46 Act of Feb. 25, 1865, ch. 54, 13 Stat. 438 (creating the Eastern District of New York); *see History of Nassau County, supra* intro. note 22.

47 Act of Feb. 25, 1865, ch. 54, 13 Stat. 438 (creating the Eastern District of New York); *see* A HISTORY OF THE UNITED STATES COURT FOR THE EASTERN DISTRICT OF NEW YORK 7-8 (S. Duberstein, Ed., Fed. Bar Ass'n of N.Y., N.J. & Ct 1965) *available at* https://img.nyed.uscourts.gov/files/local_rules/EDNY%20History%201865-1965%20Centennium.pdf [http://perma.cc/KH9C-5VYF].

48 Judiciary Act, ch. 22, 16 Stat. 44 (1869).

49 Burrows & Wallace, *supra* ch. 2 note 41, at 942.

50 Act of Feb. 9. 1903, ch. 527, 32 Stat. 805; Act of May 26, 1906, ch. 2257, 34 Stat. 202; Act of March 2, 1909, ch. 242, 35 Stat. 685; *see U.S. District Courts for the Districts of New York, Legislative History,* http://www.fjc.gov/history/home.nsf/page/courts_district_ny.html [http://perma.cc/VE8C-MNJZ] [hereinafter *Legislative History*].

51 Fed. Judicial Ctr., *supra* ch. 1 note 42.

52 JOHN P. EATON & CHARLES A. HAAS, TITANIC: TRIUMPH AND TRAGEDY (2d ed. W.W. Norton & Co. 1995); INFORMATION ANNUAL, 1916 (Cumulative Digest Co. 1917); *Titanic Disaster Once More in Court,* N.Y. TIMES, June 23, 1915, at 5; *End Titanic Suits By Paying $665,000,* N.Y. TIMES, July 29, 1916, at 9.

53 *In re The Lusitania*, 251 F. 715, 736 (S.D.N.Y. 1918); AMY SHAPIRO, MILLICENT FENWICK: HER WAY (Rutgers Univ. Press 1970).

54 *See* MORRIS, *supra* intro. note 2, at 115; Goldman v. United States, 245 U.S. 474 (1918); United States v. Am. Socialist Soc'y, 260 F. 885 (S.D.N.Y. 1919).

55 Masses Pub'g Co. v. Patten, 244 F. 535 (S.D.N.Y.), *rev'd*, 246 F. 24 (2d Cir. 1917); *see* MORRIS, *supra* intro. note 2, at 119.

56 Masses Pub'g Co. v. Patten, 246 F. 24 (2d Cir. 1917).

57 Act of Sept. 14, 1922, ch. 306, 42 Stat. 837; Act of Feb. 26, 1929, ch. 334, 45 Stat. 1317; Act of June 15, 1936, ch. 544, 49 Stat. 1491; *see Legislative History, supra* ch. 2 note 50.

58 *The Mullet Post Office Site, supra* ch. 1 note 3.

59 *See* MORRIS, *supra* intro. note 2, at 156-57; United States v. Hiss, 185 F.2d 822 (2d Cir. 1947).

60 Transcript of Record at 226, United States v. Julius Rosenberg, et al., No. c 134-245 (S.D.N.Y.) (March 6, 1951), *available at* http://www.law.umkc.edu/faculty/projects/FTrials/Rosenberg/RosenbergTrial.pdf [http://perma.cc/H884-JQFF].

61 *Id.* at 230.

62 *Id.* at 1614.

63 Sidney Zion, *Roy Cohn No Fingerprints*, THE DAILY NEWS, May 3, 1999, *available at* http://www.nydailynews.com/archives/news/roy-cohn-fingerprints-article-1.832049 [http://perma.cc/PZ3H-PYTG].

64 Interview with Elkan Abramowitz, Esq., former law clerk to Judge Inzer B. Wyatt, and former Assistant U.S. Attorney, in New York, NY (April, 2010).

65 United States v. Yousef, 327 F.3d 56, 79 (2d Cir. 2003).

66 United States v. Salameh, 152 F.3d 88 (2d Cir. 1998) (*Salameh I*).

67 *See* United States v. Yousef, 925 F. Supp. 1063, 1065-66 (S.D.N.Y. 1996).

68 Benjamin Weiser, *Mastermind Gets Life for Bombing of Trade Center*, N.Y. Times, Jan. 9, 1998, at A1.

69 *Yousef*, 327 F.3d at 80.

70 United States v. Rahman, 189 F.3d 88, 103-11 (2d Cir. 1999), United States v. Salameh, 261 F.3d 271, 274-75 (2d Cir. 2001), *cert. denied sub. nom.*, Abouhalima v. United States, 122 S. Ct. 2681 (2002), *cert. denied*, 123 S. Ct. 187 (2002) (*Salameh II*); In re Terrorist Bombings of U.S. Embassies in East Africa, 552 F.3d 93, 101-02, 107 (2d Cir. 2008); United States v. Bin Laden, 397 F. Supp. 2d 465, 473 (S.D.N.Y. 2005); United States v. Bin Laden, 160 F. Supp. 2d 670, 673 n.5 (S.D.N.Y. 2001); United States v. Bin Laden, 156 F. Supp. 2d 359, 361, 363 (S.D.N.Y. 2001); Benjamin Weiser, *4 Guilty in Terror Bombings of 2 U.S. Embassies in Africa*, N.Y. Times, May 30, 2001, at A1.

71 Sandy Smith & William Lambert, *The Mob Finds a 'Patsy' in a Mayor's Inner Circle*, Life, Jan. 5, 1968, at 46.

72 *Id.* at 46, 50.

73 *Id.* at 46.

74 United States v. Corallo, 413 F.2d 1306, 1307 (2d. Cir. 1969).

75 *Id.* at 1332.

76 United States v. Casamento, 887 F.2d 1141 (2d Cir. 1989); Frank J. Prial, *U.S. Seeks Long Terms This Week for 16 in 'Pizza Connection' Case*, N.Y. Times, June 21, 1987, http://www.nytimes.com/1987/06/21/nyregion/us-seeks-long-terms-this-week-for-16-in-pizza-connection-case.html [http://perma.cc/LD8M-MSYA].

77 N.Y. Times Mag., June 5, 1977, cover; *see* Trang Chuong, *Leroy "Nicky" Barnes: Godfather or Snitch?*, Blackbook, Nov. 1, 2007, *available at:* http://www.bbook.com/article/leroy-nicky-barnes-godfather-or-snitch/ [http://perma.cc/J5GB-VY6V].

78 *Nicky Barnes Biography,* http://www.biography.com/people/nicky-barnes-481806#awesm=~oIvGS2XjzghmDp [http://perma.cc/884W-A7CC].

79 *See* United States v. Barnes, 604 F.2d 121, 139 (2d Cir. 1979).

80 *Id.* at 133.

81 Grove Press, Inc. v. Christenberry, 175 F. Supp. 488, 489, 502-03 (footnote omitted) (S.D.N.Y. 1959), *aff'd*, 275 F.2d 433 (2d Cir. 1960).

82 Floyd Abrams, Freely Speaking: Trials of the First Amendment ch. I at 18 (Viking 2005).

83 United States v. New York Times Co., 328 F. Supp. 324, 327 (S.D.N.Y.), *rev'd*, 444 F.2d 544 (2d Cir.); *rev'd,* 403 U.S. 713 (1971).

84 Ben Barna, *Legendary Paparazzo Ron Galella Picks His Modern-Day Jackie Onassis*, Blackbook, Aug. 4, 2010, *available at* http://www.bbook.com/legendary-paparazzo-ron-galella-picks-his-modern-day-jackie-onassis/ [http://perma.cc/62SC-8CPS].

85 *See id.*; *see also Smash His Camera* (HBO broadcast Aug. 4, 2010), *available at* http://www.hbo.com/documentaries/smash-his-camera/index.html [http://perma.cc/4LJB-8UR4].

86 *See* David Hinckley, *Infamous Jackie Onassis photog Ron Galella's artistic legacy picture perfect in 'Smash His Camera,'* NYDailyNews.com, June 7, 2010, http://www.nydailynews.com/entertainment/tv/2010/06/07/2010-06-07_a_paparazzo_sits_for_his_portrait.html [http://perma.cc/EMK5-66FV].

87 Galella v. Onassis, 353 F. Supp. 196, 199, 239 (S.D.N.Y. 1972).

88 Galella v. Onassis, 487 F.2d 986, 1000 (2d. Cir. 1973); *Galella*, 353 F. Supp. 196 at 226.

89 *Galella*, 353 F. Supp. at 241.

90 *Onassis*, 487 F.2d at 998.

91 *Id.* at 991-2.

92 *Id.*

93 Albert Krebs, *Notes on People: Lennons Love U.S.*, N.Y. Times, Mar. 17, 1972, at 47.

94 *Id.*; *see also* Laurie Johnson, *Lennon Sees a Wide Impact in Ouster*, N.Y. Times, Apr. 3, 1973, at 40.

95 Lennon v. Immigration & Naturalization Serv., 527 F.2d 187, 190 (2d. Cir. 1975); Joel Siegel, *Lennon: Back in the U.S.S.A.*, ROLLING STONE, Oct. 10, 1974, at 11.

96 Joe Treen, *Justice for a Beatle: The Illegal Plot to Prosecute and Oust John Lennon*, ROLLING STONE, Dec. 5, 1974, at 9.

97 *Id.*

98 *Lennon*, 527 F.2d at 188.

99 *Id.* at 195.

100 Grant v. Esquire, Inc., 367 F. Supp. 876 (S.D.N.Y. 1973); Groucho Marx Prods., Inc. v. Day & Night Co., 523 F. Supp. 485 (S.D.N.Y. 1981); Allen v. Nat'l Video, Inc., 610 F. Supp. 612 (S.D.N.Y. 1985); Allen v. Men's World Outlet, Inc., 679 F. Supp. 360 (S.D.N.Y. 1988).

101 Warner Bros. Entm't Inc. v. RDR Books, 575 F. Supp. 2d 513 (S.D.N.Y. 2008); Scholastic, Inc. v. Stouffer, 221 F. Supp. 2d 425 (S.D.N.Y. 2002); Westmoreland v. CBS Inc., 596 F. Supp. 1170 (S.D.N.Y. 1984); Sharon v. Time Inc., 575 F. Supp. 1162 (S.D.N.Y. 1983); Judge Abraham D. Sofaer, *Jury Management in Sharon v. Time, Inc.*, 8 U. Bridgeport 445 (1987), *available at* http://www.quinnipiac.edu/prebuilt/pdf/SchoolLaw/LawReviewLibrary/38_8UBridgeportLRev445(1987).pdf [http://perma.cc/2EPF-Z2K5]; Sanders v. Madison Square Garden, L.P., 525 F. Supp. 2d 364 (S.D.N.Y. 2007).

102 Meryl Gordon, *Queen of Mean Dethroned; "Little People" Rejoice*, N.Y. MAGAZINE, April 1, 2012, *available at* http://nymag.com/news/features/scandals/leona-helmsley-2012-4/ [http://perma.cc/LPY4-YFUV].

103 United States v. Stewart, 433 F.3d 273 (2d Cir. 2006); Krysten Crawford, *Martha: I Cheated No One*, CNN/MONEY, *available at* http://money.cnn.com/2004/07/16/news/newsmakers/martha_sentencing/ [http://perma.cc/3KWX-BU9C].

104 Fed. Magistrates Act, Public Law 90-578, 82 Stat. 1107 (1968); Bankruptcy Reform Act, Public Law 95-598, 92 Stat. 2657 (1978).

105 Geoffrey Blodgett, *The Politics of Public Architecture*, in CASS GILBERT, LIFE AND WORK 62, 66-67 (Barbara S. Christen & Steven Flanders, eds., 2001).

106 Interview with Clifford Kirsch, S.D.N.Y. District Executive ("The budget from the General Services Administration was $354 million."); *see* United States Courthouse, 500 Pearl Street, New York, New York, *Dedication Ceremony*, June 3, 1996, at 13.

107 Alan S. Osler, *A Spur to Slow Construction*, N.Y. TIMES, Apr. 28, 1991, at R5.

108 *See* Adam Clymer, *Daniel Patrick Moynihan Is Dead; Senator From Academia Was 76*, N.Y. TIMES, March 27, 2003, *available at* http://www.nytimes.com/2003/03/27/nyregion/daniel-patrick-moynihan-is-dead-senator-from-academia-was-76.html?ref=danielpatrickmoynihan&pagewanted=1 [http://perma.cc/2AKU-3X34].

109 NATHAN GLAZER & DANIEL PATRICK MOYNIHAN, BEYOND THE MELTING POT (MIT Press 2d ed. 1970).

110 Nathan Glazer, *Daniel Patrick Moynihan and Federal Architecture, in* CELEBRATING THE COURTHOUSE, *supra* intro. note 28, at 226-230.

111 *See* Kohn Pederson Fox Assoc., *Daniel Patrick Moynihan U.S. Courthouse*, http://www.kpf.com/project.asp?T=13&ID=117 [http://perma.cc/2M25-WQB9].

112 *Id.*

113 David W. Dunlap, *Putting a New Face on Justice*, N.Y. TIMES, July 19, 1998, *available at* http://www.nytimes.com/1998/07/19/realestate/putting-a-new-face-on-justice.html?pagewanted=all&src=pm [http://perma.cc/4NGT-RE84].

114 Benjamin Weiser, *Abduwali Abdukhadir Muse*, N.Y. TIMES, Feb. 17, 2011, *available at* http://query.nytimes.com/gst/fullpage.html?res=9903E2D9103DF934A25751C0A9679D8B63 [http://perma.cc/9DJZ-N4X5].

115 Peter Lattman, *11 Years in Jail For Fund Chief In Stock Deals*, N.Y. TIMES, October 14, 2011, *available at* http://query.nytimes.com/gst/fullpage.html?res=9401E2D61538F937A25753C1A9679D8B63&module=Search&mabReward=relbias%3As%2C%7B%221%22%3A%22RI%3A10%22%7D [http://perma.cc/NSJ2-6TUL].

116 Judge Charles L. Brieant, *The Federal Court in White Plains After Twenty-One Years*, WESTCHESTER BAR JOURNAL, Volume 32 No. 1, Spring Summer 2005, at 19.

117 *Id.*

118 U.S. District Court, S.D.N.Y., *Charles L. Brieant, Jr. U.S. Courthouse Fast Facts*, http://www.nysd.

uscourts.gov/docs/publications/site_wpfacts.pdf [http://perma.cc/UE3L-2KCB]; U.S. Dep't of Commerce, U.S. Census Bureau, *State & County QuickFacts*, http://quickfacts.census.gov/qfd/states/36000.html [http://perma.cc/YD7Y-RXJH] (select each county for population information) [http://perma.cc/8TNY-9Z8L (Westchester); http://perma.cc/3CFY-UUAV (Rockland); http://perma.cc/LKW9-XVG3 (Putnam); http://perma.cc/L3LJ-FG4L (Orange); http://perma.cc/KLN8-CBU7 (Dutchess); http://perma.cc/QA5W-AWTY (Sullivan)].

119 Brieant, *supra* ch. 2 note 116, at 19.

120 Interview with Clifford Kirsch; interview with Mag. Judge Mark Fox.

121 Interview with Clifford Kirsch; interview with Mag. Judge Mark Fox.

122 Brieant, *supra* ch. 2 note 116, at 19-20.

123 *Id.*

124 *Id.* at 20.

125 *Id.*

126 *See Barenet Schecter, TCa BaOOGa AJM NaR YJMF 231-242 (Walker & Co. 2002).*

127 Dunlap, *supra* ch. 2 note 113.

128 *Hudson River Brickmaking*, http://brickcollecting.com/hudson.htm [http://perma.cc/WTR4-WDDR].

129 *Id.*

130 Thomas E. Rinaldi & Robert J. Yasinac, HUDSON VALLEY RUINS 31 (Univ. Press of England 2006); Brieant, *supra* ch. 2 note 116, at 20 (obtained brick from last functioning brickyard on Hudson).

131 Site visit; interview with Alice Coma, Judge Brieant's former deputy.

132 Jone Johnson Lewis, *Sybil Ludington*, http://womenshistory.about.com/od/waramrevolution/p/ludington_ride.htm [http://perma.cc/D75W-787T].

133 Interview with Clifford Kirsch, S.D.N.Y. District Executive; White Plains Federal Courthouse Fast Facts.

134 Interview with Clifford Kirsch and Michael McMahon.

135 Interview with Clifford Kirsch; interview with Mag. Judge Mark Fox.

136 Site visit; interview with Alice Coma.

137 White Plains Federal Courthouse Fast Facts, United States District Court, Southern District of New York.

138 Interview with Mag. Judge Paul Davison; interview with Mag. Judge Mark Fox; interview with Clifford Kirsch.

139 Timothy O'Connor, *Courthouse in White Plains named for Judge Brieant*, THE JOURNAL NEWS, Nov. 13, 2008, *available at* http://archive.lohud.com/article/20081113/NEWS02/811130431/Courthouse-White-Plains-named-Judge-Brieant [http://perma.cc/V5TF-V3Y5]; interview with Mag. Judge Fox; FEDERAL BAR COUNCIL, SECOND CIRCUIT REDBOOK, 169 (2003-2004).

140 Dennis Hevesi, *Charles L. Brieant, Jr. Longtime Federal Judge Dies at 85,* N.Y. TIMES, July 27, 2008, at A24.

141 Interview with Mag. Judge Davison; Hevesi, *supra* ch. 2 note 140.

142 Tamar Lewin, *Pennzoil-Texaco Fight Raised Key Questions*, N.Y. TIMES, Dec. 19, 1987.

143 *Id.*; Hevesi, *supra* ch. 2 note 140.

144 Lewin, *supra* ch. 2 note 142; Hevesi, *supra* ch. 2 note 140; *Pennzoil Co. v. Texaco, Inc*, 481 U.S. 1 (1987).

145 Lewin, *supra* ch. 2 note 142.

146 Debra Whitefield, *Pennzoil and Texaco Reach Tentative Pact*, L.A. TIMES, Dec. 19, 1987.

147 Thomas S. Mulligan and Chris Kraul, *Texaco Settles Race Bias Suit For $176 Million,* L.A. TIMES, Nov. 16, 1996.

148 *Id.*; Angela G. King, *Coca-Cola takes the high road*, Black Enterprise, Feb. 1, 2001.

149 Interview with Judge Cathy Seibel; Joseph Berger, *Woman Sentenced to Life For Ax Killing of Husband*, N.Y. TIMES, May 1, 1997, *available at* http://www.nytimes.com/1997/05/01/nyregion/woman-sentenced-to-life-for-ax-killing-of-husband.html [http://perma.cc/24DE-QRPP]. *See Gluzman*, 154 F.3d 49.

150 Greg B. Smith, *Pirro's Hubby Guilty of Being a Tax Cheat*, N.Y. DAILY NEWS, June 23, 2000, *available at* http://www.nydailynews.com/archives/news/pirro-hubby-guilty-tax-cheat-article-1.868223 [http://perma.cc/ZU66-HS37].

151 U.S. Gen. Servs. Admin., *Alexander Hamilton U.S. Custom House, New York, NY, Building Overview*, http://www.gsa.gov/portal/ext/html/site/hb/

category/25431/actionParameter/exploreByBuilding/buildingId/644 [http://perma.cc/R76A-STYG] [hereinafter GSA *Alexander Hamilton Website*]. The Southern District Bankruptcy Court also has locations in Poughkeepsie and White Plains.

152 *See* Blodgett, *supra* ch. 2 note 105, at 66-67; GSA *Alexander Hamilton Website*, *supra* ch. 2 note 151, "Overview" section.

153 *See* Blodgett, *supra* ch. 2 note 105, at 66-67.

154 GSA *Alexander Hamilton Website*, *supra* ch. 2 note 151, "Significance" section; National Register of Historic Places Nomination Form.

155 GSA *Alexander Hamilton Website*, *supra* ch. 2 note 151, "Overview" section.

156 *See* Blodgett, *supra* ch. 2 note 105, at 69.

157 GSA *Alexander Hamilton Website*, *supra* ch. 2 note 151, "Significance" section.

158 *Id.*

159 *Id.* at "Overview" section.

160 Interview with Bankruptcy Judge Burton R. Lifland (Chief Judge during move and flood), and interview with Bankruptcy Judge Cecelia G. Morris (Clerk of Court at time of flood, now Chief Judge).

161 Clive Irving, In Their Name (Random House 1995).

162 *See* Nick Brown, *Manhattan Bankruptcy Court to Reopen on Tuesday*, Chi. Trib., Nov. 12, 2012, *available at* articles.chicagotribune.com/2012-11-12/news/sns-rt-us-storm-sandy-bankruptcy-courtbre8ac00o-20121112_1_court-employees-court-order-bankruptcy-court.

163 *See* United States Bankruptcy Court, Southern District of New York, *Mega Cases*, http://www.nysb.uscourts.gov/cgi-bin/megaCases.pl [http://perma.cc/C8UJ-97NQ].

164 United States Courts, *Statistics*, http://www.uscourts.gov/Statistics/BankruptcyStatistics.aspx [http://perma.cc/X3VH-QK7N].

CHAPTER 3

1 The locations to be designated for court sittings evolved over time with the changing geography of the District. Originally, court sessions were to be held in Utica, Canandaigua and Salem. By 1818, the counties of Rensselaer, Albany, Schenectady, Schoharie, and Delaware and the remainder of New York State lying north of those counties were included in the Northern District and Congress had designated Albany and Utica as places for holding court. In 1864 Auburn was added as a place for holding court, with the term to be designated in the judge's discretion.

2 Act of April 9, 1814, ch. 49, 3 Stat. 120.

3 *Id.* at § 2.

4 Roger J. Miner, *United States District Court for the Northern District of New York, Its History and Antecedents, in* United States Courts in the Second Circuit, A Collection of History Lectures Delivered by Judges of the Second Circuit 73-74 (Fed. Bar Found. 1992).

5 *See infra* Chapter 5 for courthouses of the Western District of New York.

6 Miner, *supra* ch. 3 note 4, at 86.

7 *Id.* at 91.

8 *Sargol Trial at an End With Verdict of Guilty*, Auburn Citizen, Jan. 30, 1917, at 6.

9 *Jones Had An Interest in Obesity Remedy Too*, Auburn Citizen, Jan. 23, 1917, at 8.

10 *With Whom Did This Sargol Witness Talk?*, Auburn Citizen, Jan. 3, 1917, at 6.

11 *Cregg Talked All Day; His Voice Almost Gone*, Auburn Citizen, Jan. 27, 1917, at 6.

12 *Says Fight Films May Be Shown in N.Y.*, Auburn Citizen, Oct. 24, 1927, at 6.

13 Tom Wells, The War Within: America's Battle over Vietnam 124-25 (1994).

14 *Draft Card Destroyer Sentenced in Auburn*, Auburn Citizen-Advertiser, Nov. 14, 1968, at 3.

15 United States v. Dancis, 406 F.2d 729, 731 (2d Cir. 1969).

16 Albert S. Kurek, the Troopers Are Coming II: New York Troopers 1943-1985, at 193-94 (2007); *Gas Quells Prison Riot At Auburn*, Lockport Union-Sun & J., Dec. 21, 1970, at 14.

17 *You Don't Mind the Language, Your Honor?*, Auburn Citizen-Advertiser, Mar. 12, 1971, at 11.

18 *Auburn Six Inmates Transferred 'Outside'*, Auburn Citizen-Advertiser, July 7, 1971, at 3.

19 *'Auburn Six' Inmate Serving Three Months In County Jail*, Auburn Citizen-Advertiser, May 3, 1972, at 13.

20 *See* U.S. Gen. Servs. Admin., *James T. Foley U.S. Post Office and Courthouse, Albany, NY*, http://www.gsa.gov/portal/content/104832 (follow "Find a Building" hyperlink, then under "Search by City" choose Albany and the "Find All Buildings in City" hyperlink) [http://perma.cc/4UF8-NKGK] [hereinafter GSA *Foley Website*].

21 *Id.*

22 Interview with John M. Domurad, Chief Deputy and member of the Albany Historical Society, in Albany, NY (April 5, 2010).

23 Bureau of Engraving & Printing, U.S. Dep't of the Treasury, *$100 Note*, http://www.moneyfactory.gov/small100denom.html [http://perma.cc/P4BS-ZRXZ].

24 GSA *Foley Website*, *supra* ch. 3 note 20.

25 *See* Alfonso A. Narvaez, *James Thomas Foley Dies at 80; U.S. Judge in Albany Since 1949*, N.Y. Times, Aug. 18, 1990, *available at* http://www.nytimes.com/1990/08/18/obituaries/james-thomas-foley-dies-at-80-us-judge-in-albany-since-1949.html [http://perma.cc/R6G2-2EJZ].

26 Judge Roger J. Miner Speech at the Dedication of the James T. Foley U.S. Courthouse (Oct. 27, 1988) (provided by Judge Miner, January 29, 2010).

27 Chuck Miller, *Rugby in the National Spotlight: The 1981 USA Tour of the Springboks, How a Traveling National Rugby Team Became a Lightning Rod for the Policies of Apartheid*, Rugby Magazine, Apr. 10, 1995, *available at* http://www.chuckthewriter.com/springboks.html [http://perma.cc/9ZY5-SQPS].

28 *Id.*

29 Selfridge v. Carey, 522 F. Supp. 693, 695 (N.D.N.Y. 1981).

30 Selfridge v. Carey, 660 F.2d 516, 516 (2d Cir. 1981) (per curiam).

31 Paul L. Montgomery, *Protestors in Albany Shout as Springboks Triumph in Rainfall*, N.Y. Times, Sept. 23, 1981, *available at* http://www.nytimes.com/1981/09/23/nyregion/protesters-in-albany-shout-as-springboks-triumph-in-rainfall.html [http://perma.cc/Y4R6-Z9PM].

32 Jesse McKinley, *Ex-State Senate Chief Acquitted of Fraud in Retrial, "This System, It Works," He Says*, N.Y. Times, May 16, 2014, *available at* http://www.nytimes.com/2014/05/17/nyregion/joseph-bruno-former-state-senate-leader-is-acquitted.html [http://perma.cc/2ZQN-8B8D].

33 United States v. New York, No. 1:10-cv-1214, 2012 WL 254263 (N.D.N.Y. Jan. 27, 2012).

34 Edith M. Scully, *New PO, U.S. Building OKd*, Syracuse Post-Standard, Sept. 10, 1966, at 1.

35 *Id.*

36 *Move-in starts May 7*, Syracuse Herald-Journal, Apr. 14, 1976, at 27.

37 Eric Pace, *James M. Hanley, 83, Dies; Served 8 Terms in Congress*, N.Y. Times, Oct. 27, 2003, *available at* http://www.nytimes.com/2003/10/27/nyregion/james-m-hanley-83-dies-served-8-terms-in-congress.html [http://perma.cc/4738-9GGJ].

38 *Id.*

39 Evamaria Hardin, Onondaga Historical Ass'n, Syracuse Landmarks: an AIA Guide to Downtown and Historic Neighborhoods 43 (1993).

40 U.S. Gen. Servs. Admin., *First Impressions Program Overview*, http://www.gsa.gov/portal/category/27234 [http://perma.cc/WFY5-3JR3].

41 *See* Smithsonian Am. Art Museum & The Renwick Gallery, *Maquette for One, Two, Three*, http://americanart.si.edu/collections/search/artwork/?id=14689 [http://perma.cc/2E7F-VK3R].

42 U.S. Gen. Servs. Admin., *More Good News from Syracuse*, in Urban Development Enews Archive FY2002 (Nov. 2002), http://www.gsa.gov/portal/content/100867 [http://perma.cc/VMR3-NAVD].

43 Charley Hannagan, *A Community Garden Blooms at Syracuse Federal Building*, Syracuse Post-Standard, July 14, 2010, *available at* http://www.syracuse.com/news/index.ssf/2010/07/a_community_garden_blooms_at_s.html [http://perma.cc/3JME-MNUB].

44 Charles McChesney, *Calling for Respect for the Constitution, Tea Partiers Protest on Tax Day*, Syracuse Post-Standard, Apr. 15, 2010, *available at* http://www.syracuse.com/news/index.ssf/2010/04/calling_for_respect_for_the_co.html [http://perma.cc/82Q2-CH24]; Charley Hannagan, *Planned Parenthood to Hold Rally This Afternoon to Keep Federal Funding*, Syracuse Post-Standard, Feb. 23. 2011, *available at* http://www.syracuse.com/news/index.ssf/2011/02/planned_parenthood_to_hold_syr.html [http://perma.cc/D7QS-LFK6]; John Mariani, *Occupy Syracuse Seeks Common Council Backing for Constitutional*

Amendment Against 'Corporate Personhood,' Syracuse Post-Standard, Jan. 20, 2012, *available at* http://www.syracuse.com/news/index.ssf/2012/01/occupy_syracuse_seeks_common_c.html [http://perma.cc/6MDX-KEEK].

45 *Rafil A. Dhafir*, Wikipedia, http://en.wikipedia.org/wiki/Rafil_A._Dhafir [http://perma.cc/6N3H-99XW].

46 Cornell Univ. v. Hewlett-Packard Co., 609 F. Supp. 2d 279, 293 (N.D.N.Y. 2009).

47 Much of the information for this section comes from U.S. Gen. Servs. Admin., *Federal Building/U.S. Courthouse, Binghamton, NY*, http://www.gsa.gov/portal/ext/html/site/hb/category/25431/actionParameter/exploreByBuilding/buildingId/278 [http://perma.cc/S4SW-WJYM].

48 *See* Nancy Dooling, *The St. Patrick's Four Verdict*, Press & Sun-Bulletin, Sept. 27, 2005, at 1A.

49 Much of the information for this section comes from U.S. Gen. Servs. Admin., *Alexander Pirnie Federal Building, Utica, NY*, http://www.gsa.gov/portal/content/104832 (follow "Find a Building" hyperlink, then under "Search by City" choose Utica and the "Find All Buildings in City" hyperlink) [http://perma.cc/A4P7-CAJD].

50 Gambino v. U.S., 275 U.S. 310 (1927).

51 Reitz v. Mealey, 34 F. Supp. 532, 534-35 (N.D.N.Y. 1940).

52 Reitz v. Mealey, 314 U.S. 33, 40 (1941), *overruled by* Perez v. Campbell, 402 U.S. 637 (1971).

CHAPTER 4

1 H.R. 184, 38th Cong. (1st Sess. 1864).

2 Act of Feb. 25, 1865, ch. 54, 13 Stat. 438 (creating the Eastern District of New York).

3 Bernard A. Grossman, *A Court is Born* and *The Homes of the Court*, *in* A History of the United States Court for the Eastern District of New York 7, 8-10 (Samuel C. Duberstein, ed., 1965), *available at* https://img.nyed.uscourts.gov/files/local_rules/EDNY%20History%201865-1965%20Centennium.pdf [http://perma.cc/789X-ZTCR].

4 Sidney Goldstein, *The Development of the District and the Growth of the Court*, *in* A History of the United States Court for the Eastern District of New York, *supra* ch. 4 note 3, at 39–40.

5 Norval White & Elliot Willensky, AIA Guide to New York City, 898–99 (3d ed. 1988); David McCullough, the Great Bridge: the Epic Story of the Building of the Brooklyn Bridge 426 (1972).

6 U.S. Gen. Servs. Admin., *Conrad B. Duberstein U.S. Bankruptcy Courthouse, Brooklyn, NY*, http://www.gsa.gov/portal/ext/html/site/hb/category/25431/actionParameter/exploreByBuilding/buildingId/2 [http://perma.cc/K5CS-P5EA], [hereinafter GSA *Duberstein Website*].

7 David Rohde, *As Courthouse Gets Go-Ahead, Lawsuit May Be One Step Behind*, N.Y. Times, Mar. 16, 1997, at C11.

8 Hadiya Strasberg, *Superior Court*, Traditional Building, Apr. 2007, *available at* http://www.traditional-building.com/Previous-Issues-07/AprilProject07SuperiorCourt.htm [http://perma.cc/DZ5J-VYVM].

9 GSA *Duberstein Website*, *supra* ch. 4 note 6.

10 National Prohibiton (Volstead) Act, ch. 85, 41 Stat. 305 (1919).

11 Cornelius W. Wickersham, Jr., *The Criminal Division of the Court*, *in* A History of the United States Court for the Eastern District of New York, *supra* ch. 4 note 3, at 29; United States v. Lang, 73 F. Supp 561, 561-62 (E.D.N.Y. 1947).

12 United States v. Heine, 151 F.2d 813, 814–17 (2d Cir. 1945).

13 The House on 92nd Street (Twentieth Century-Fox 1945).

14 United States v. Monti, 168 F. Supp. 671, 672–75 (E.D.N.Y. 1958).

15 United States v. Abel, 258 F.2d 485, 487–502 (2d Cir. 1958).

16 The FBI Story (Warner Bros. 1959).

17 James B. Donovan, Strangers on A Bridge (1964).

18 Allegheny Airlines, Inc. v. Village of Cedarhurst, 238 F.2d 812, 814–17 (2d Cir. 1956).

19 In re Air Disaster at Lockerbie, 709 F. Supp 231 (J.P.M.L. 1989).

20 Edward L. Dubroff, *Nationality and Naturalization*, *in* A History of the United States Court for the Eastern District of New York, *supra* ch. 4 note 3, at 34.

21 Bernard A. Grossman, *A Court is Born*, *in* A History of the United States Court for the Eastern District of New York, *supra* ch. 4 note 3, at 11.

22 *See* History, Art & Archives: U.S. House of Representatives, *Celler, Emanuel*, http://history.house.gov/People/Detail?id=10788 [http://perma.cc/X7HN-DQUX]; *see also* Emanuel Celler, You Never Leave Brooklyn: the Autobiography of Emanuel Celler (1953).

23 N.Y.S. Ass'n for Retarded Children, Inc. v. Rockefeller, 357 F. Supp. 752 (E.D.N.Y. 1973); *State and Families Reach Final Accord Over Willowbrook*, N.Y. Times, Mar. 3, 1987, at B4.

24 Jeffrey B. Morris, To Administer Justice on Behalf of All the People: the United States District Court for the Eastern District of New York, 1965-1990, at 45 (1992).

25 N.Y.S. Ass'n for Retarded Children, *supra* ch. 4 note 23, 357 F. Supp. at 758.

26 Berkman v. City of New York, 536 F. Supp. 177 (E.D.N.Y. 1982), *aff'd*, 705 F.2d 584 (2d Cir. 1983).

27 Able v. United States, 847 F. Supp. 1038, 1045-46 (E.D.N.Y. 1994), *rev'd*, 155 F.3d 628 (2d Cir. 1998).

28 United States v. Volpe, 224 F.3d 72 (2d Cir. 2000); Mike Cluffey, *Eugene Nickerson, Louima Judge, Dies*, N.Y. Daily News, Jan. 3, 2002, *available at* http://www.nydailynews.com/archives/news/eugene-nickerson-louima-judge-dies-article-1.487735 [http://perma.cc/443L-5BPK].

29 Louima v. City of N.Y., No. 98CV5083(SJ), 2004 U.S. Dist. LEXIS 13707 (E.D.N.Y. July 21, 2004); Sewell Chan, *The Abner Louima Case, 10 Years Later*, N.Y. Times City Room (Aug. 9, 2007), http://cityroom.blogs.nytimes.com/2007/08/09/the-abner-louima-case-10-years-later/ [http://perma.cc/Q39J-9GS6].

30 *See* Alan Vinegrad, *Prosecutions of Lemrick Nelson Jr.*, N.Y. Law Journal, May 23, 2003, at 1.

31 Hornell Brewing Co., Inc. v. Brady, 819 F. Supp. 1227, 1245–46 (E.D.N.Y. 1993).

32 Airport Transp. Ass'n of Am. v. PATCO, 453 F. Supp. 1287 (E.D.N.Y. 1978), *aff'd*, 594 F. 2d 851 (2d Cir. 1978), *cert. denied*, 441 U.S. 944 (1979); *see also* Airport Transp. Ass'n of Am. v. PATCO, 516 F. Supp. 1108 (E.D.N.Y. 1981).

33 In re Agent Orange Prod. Liab. Litig., 597 F. Supp. 740 (E.D.N.Y. 1984), *aff'd*, 818 F.2d 146 (2d Cir. 1987).

34 Elizabeth Stull, *Judge Weinstein's 40th Anniversary on the Bench*, Brooklyn Daily Eagle, April 24, 2007, *available at* http://50.56.218.160/archive/category.php?category-id=4&id=12473 [http://perma.cc/RQP9-VQWQ].

35 William K. Rashbaum, *Mob Figure Sentenced In Fraud Scheme*, N.Y. Times, Jan. 31, 2006, at B4.

36 *See* United States v. Thai, 29 F.3d 785, 794 (2d Cir. 1994).

37 United States v. Levasseur, 816 F.2d 37 (2d Cir. 1987); United States v. Gotti, 6 F.3d 924, 929 (2d Cir. 1986).

38 Michael Cooper, *For Medellin Assassin, 10 Life Sentences*, N.Y. Times, May 6, 1995, at A23.

39 Press Release, New York City Police Dep't, New York City Police Commissioner Raymond W. Kelly Dedicates Police Headquarters Visitor's Entrance to Retired Detectives Injured in a Terrorist Attack on One Police Plaza 25 Years Ago (Dec. 31, 2007) (on file with author).

40 Pelli Clarke Pelli Architects, *Awards*, http://pcparch.com/firm/awards [http://perma.cc/SE5J-JNQM].

41 Steel Institute of New York, *U.S. District Courthouse, Cadman Plaza*, Metals in Construction, Spring 2007, at 46.

42 Interview with the Judge Raymond J. Dearie, Senior U.S. Dist. Judge, E.D.N.Y., and James E. Ward, Jr., Dist. Exec., U.S. Dist. Court, E.D.N.Y., in Brooklyn, N.Y. (June 9, 2011) ("Dearie and Ward Interview").

43 *Id*.

44 *See* Stephanie Smith, Cong. Research Serv., RS22121, the Interagency Security Committee and Security Standards for Federal Buildings 2–3 (2007).

45 Daniel Watch & Deepa Tolat, *Retrofitting Existing Buildings to Resist Explosive Threats*, Whole Building Design Guide (Oct. 19, 2011), *available at* http://www.wbdg.org/resources/retro_rstexplo.php [http://perma.cc/N6YS-J4CZ].

46 Dearie and Ward Interview, *supra* ch. 4 note 42.

47 Rohde, *supra* ch. 4 note 7.

48 *Judge Upholds Plan for New Courthouse*, N.Y. Times, July 26, 1997, at A1.

49 U.S. Gen. Servs. Admin., United States Courthouse, Brooklyn, New York 26 (2006) [hereinafter U.S. Courthouse, Brooklyn].

50 *Id*. at 24.

51 Dearie and Ward Interview, *supra* ch. 4 note 42.

52 Lynda Richardson, *Revised Plan for Criticized Courthouse*, N.Y. Times, July 19, 1996.

53 *Id.*

54 U.S. Courthouse, Brooklyn, *supra* ch. 4 note 49, at 6–7.

55 Dearie and Ward Interview, *supra* ch. 4 note 42.

56 Jason Grant, *U.S. Courthouse is Named for Theodore Roosevelt*, N.Y. Times City Room (Dec. 30, 2008), http://cityroom.blogs.nytimes.com/2008/12/30/us-courthouse-is-named-for-theodore-roosevelt/ [http://perma.cc/2J9Q-A79D].

57 United States v. Defreitas, 701 F. Supp. 2d 297 (E.D.N.Y. 2010).

58 *See* United States v. Siraj, 533 F.3d 99, 100 (2d Cir. 2008).

59 Arar v. Ashcroft, 414 F. Supp. 2d 250, 287–88 (E.D.N.Y. 2006).

60 *See, e.g.,* United States v. City of N.Y., No. 07CV2067(NGG), 2010 U.S. Dist. LEXIS 111064 (E.D.N.Y. Oct. 19, 2010). The long-running case also received consideration in the Second Circuit and ultimately was settled after New York City Mayor de Blasio took office in 2014. *See* Edward Sandoval & John Marzulli, *New York City to pay $98 Million to Settle Case Alleging FDNY Discriminated against minority applicants*, N.Y. Daily News (March 18, 2014), *available at* http://www.nydailynews.com/new-york/city-pay-98-million-fdny-discrimination-case-article-1.1725702 [http://perma.cc/HG9J-U8C2].

61 GSA *Duberstein Website*, *supra* ch. 4 note 6.

62 Conrad B. Duberstein, Acceptance Remarks *in A Tribute to the Honorable Conrad B. Duberstein*, Emory Bankruptcy Developments Journal, Vol 22 at 5-11 (2005).

63 Conrad B. Duberstein, Remarks *in Dedication Ceremony for the Conrad B. Duberstein Bankruptcy Courthouse*, 13 Am. Bankr. Inst. L. Rev 1 at pages 21-22 (2005).

64 While the 2010 United States Census reported a population of over 2.8 million residents in Nassau and Suffolk Counties, the courthouse is served by only three active District Judges, four Senior Judges (who maintain virtually full dockets), and four Magistrate Judges.

65 By happenstance, the dedication of the Courthouse occurred on the same day that a TWA Flight 800 memorial took place nearby in Heckscher State Park.

66 Senior District Judge Leonard D. Wexler was chair of the Eastern District's committee that oversaw the Courthouse's design and construction, and he sat on the architect selection committee. He is widely recognized as an important inspiration behind the Courthouse.

67 Much of the information in this section is based on an April 14, 2011 interview with Judge Leonard D Wexler in Central Islip, a site tour of the courthouse, and discussions with other judges of the Eastern District, including Judges Joseph F. Bianco, Thomas C. Platt, Joanna Seybert, Arthur D. Spatt, and Magistrate Judge James Orenstein.

68 Dubroff, *supra* ch. 4 note 20.

69 Press Release, United States Attorney's Office, Eastern District of New York, Members And Associates Of The Pagans Outlaw Motorcycle Gang Arrested In Tri-State Area Sweep (Sept. 15, 2010); Charlie LeDuff, *Prosecutors Say Doctor Killed to Feel a Thrill*, N.Y. Times, Sept. 7, 2000.

70 *Life in Jail for Poison Doctor* (CBS news broadcast, July 12, 2000), *available at* http://www.cbsnews.com/news/life-in-jail-for-poison-doctor/ [http://perma.cc/F35Q-LDVQ].

71 Press Release, United States Attorney's Office, Eastern District of New York, Columbian Drug Trafficker Sentenced to 40 Years for International Cocaine Distribution Conspiracy (Apr. 25, 2012).

CHAPTER 5

1 Act of May 12, 1900, ch. 391, 31 Stat. 175 (creating the Western District of New York). *See also* Western District of N.Y., *Court/District History*, www.nywd.uscourts.gov/courtdistrict-history.

2 Much of the history of the Western District provided in this section is derived from an April 22, 1986 lecture given by District Judge John T. Curtin. *See* John T. Curtin, *United States District Court for the Western District of New York, in* United States Courts in the Second Circuit: A Collection of History Lectures Delivered by Judges of the Second Circuit 124–137 (Fed. Bar Found. 1992).

3 Wright v. Herring-Curtiss Co., 211 F. 654, 655 (2d Cir. 1914).

4 *See* Joseph W. Barnes, *Rochester's City Halls*, 40 Rochester History, no. 2, April 1978, at 1, 12.

5 *Id.* at 13.

6 United States v. Glick, 463 F.2d 491, 495 (2d Cir. 1972).

7 *See* Barnes, *supra* ch. 5 note 4, at 20-22.

8 Edward R. Korman & Abbott A. Leban, *Kenneth Barnard Keating*, http://www.nycourts.gov/history/

legal-history-new-york/luminaries-court-appeals/keating-kenneth.html [http://perma.cc/7DLN-6YN4].

9   The Attica case has generated a great deal of litigation over many years, covered in many reported cases and news stories. This account is largely drawn from a telephone interview with Judge Michael A. Telesca, Senior U.S. Dist. Judge, W.D.N.Y (July 27, 2010). The settlement and its background are also detailed in David W. Chen, *Compensation Set On Attica Uprising*, N.Y. Times, Aug. 29, 2000, at B5, *available at* http://www.nytimes.com/2000/08/29/nyregion/compensation-set-on-attica-uprising.html?pagewanted=1 [http://perma.cc/K2YY-KVQP].

10 Eastman Kodak Co. v. Apple, Inc., No. 12-06020 (W.D.N.Y., filed Jan. 10, 2012); Eastman Kodak Co. v. HTC, No. 12-06021 (W.D.N.Y., filed Jan. 10, 2012); *see In re* Eastman Kodak Co., No. 12-10202 (Bankr. S.D.N.Y. Jan. 11, 2013) (approval of sale by U.S. Bankruptcy Judge Allan Gropper); Beth Jinks, *Apple, Google in Group Buying Kodak Patents*, Bloomberg (Dec. 19, 2012, 12:36 PM), www.bloomberg.com/news/2012-12-19/kodak-agrees-to-sell-imaging-patents-for-525-million.html [http://perma.cc/6BYK-QN2T].

11 President Franklin D. Roosevelt, Address at the Dedication of the Federal Building in Buffalo (Oct. 17, 1936), *available at* www.presidency.ucsb.edu/ws/?pid=15194 [http://perma.cc/7C5T-JTUJ].

12 The history of Love Canal and its environmental issues and the resulting cases has been extensively documented. For an overview, *see Love Canal*, http://en.wikipedia.org/wiki/Love_Canal [http://perma.cc/C5JN-LJBT].

13 United States v. Hooker Chems. & Plastics Corp., 850 F. Supp. 993, 1069 (W.D.N.Y. 1994).

14 *See* Matt Chandler, *Love Canal: A Landmark Case with Lasting Impact*, Buffalo Law Journal, Jan. 12, 2009, *available at* http://www.bizjournals.com/buffalo/blog/buffalo-law-journal/2009/01/love-canal-a-landmark-case-with-lasting-impact.html [http://perma.cc/GA4V-DLS2].

15 *See In re* Kinsman Transit, 338 F.2d 708, 721–27 (2d Cir. 1964).

16 *Id.* at 714.

17 Arthur v. Nyquist, 415 F. Supp. 904, 969 (W.D.N.Y. 1976), *aff'd in part, rev'd in part*, 573 F.2d 134 (2d Cir. 1978).

18 *See The Buffalo Nine*, http://en.wikipedia.org/wiki/The_Buffalo_Nine [http://perma.cc/LT77-3G6M].

19 Telephone interview with then Chief Judge William M. Skretny, W.D.N.Y (Oct. 12, 2011).

20 Barry A. Muskat, *So Far, So Good: The New Federal Courthouse*, Buffalo Spree, Dec. 2009, *available at* www.buffalospree.com/buffalospreemagazine/archives/2009_12/1209architecture.html [http://perma.cc/KB8S-FTAD].

21 James Fink, *Buffalo Courthouse is Topped Off*, Buffalo Business First, Apr. 17, 2009, *available at* www.bizjournals.com/buffalo/stories/2009/04/13/daily47.html [http://perma.cc/577Z-YDEV].

22 *See* Muskat, *supra* ch. 5 note 17.

CHAPTER 6

1   Judge José A. Cabranes, *Notes on the History of the Federal Court of Connecticut*, in United States Courts in the Second Circuit: A Collection of History Lectures Delivered by Judges of the Second Circuit 38–61 (Fed. Bar Found. 1992); Judge Cabranes' April 21, 1983 speech is also found in 57 Conn. B.J. 351 (1983). Much of the early history of the district is drawn from this source.

2   Cabranes, *supra* ch. 6 note 1, at 39, 44.

3   Charles Hopkins Clark, *Capitals and Statehouses of Connecticut*, in State of Connecticut, the One Hundredth Anniversary of the First Meeting of the General Assembly, Under the Present Constitution and the Second General Legislative Reunion 41, 44 (William Harrison Taylor ed., 1919).

4   Henry Peck & George H. Coe, The New Haven State House with Some Account of the Green 7–8 (1889); *See also* Priscilla Searles, *When We Were Kings*, Business New Haven, February 23, 1998; David M. Roth, Connecticut: A Bicentennial History 6 (1979).

5   Peck & Coe, *supra* ch. 6 note 4, at 8.

6   *Id.* at 9.

7   *Id.*

8   *Id.* at 17.

9   Clark, *supra* ch. 6 note 3, at 44.

10 Peck & Coe, *supra* ch. 6 note 4, at 33.

11 *Id.* at 17.

12 *Id.* at 15.

13 *Id.*

14 *Id.* at 35.

15 *New Haven's State House Going*, N.Y. Times, July 13, 1889, at 1.

16 Peck & Coe, *supra* ch. 6 note 4, at 12, 60–62.

17 *Id.* at 12–13; *see also New Haven's State House Going*, *supra* ch. 6 note 15.

18 Peck & Coe, *supra* ch. 6 note 4, at 12.

19 *Id.* at 18.

20 Clark, *supra* ch. 6 note 3, at 44; Peck & Coe, *supra* ch. 6 note 4, at 38, 44.

21 Clark, *supra* ch. 6 note 3, at 44.

22 *Id.* at 44–45; *see also New Haven's State House Going*, *supra* ch. 6 note 15.

23 *New Haven's State House Going*, *supra* ch. 6 note 15.

24 Peck & Coe, *supra* ch. 6 note 4, at 155.

25 Clark, *supra* ch. 6 note 3, at 44–45; Peck & Coe, *supra* ch. 6 note 4, at 18; *New Haven's State House Going*, *supra* ch. 6 note 15.

26 Marlene Clark, *A Capitol Idea: Moving the State Capital to Hartford*, Hartford Courant, Jan. 3, 2007, at B2.

27 Peck & Coe, *supra* ch. 6 note 4, at 18, 25, 33.

28 Douglas O. Linder, *The Amistad Case*, Soc. Sci. Res. Network, Oct. 15, 2007, http://papers.ssrn.com/sol3/papers.cfm?abstract_id=1021314 [http://perma.cc/4G27-FVAC].

29 Margaret B. Wilson & Diane R. Gatewood, *From* Amistad *to* Brown: *The March for Justice in the Courts*, 23 Update on L. Related Educ. 14, 15 (1999); *see also* Helen Kromer, Amistad: the Slave Uprising Aboard the Spanish Schooner 15 (1997).

30 Linder, *The Amistad Case*, *supra* ch. 6 note 28, at 2.

31 Kromer, *supra* ch. 6 note 29, at 19.

32 Kromer, *supra* n ch. 6 note 29, at 19; *see also* Douglas O. Linder, *Salvaging Amistad*, 31 J. Mar. L. & Com. 559, 565 (2000); Wilson & Gatewood, *supra* ch. 6 note 29, at 15.

33 Kromer, *supra* ch. 6 note 29, at 18-19; *see also* Linder, *The Amistad Case*, *supra* ch. 6 note 28, at 1–2.

34 Linder, *The Amistad Case*, *supra* ch. 6 note 28, at 2.

35 Linder, *Salvaging Amistad*, *supra* ch. 6 note 32, at 560, 565.

36 Perry Walton, *The Mysterious Case of the Long, Low, Black Schooner*, 6 New Eng. Q. 353, 358 (1933).

37 Linder, *The Amistad Case*, *supra* ch. 6 note 28, at 1; *see also* Ted Widmer, Martin Van Buren 121 (2005).

38 Walter Dean Myers, Amistad: A Long Road to Freedom 40 (1998); *see also* Linder, *Salvaging Amistad*, *supra* ch. 6 note 32, at 565.

39 Linder, *Salvaging Amistad*, *supra* ch. 6 note 32, at 570.

40 Linder, *Salvaging Amistad*, *supra* ch. 6 note 32, at 569; *see also* Michael Daly Hawkins, *John Quincy Adams and the Antebellum Maritime Slave Trade: The Politics of Slavery and the Slavery of Politics*, 25 Okla. City U. L. Rev. 1, 37 (2000).

41 Cabranes, *supra* ch. 6 note 1, at 48.

42 Donald Dale Jackson, *Mutiny on the Amistad*, Smithsonian Mag., Dec. 1997, at 115–17; *see also* Sidney Kaplan and J.W. Barber, *Black Mutiny on the Amistad*, 10 Mass. Rev. 493, 521 (1969) (note that due to an error in the print volume, pages 493–532 of this article are incorrectly printed as pages "291–298, 1–32" on the physical page).

43 Linder, *The Amistad Case*, *supra* ch. 6 note 28, at 3; *see also* Jackson, *supra* ch. 6 note 42, at 115–17.

44 Linder, *The Amistad Case*, *supra* ch. 6 note 28, at 3.

45 *Id.*; Peck & Coe, *supra* ch. 6 note 4, at 67.

46 Linder, *The Amistad Case*, *supra* ch. 6 note 28, at 3–6.

47 R. Earl McClendon, *The Amistad Claims: Inconsistencies of Policy*, 48 Pol. Sci. Q. 386, 388 (1933).

48 Linder, *The Amistad Case*, *supra* ch. 6 note 28, at 3; *see also* Hawkins, *supra* ch. 6 note 40, at 38–39.

49 Linder, *The Amistad Case*, *supra* ch. 6 note 28, at 3–4; *see also* William M. Wiecek, *Slavery and Abolition Before the United States Supreme Court, 1820-1860*, 65 J. Am. Hist. 34, 41 (1978).

50 *See* United States v. Libellants & Claimants of The Schooner Amistad, 40 U.S. 518, 525 (1841).

51 Wiecek, *supra* ch. 6 note 49, at 41–42.

52 Linder, *The Amistad Case, supra* ch. 6 note 28, at 4.

53 Linder, *Salvaging Amistad, supra* ch. 6 note 32, at 573–575.

54 Wiecek, *supra* ch. 6 note 49, at 42.

55 *See Libellants & Claimants of the Schooner Amistad*, 40 U.S. at 596–97.

56 Linder, *Salvaging Amistad, supra* ch. 6 note 32, at 575–76.

57 *See Libellants & Claimants of the Schooner Amistad*, 40 U.S. at 518.

58 Linder, *The Amistad Case, supra* ch. 6 note 28, at 5–6.

59 *Id.* at 6.

60 *Id.*

61 *See Libellants & Claimants of the Schooner Amistad*, 40 U.S. at 567–80 (summarizing the Attorney General's argument); *see also* Wiecek, *supra* ch. 6 note 49, at 42–43.

62 Linder, *The Amistad Case, supra* ch. 6 note 28, at 6; *see also* Joseph K. Adjaye, *Amistad and the Lessons of History*, 29 J. Black Stud. 455, 456 (1999); Patricia Roberts-Miller, *John Quincy Adams's Amistad Argument: The Problem of Outrage; Or, the Constraints of Decorum*, 32 Rhetoric Soc'y Q. 5, 14–23 (2002).

63 Linder, *The Amistad Case, supra* ch. 6 note 28, at 7.

64 President William Howard Taft, Address at the Laying of the Cornerstone, *in* New Haven, Conn. Federal Building: Cornerstone Laid June 4, 1914, at 13, 17 (New Haven Chamber of Commerce), *available at* http://cdm15019.contentdm.oclc.org/cdm/singleitem/collection/p4005coll11/id/473/rec/1 [http://perma.cc/TE8U-BMWE].

65 George Nichols, *The New Haven Post Office and Court House*, 31 Architectural F. 85, 86 (1919).

66 Charles C. Goetsch, *A Short History of the New Haven Courthouse, in* Ceremony of Rededication, United States District Courthouse, New Haven, Connecticut, September 27, 1985.

67 *Id.*

68 Paul Von Zielbauer, *Richard C. Lee, 86, Mayor Who Revitalized New Haven*, N.Y. Times, Feb. 4, 2003, at C15.

69 SCM Corp. v. Xerox Corp., 463 F. Supp. 983 (D. Conn. 1978), *aff'd after remand,* 645 F.2d 1195, (2d Cir. 1981).

70 *SCM Corp.,* 463 F.Supp. at 985-90, 1014, and 1019-20.

71 *See* SCM Corp. v. Xerox Corp., 645 F.2d 1195 (2d Cir. 1981), *cert. denied,* 455 U.S. 1016 (1982).

72 Ricci v. DeStefano, 557 U.S. 557 (2009).

73 Ricci v. DeStefano, 554 F. Supp. 2d 142 (D. Conn. 2006), *aff'd,* 264 F. App'x 106 (2d Cir.), *and summary order withdrawn and aff'd,* 530 F.3d 87 (2d Cir. 2008), *rev'd,* 557 U.S. 557 (2009).

74 Rick Lyman, *At N.Y. Corruption Trial, A Former Official Recounts Bribery Schemes*, Philly.com, http://articles.philly.com/1986-10-06/news/26060289_1_corruption-trial-corruption-scandal-bribery [http://perma.cc/X87J-9MEJ].

75 U.S. Gen. Servs. Admin., Abraham A. Ribicoff Federal Building and Courthouse, *available at* www.gsa.gov/graphics/regions/Ribicoffmore.pdf.

76 Nat'l Park Serv., U.S. Department of the Interior, National Register of Historic Places InventoryNomination Form Apr. 14, 1977 (for Buckingham Square District).

77 *Federal Building to Get Seal of Commendation*, Hartford Courant, June 4, 1963, at 30A.

78 *Shelter Possible in New Federal Office Building*, Hartford Courant, May 20, 1962, at 3B.

79 *Razing to Start on Site of New Federal Building*, Hartford Courant, Dec. 11, 1960, at 10B.

80 *Id.*; U.S. Gen. Servs. Admin., *A.A. Ribicoff Fed. Bldg.*, Hartford Field Office Newsletter (Fall 1994).

81 Robert Byrnes, *Washington Report: House Unit Approves $7,636,400 for Hartford Federal Building*, Hartford Courant, Apr. 15, 1960, at 2A.

82 *Contracting Bids are Being Sought for New Federal Building in City*, Hartford Courant, Aug. 28, 1960, at 1B; *Federal Building*, Hartford Courant, Nov. 12, 1961, at 1D.

83 *Federal Building*, Hartford Courant, Nov. 12, 1961, at 1D.

84 *Federal Building Dedication Today*, Hartford Courant, June 17, 1963, at 12A.

85 Martin Weil, *Abraham Ribicoff, 87, Dies; Senator, HEW Chief*, Wash. Post, Feb. 23, 1988, at D06.

86 Unless otherwise specified, biographical information about Abraham Ribicoff comes from U.S. Congress, *Ribicoff, Abraham Alexander*, Biographical Directory of the United States Congress 1774 - Present, http://bioguide.congress.gov/scripts/biodisplay.pl?index=R000191 [http://perma.cc/TDM3-AY6S].

87 *Ribicoff of Connecticut Dies; Governor and Senator Was 87*, N.Y. Times, Feb. 23, 1988, at A1.

88 *Id.*

89 GSA, *Abraham A. Ribicoff Federal building and Courthouse*, http://www.gsa.gov/graphics/regions/Ribicoffmore.pdf [http://perma.cc/9QK7-5UCU].

90 William Cockerham, *Era Ends as Annex Opens*, Hartford Courant, Apr. 13, 1992, at B1.

91 *Id.*

92 Richard L. Madden, *Wells Fargo Robbery Case Takes a Long Route to Trial*, N.Y. Times, Dec. 28, 1987, at B1.

93 Marisa O. Colon, *Motives Still Debated, 10 Years After Heist*, Hartford Courant, Sept. 12, 1993, at A1.

94 United States v. Ojeda Rios, 495 U.S. 257 (1990).

95 18 U.S.C. § 2518 (2012).

96 Edmund H. Mahony, *Elusiveness Has Its Cost, Suspect In '83 Wells Fargo Robbery Denied Bail*, Hartford Courant, Apr. 16, 2008, at A1.

97 *Puerto Rican Pleads Guilty to 1983 Conn. Robbery*, New Haven Register, Feb. 5, 2010.

98 Alaine Griffin, *Machetero Gets 7 Years*, Hartford Courant, May 27, 2010, at B1.

99 Edmund H. Mahony, *Not Guilty Plea in Heist*, Hartford Courant, May 21, 2011, at A1; Edmund H. Mahony, *Longtime Fugitive Gets 5 Years in Jail*, Hartford Courant, Nov. 14, 2012, at B1.

100 Conn. Gen. Stat. Ann. § 17-2d (Supp. 1965).

101 *Id.*; *see also* Shapiro v. Thompson, 394 U.S. 618, 623 (1969).

102 *Thompson v. Shapiro*, 270 F. Supp. 331 (D. Conn. 1967), aff'd 394 U.S. 618, 623 (1969). A three-judge panel was convened for the challenge to the constitutionality of the state law, drawing on the procedure for challenges to the constitutionality of an act of Congress.

103 *Id.* at 336.

104 *Id.*

105 *Id.* at 336–38 (holding the purpose of the law invalid and the classifications drawn by the law unreasonable).

106 *Id.* at 338-41.

107 *Shapiro v. Thompson*, 394 U.S. 618 (1969).

108 *Id.* at 641–42.

109 Interview with Mag. Judge Holly B. Fitzsimmons.

110 142 Cong. Rec. No. S8370 (July 19, 1996, remarks of Senator Dodd) *available at*. http://www.gpo.gov/fdsys/pkg/CREC-1996-07-19/pdf/CREC-1996-07-19-pt1-PgS8370-4.pdf#page=1 [http://perma.cc/MB4X-LFE5].

111 Northeastern Tel. Co. v. AT&T, 497 F. Supp. 230 (D. Conn. 1980).

112 Interview with Mag. Judge Fitzsimmons, *supra* ch. 6 note 109; *see* United States v. Giordano, 442 F.3d 30 (2d Cir. 2006).

CHAPTER 7

1 During various periods in its history, Vermont's federal courts also have sat in locations in Windsor, Montpelier, Newport, Saint Johnsbury and Bennington. A number of those historic buildings now house public libraries or post offices. Remarkably, in Vermont's 222-year history, a total of only nineteen judges have served its District Courts.

2 Albert W. Coffrin, The United States District Court for the District of Vermont—Its Background, History and Judicial Heritage (1985) (unpublished manuscript) at 1-2.

3 *Id.* at 2.

4 *Id.*

5 *Id.*

6 *Id.* at 3.

7 *Id.*

8 Editorial, Burlington Free Press, January 15, 1993.

9 Chief Judge Franklin S. Billings Jr., Chief Judge of the Second Circuit James L. Oakes, and Senior Judge James S. Holden, Testimonial, In Re Honorable

Albert W. Coffrin, at a Special Session of the U.S. District Court for the District of Vermont 10 (Feb. 10, 1989) (transcript available in Judge Coffrin's papers at the District of Vermont).

10 Coffrin, *supra* ch. 7 note 2, at 9.

11 *Id.* at 4-5.

12 *Id.* at 5.

13 *Id.* at 6.

14 *Id.* at 6-7.

15 Franklin Bowditch Dexter, 3 Biographical Sketches of the Graduates of Yale College May 1763- July 1778, at 661.

16 Coffrin, *supra* ch. 7 note 2, at 7.

17 *Id.* at 9.

18 *Id.* at 10.

19 *Id.*

20 Francis Wharton, *Trial of Matthew Lyon for a Seditious Libel*, in State Trials of the United States 333.

21 *Id.*

22 *Id.* at 339.

23 *Id.* at 339-342.

24 *Id.* at 341.

25 *Id.*

26 *Id.* at 336.

27 Coffrin, *supra* ch. 7 note 2, at 11.

28 Wharton, *supra* ch. 7 note 20, at 342.

29 *Id.* at 342-343.

30 *Id.* at 343.

31 *Id.*

32 *Id.* at 344.

33 Coffrin, *supra* ch. 7 note 2, at 12.

34 *Id.* at 12-13.

35 *Id.* at 13-14.

36 *United States v. Frederick Hoxie*, 1 Paine's Reports 34 (1827).

37 Coffrin, *supra* ch. 7 note 2, at 17-18.

38 *Id.* at 16-17.

39 *Ex Parte* Field, 9 F. Cas. 1, 5 (C.C.D.Vt. 1862) (No. 4,761).

40 In 1988, the courthouse and post office in Rutland was named for Robert T. Stafford, a former Vermont Congressman, Governor and Senator.

41 Account taken from Gene Sessions, *Espionage in Windsor: Clarence Waldron and Patriotism in World War I*, 61 Vt. History 133 (Vt. Hist. Soc. 1993).

42 Coffrin, *supra* ch. 7 note 2, at 23.

43 *Id.* at 26.

44 *Id.* at 23-24.

45 *Vermonter of the Year*, Vt. Sunday Magazine, December 27, 1992, at 13.

46 Burlington Free Press, December 11, 1958.

47 Achilles v. New England Tree Co., 369 F.2d 72, 73 (2d Cir. 1966).

48 Pereza v. Mark, 423 F.2d 149, 150-51 (2d Cir. 1970).

49 Coffrin, *supra* ch. 7 note 2, at 32.

50 *In re* Parrottee, 22 F.3d 472 (2d. Cir. 1994).

51 414 U.S. 291 (1973).

52 Int'l Dairy// Foods Ass'n v. Amestoy, 92 F.3d 67 (2d. Cir. 1996).

53 Nat'l Elec. Mfrs. Ass'n v. Sorrell, 272 F.3d 104 (2d Cir. 2000).

54 IMS Health Inc. v Sorrell, 630 F.3d 263 (2d. Cir. 2010), *aff'd*, 131 S. Ct. 2653 (2011).

55 Eizabeth York, *The Honorable James L. Oakes: A Tribute*, Vt. Bar J., Fall 2007, at 33, 34.

PICTURE CREDITS

Front and back cover photos by Timothy Schenck.

2   Courtesy of GSA (U.S. General Services Administration).

8   Courtesy of U.S. Court of Appeals for the Second Circuit.

16   Courtesy of GSA.

20   Map courtesy of Loeb & Loeb (Juan Pla, graphics).

CHAPTER 1

30   From James Stewart & Company, *A Century in Construction*, p. 22 (Privately Printed, New York, 1944).

32   From *New York Is a City of Superlatives* (L.H. Nelson Co., Portland, ME 1900).

33   Top, from Photo Engraving Co., *Scientific American*, Sept. 18, 1875, Picture Collection, The New York Public Library, Astor, Lenox and Tilden Foundations; Bottom, U.S. Patent & Trademark Office.

34   From Vol. 2, Martha J. Lamb, *History of the City of New York* (Valentine's Manual 1921), p. 423 (left) and 424 (right); digital imaging by Anthony Troncale.

35   Gustavus W. Pach, View in the Five Points (1875). Robert N. Dennis Collection of Stereoscopic Views, Miriam and Ira D. Wallach Division of Art, Prints and Photographs, The New York Public Library, Astor, Lenox and Tilden Foundations.

37   Courtesy of the Federal Bar Council, George J. Atwell Foundation Co.

38   Courtesy of GSA.

39   Courtesy of GSA (all photos).

40   Courtesy of U.S. Court of Appeals for the Second Circuit (all photos).

41   Timothy Schenck.

42   Courtesy of U.S. Court of Appeals for the Second Circuit.

43   Courtesy of U.S. Court of Appeals for the Second Circuit (all photos).

44   Timothy Schenck.

46   Timothy Schenck.

47   Timothy Schenck.

48   Courtesy of U.S. Court of Appeals for the Second Circuit (all photos).

52   Top, Courtesy of the Lend Lease Corporation; Bottom, Courtesy of U.S. Court of Appeals for the Second Circuit.

CHAPTER 2

54   Top left, Daniel Acker/Bloomberg/Getty Images; Top right, Rick Kopstein; Bottom right, Courtesy of the National Museum of the American Indian; Bottom left, Courtesy of GSA.

56   From Vol. 2, Martha J. Lamb, *History of the City of New York*, p. 634 (Valentine's Manual 1921); digital imaging by Anthony Troncale.

57   Left, Picture Collection, The New York Public Library, Astor, Lenox and Tilden Foundations; Right, Archibald Robertson, View up Wall Street with City Hall [Federal Hall] and Trinity Church, New York City, 1798, graphite, watercolor, pen and ink on paper, 8.5 x 11.25 inches, Luce Center, Object No. 1864.14, New-York Historical Society.

58   From Stephen Jenkins, *The Greatest Street in the World – Broadway*, p. 26 (G.P. Putnam's Sons, New York 1911); digital imaging by Anthony Troncale.

59   From Charles Haynes Haswell, *Reminiscences of New York by an Octogenarian*, p. 83 (Harper & Brothers, New York 1896); digital imaging by Anthony Troncale.

60   Alexander Jackson Davis, Residence of John Cox Stevens New York City, Watercolor, black ink, and graphite, Object Number 1908.27, New-York Historical Society.

61 From Arthur Hornblow, Vol. 2, *A History of the Theatre in America from its Beginnings to the Present Time*, p. 122 (J. Lippincott & Co., Philadelphia & London 1919); digital imaging by Anthony Troncale.

63 Ewing Galloway, from Nathan Silver, *Lost New York* (Houghton Mifflin 1967).

64 Top, Frank Walts, A Cryptic Study of Mae Marsh's Features, Bottom, Henry J. Glintenkamp, Conscription; both from *The Masses*, Vol. 9, No. 10, August 1917 (The Masses Publishing Co.).

66 Wurts Brothers (Photographer), Collection of Photographs of New York City, The New York Public Library, Irma and Paul Milstein Division of United States History, Local History and Genealogy.

67 Top, from *American Heritage*, August/September 1981, Vol. 32, no. 5 © American Heritage Publishing. Reprinted by permission; Bottom, Library of Congress, Prints & Photographs Division, NYWT&S Collection, LC-USZ62-117772.

68 © Christine Cornell.

69 Alex Webb, Magnum Photos. From The New York Times, June 5, 1977 © 1977 The New York Times. All rights reserved.

70 From The New York Times, June 13, 1971 © 1971 The New York Times. All rights reserved.

72 Top, JOHN MARSHALL MANTEL/The New York Times, May 18, 2009 © 2009 The New York Times. All rights reserved; Middle and Bottom, © Christine Cornell.

73 Associated Press Bebeto Matthews, © 2004 Associated Press.

74 Taylor Lednum, GSA Design Excellence Program.

75 Taylor Lednum, GSA Design Excellence Program.

76-77 Daniel Acker/Bloomberg/Getty Images.

78 Taylor Lednum, GSA Design Excellence Program.

79 Rick Kopstein.

80 Library of Congress, Prints & Photographs Division, photograph by Carol M. Highsmith, LC-DIG-highsm-02731; Sculpture *Sounding Stones* © Maya Lin.

81 Library of Congress, Prints & Photographs Division, photograph by Carol M. Highsmith, LC-DIG-highsm-02735, Sculpture *Justice* © Raymond Kaskey 1996.

82 Andrew Burton/Getty Images.

83 Courtesy of GSA.

84 Marjorie Press Lindblom.

85 Marjorie Press Lindblom.

86 Marjorie Press Lindblom.

87 © Christine Cornell.

88-89 Courtesy of the National Museum of the American Indian.

90 Library of Congress, Prints & Photographs Division, photographs by Carol M. Highsmith, LC-DIG-highsm-02714 (top), LC-DIG-highsm- 02828 (bottom).

91 Library of Congress, Prints & Photographs Division, photograph by Carol M. Highsmith, LC-DIG-highsm-02691.

92 Library of Congress, Prints & Photographs Division, photograph by Carol M. Highsmith, LC-DIG-highsm-02709.

93 Associated Press Mark Lennihan.

CHAPTER 3

94 Top, Library of Congress, Prints & Photographs Division, photograph by Carol M. Highsmith, LC-DIG-highsm-02267; Second from top, John Cahill/Phorio; Third from top and Bottom, Library of Congress, Prints & Photographs Division, photographs by Carol M. Highsmith, LC-DIG-highsm-10479 (third from top), LC-DIG-highsm-10920 (bottom).

96 National Archives, RG 121-BS, Box 59, Auburn Folder.

97 Library of Congress, Chronicling America: Historic American Newspapers, The Washington Times, May 12, 1912.

99 National Archives, RG121-BS, Box 59, Albany Folder.

100 Library of Congress, Prints & Photographs Division, photograph by Carol M. Highsmith, LC-DIG-highsm-02265.

101 Top left and Bottom right, John Domurad, U.S. District Court for the Northern District of New York; Top right and Bottom left, Rick Kopstein.

102 Rick Kopstein (all photos).

103 Library of Congress, Prints & Photographs Division, photographs by Carol M. Highsmith, LC-DIG-highsm-02277 (top), LC-DIG-highsm-02279 (bottom center); Bottom left and right, Rick Kopstein.

104 Top, Rick Kopstein; Bottom, Library of Congress, Prints & Photographs Division, photographs by Carol M. Highsmith, LC-DIG-highsm-02272 (left) and LC-DIG-highsm-02269 (right).

106 Photo Courtesy of GSA; Sculpture *One, Two, Three* © Estate of Sol LeWitt, 2014.

107 John Berry/The Post-Standard.

108 Lawrence Baerman, U.S. District Court for the Northern District of New York.

109 Lawrence Baerman, U.S. District Court for the Northern District of New York.

110 National Archives, RG 121-BS, Box 59, Binghamton Folder.

111 Library of Congress, Prints & Photographs Division, photographs by Carol M. Highsmith, LC-DIG-highsm-10465 (top left), LC-DIG-highsm-10483 (bottom left), LC-DIG-highsm-10474 (top right), LC-DIG-highsm-10477 (center right), LC-DIG-highsm-10470 (bottom right).

112-113 Library of Congress, Prints & Photographs Division, photograph by Carol M. Highsmith, LC-DIG-highsm-10469.

113 Library of Congress, Prints & Photographs Division, photographs by Carol M. Highsmith, LC-DIG-highsm-10467 (top right), LC-DIG-highsm-10468 (bottom right).

114 Library of Congress, Prints & Photographs Division, photographs by Carol M. Highsmith, LC-DIG-highsm-11080 (top left), LC-DIG-highsm-11078 (top right), LC-DIG-highsm-11083 (bottom left); LC-DIG-highsm-11084 (bottom right).

116 National Archives, RG 121-C, Box 23, Folder H. Print 2.

117 Library of Congress, Prints & Photographs Division, photograph by Carol M. Highsmith, LC-DIG-highsm-10923.

118 Library of Congress, Prints & Photographs Division, photograph by Carol M. Highsmith, LC-DIG-highsm-10921.

119 Top, Library of Congress, Prints & Photographs Division, photograph by Carol M. Highsmith, LC-DIG-highsm-10928; Bottom, Rick Kopstein.

CHAPTER 4

120 Top, Douglas C. Palmer, U.S. District Court for the Eastern District of New York; Center, Trix Rosen Photography/GSA; Bottom, Taylor Lednum, GSA Design Excellence Program.

122 Library of Congress, Prints & Photographs Division, NYWT&S Collection, LC-USZ62-136140.

123 Library of Congress, Prints & Photographs Division, NYWT&S Collection, LC-USZ62-128525.

124 Courtesy of GSA.

126 © Bettmann/Corbis.

127 © Christine Cornell.

128 Rick Kopstein.

130 Douglas C. Palmer, U.S. District Court for the Eastern District of New York.

131 Photo, Douglas C. Palmer, U.S. District Court for the Eastern District of New York; Sculpture *Beacon* by Lisa Scheer.

132 Rick Kopstein.

133 Douglas C. Palmer, U.S. District Court for the Eastern District of New York.

134 Rick Kopstein.

135 Douglas C. Palmer, U.S. District Court for the Eastern District of New York.

136-137 Trix Rosen Photography/GSA.

138 Douglas C. Palmer, U.S. District Court for the Eastern District of New York.

139 Douglas C. Palmer, U.S. District Court for the Eastern District of New York.

140-141 Rick Kopstein.

142 Taylor Lednum, GSA Design Excellence Program.

143 Taylor Lednum, GSA Design Excellence Program.

144 Photo, Rick Kopstein; *Hooloomooloo IV* © 2014 Frank Stella/Artists Rights Society (ARS), New York.

145 Top, Photo, Douglas C. Palmer, U.S. District Court for the Eastern District of New York; *Hooloomooloo IV* (detail) © 2014 Frank Stella/Artists Rights Society (ARS), New York; Bottom, Douglas C. Palmer, U.S. District Court for the Eastern District of New York; *Joatinga* © 2014 Frank Stella/Artists Rights Society (ARS), New York.

146 Douglas C. Palmer, U.S. District Court for the Eastern District of New York.

147 Taylor Lednum, GSA Design Excellence Program.

CHAPTER 5

148 Top, Patricia A. McGovern; Bottom, Taylor Lednum, GSA Design Excellence Program.

150 U.S. Patent & Trademark Office.

151 National Park Service, http://perma.cc/92EX-KAB6 (which credits the Nashville, Tennessee News, October 13, 1901).

152 Library of Congress, Prints & Photographs Division, HABS, Reproduction number HABS NY, 28-ROCH, 21-7.

153 Library of Congress, Prints & Photographs Division, HABS, Reproduction number HABS NY, 28-ROCH, 21-17.

154 Library of Congress, Prints & Photographs Division, HABS, Reproduction number HABS NY, 28-ROCH, 21-4.

155 Courtesy of GSA.

156 Courtesy of GSA; Sculpture *Equilateral Six* Duane Hatchett.

157 U.S. Court of Appeals for the Second Circuit, Scott Teman, Circuit Architect.

158 *Times Union*, September 14, 1971.

159 Taylor Lednum, GSA Design Excellence Program.

160 Courtesy, University Archives, University at Buffalo, The State University of New York.

161 Taylor Lednum, GSA Design Excellence Program.

162 Taylor Lednum, GSA Design Excellence Program.

163 Taylor Lednum, GSA Design Excellence Program.

164 Taylor Lednum, GSA Design Excellence Program.

165 Taylor Lednum, GSA Design Excellence Program.

166-167 Photo, Taylor Lednum, GSA Design Excellence Program; Panels © Robert Mangold.

168 Taylor Lednum, GSA Design Excellence Program.

169 Taylor Lednum, GSA Design Excellence Program.

CHAPTER 6

170 Top, Carol M. Highsmith Photography, Inc./Courtesy of GSA Center for Historic Buildings; Middle, Rick Kopstein; Bottom, Courtesy of GSA.

172 Courtesy Connecticut General Assembly.

173 Demolishing the Old State House on the New Haven Green, 1889, PG 300, Connecticut Cities and Towns Collection, ca. 1885-1965, Box 6, Folder "New Haven," State Archives, Connecticut State Library.

175 Wikimedia; New Haven Museum.

176 Courtesy of Collection of Talladega College, Talladega, Alabama. © Talladega College; Photo Courtesy High Museum of Art, Atlanta/Peter Harholdt.

178-179 Courtesy of Collection of Talladega College, Talladega, Alabama. © Talladega College; Photo Courtesy High Museum of Art, Atlanta/Peter Harholdt.

180 NARA Record Group 267, Records of the United States Supreme Court, Appellate Case File #2161, United States v. Libellants and Claimants of the Schooner Amistad, John Q. Adams' request for papers relating to the lower court trials of the *Amistad* Africans, January 23, 1841.

181 NARA Record Group 267, Records of the United States Supreme Court, Appellate Case File #2161, United States v. Libellants and Claimants of the Schooner Amistad, Statement of the Supreme Court to Circuit Court, March 9, 1841.

182 U.S. Treasury Department, A History of Public Buildings (Washington, D.C.: GPO, 1901): 62-63.

183 Carol M. Highsmith Photography, Inc./Courtesy of GSA Center for Historic Buildings.

184 Top, Rick Kopstein; Bottom, Carol M. Highsmith Photography, Inc./Courtesy of GSA Center for Historic Buildings.

185 Carol M. Highsmith Photography, Inc./Courtesy of GSA Center for Historic Buildings (all photos).

186-187 Carol M. Highsmith Photography, Inc./Courtesy of GSA Center for Historic Buildings.

188 Carol M. Highsmith Photography, Inc./Courtesy of GSA Center for Historic Buildings.

190 Top, Associated Press Jessica Hill; Bottom, © Christine Cornell.

191 National Archives, RG 121-C, Box 4, Folder A, Print 2.

192 Library of Congress, Prints & Photographs Division, photograph by Carol M. Highsmith, LC-DIG-highsm-02329.

193 Library of Congress, Prints & Photographs Division, photograph by Carol M. Highsmith, LC-DIG-highsm-02330.

194 Library of Congress, Prints & Photographs Division, photographs by Carol M. Highsmith, LC-DIG-highsm-02331 (top left), LC-DIG-highsm-02328 (top right), LC-DIG-highsm-02333 (bottom).

195 Library of Congress, Prints & Photographs Division, photographs by Carol M. Highsmith, LC-DIG-highsm-02342 (top), LC-DIG-highsm-02340 (middle), LC-DIG-highsm-02335 (bottom).

196-197 R.W. Sutcliffe, photographers/GSA.

198 Rick Kopstein.

200 Courtesy of GSA.

201 Rick Kopstein.

202 Photo, Rick Kopstein; Sculpture *Untitled* by Patsy Norvell.

203 Rick Kopstein.

204 Rick Kopstein.

205 © Christine Cornell.

CHAPTER 7

206 Top, Jeffrey Eaton, U.S. District Court for the District of Vermont; Middle, Rick Kopstein; Bottom, Brattleboro Historical Society.

208 National Archives, RG 121-BS, Box 89, Folder Q, Print 1.

209 Courtesy of Rutland Historical Society.

210 Postcard, Collection of Paul Rheingold.

211 U.S. District Court for the District of Vermont.

212 U.S. District Court for the District of Vermont (all photos).

213 Top, U.S. Treasury Department, *A History of Public Buildings*, p. 586-87 (U.S. Government Publishing Office, Washington, D.C. 1901); Bottom, Postcard, Collection of Paul Rheingold.

214 U.S. District Court for the District of Vermont.

216 U.S. District Court for the District of Vermont.

217 Rick Kopstein.

218 Rick Kopstein.

221 Rick Kopstein.

222 Hessler Photographers, Collection of the Supreme Court of the United States.

INDEX

Abel, Col. Rudolph I., 125
abolitionist movement, 175, 177
Abraham A. Ribicoff Federal Building and U.S. Courthouse (Hartford), 20, 27, 192; exterior of, 170–71, 194–99; interior of, 198–99; notable cases of, 199–202; renovations of, 199
Adams, John, 23, 210–11, 214
Adams, John Quincy, 179–80
Adams, Samuel H., 97
Adler, Judge Simon L., 151
admiralty cases/law, 22, 31, 33, 45, 57–58, 60, 62, 64, 122–23, 160–61, 177. *See also* Amistad Case
African Americans, 36, 74, 87, 98–99, 135, 190
African slaves, 61, 175–81
Agent Orange case, 127
Aiken, George, 219
Albany, New York, 26, 94–96, 98–107
Alexander Hamilton U.S. Custom House (Manhattan), 20, 26, 55; architect of, 35, 90; exterior of, 54, 87–91; interior of, 91–92; notable cases of, 93; restoration of, 91
Alexander Pirnie U.S. Courthouse and Federal Building (Utica), 20, 96, 115; exterior of, 94–95, 116–18; interior of, 116, 119; notable cases of, 117–18
Alfonse M. D'Amato U.S. Courthouse and Federal Building (Central Islip), 20, 28; as cultural gathering place, 142–43, 146–47; exterior of, 120–21, 140–42; interior of, 142–47; notable cases of, 146–47
Alfred P. Murrah Federal Building (Oklahoma City), 92–93, 129
Allen, Ethan, 209–10
Allen, Woody, 72–73
Amendments: Eighth, 49; Fifth, 117; First, 45, 47, 50–51, 64–65, 70–71, 97, 105–07, 127, 217, 220–21; Fourteenth, 50, 161; Fourth, 51, 117; Sixth, 49
American Institute of Architects, 25, 129
Americans with Disabilities Act, 132
Amistad Case, 175–81
Amon, Judge Carol Bagley, 127
Anthony, Susan B., 149
antitrust cases, 45–47, 50–51, 156, 189–90, 204–05
antiwar protest cases, 72, 97–98, 115, 154, 161–62, 216–17
Arcara, Judge Richard J., 163, 165
architects, 25–28, 59, 110, 182, 191. *See also* design competitions; specific firms; specific names
Architectural Forum, 183–84
art commissions, 27–28, 84–85, 108, 142, 156, 210. *See also* Art in Architecture Program; murals; sculptures

Art Deco, 26, 94, 99–101, 103–05, 110–15, 191
Art in Architecture Program, 28, 80, 108, 131, 142, 144–45, 156, 169
Art Moderne, 26, 157, 159
Arterton, Judge Janet Bond, 190
Attica Correctional Facility, 156, 158
Auburn, New York, 25, 95–99

Bacon, Robert C., 217
Baldwin, Roger, 177–79
Bankruptcy Act of 1898, 64
bankruptcy cases, 87, 93, 97–98, 115, 118, 127, 139, 156, 220
Barnes, Leroy "Nicky," 69–70
Bartels, Judge John R., 125–26
Beaux-Arts style, 26, 36, 40, 42, 54, 87–91
Belarski, Stephen J., 210, 212
Bell, Alexander Graham, 96
Bell, Mifflin E., 97, 99, 123
Benedict, Judge Charles L., 122
Benson, Judge Egbert, 23
Betts, Judge Samuel, 60–61
Beyer Blinder Belle, 53
Biafora, Enea, 103, 105
Billings, Judge Franklin S. Jr., 220
Binghamton Federal Building and U.S. Courthouse, 20, 26, 96; exterior of, 94–95, 110–11, 114; interior of, 111–15; notable cases of, 115; restoration of, 111, 115
Binghamton, New York, 20, 26, 94–98, 110–15
Bin Laden, Osama, 68, 162
Blackman, Judge Alfred, 174
Blackmun, Justice Harry A., 34
Blatchford, Judge Samuel M., 64
Bley & Lyman, 158
Blumenfeld, Judge M. Joseph, 201–02
Bohanon, Judge Richard L., 92–93
Brandeis, Justice Louis D., 117
Brattleboro U.S. Post Office and Courthouse, 20, 26, 206–07, 214–19
Brattleboro, Vermont, 26, 206–07, 214–19
Brennan, Justice William J. Jr., 202
Breyer, Justice Stephen, 28
Bridgeport, Connecticut, 20, 27, 170–71, 201–05. *See also* Brien McMahon Federal Building and U.S. Courthouse
Brieant, Judge Charles L. Jr., 28, 45, 83–84, 86–87. *See also* Charles L. Brieant Jr. Federal Building and U.S. Courthouse (White Plains)

255

Brien McMahon Federal Building and U.S. Courthouse (Bridgeport), 27; exterior of, 170–71, 200–203; horseshoe pit of, 201, 203; interior of, 203–04; notable cases of, 204–05
Brooklyn Alliance for Courthouse Alternatives, 129, 131
Brooklyn, New York, 20, 25, 28, 68, 120–41. *See also* specific courthouses
Bruno, Joseph, 107
Bryan, Judge Frederick van Pelt, 70–71
Bryant, Judge Frederick H., 97–98
Buckingham Square Historic District, 192, 194
Buffalo, New York, 20, 26, 28, 148–51, 156–69. *See also* Robert H. Jackson U.S. Courthouse
Buffalo Spree, 169
building details, 48; aluminum, 100–101, 103–05, 131, 158, 191–92, 194–95; brass, 115, 192; bronze, 42–43, 115, 158, 183–85; cast-iron, 113–15, 123, 154; ironwork, 123, 214, 216; plaster, 27, 105, 158; terra cotta, 40, 123; travertine, 158. *See also* wood details
building inscriptions, 28, 116, 158, 168, 183, 191
building materials: brick, 56, 84, 97, 116, 170–72, 174, 194, 196–97, 214, 216; brownstone, 59, 154, 172; concrete, 108, 163, 194, 217, 219; cork, 158; glass, 28, 82, 120–21, 131, 138, 142, 150, 162–68, 203, 219; granite, 25, 32, 37–38, 40, 53, 59, 79, 97, 101, 114, 118, 123, 125, 129, 138, 143, 146, 158, 170–71, 191, 194, 199; limestone, 59, 97, 114, 116, 125, 129, 131, 191, 202; marble, 25, 27, 32, 42, 59, 61, 80, 82, 99, 101, 103, 105, 111, 115, 123, 138, 154, 158, 174, 182–83, 185–87, 191, 194–95, 219; metal, 142; sandstone, 158; soapstone, 192; steel, 138, 202; stone, 25, 84, 116, 174, 182; white masonry, 26; wood, 209
Bullfinch, Charles, 172
Burger, Justice Warren, 204
Burke, Judge Harold P., 151, 160–61
Burlington Federal Building, 20, 27, 206–07, 217–21
Burlington, Vermont, 20, 27, 206–07, 215, 217–21
Burr, Aaron, 24, 56, 58–59, 171
Burton's Theatre (New York City), 61–62
Bush, George, 36
Business First (Buffalo), 163

Cabranes, Judge José A., 171–72, 189
Cadman, Rev. Doctor Samuel P., 132
Canandaigua, New York, 149
Carey, Hugh, 106, 159
Carson, Lundin & Shaw, 125
Carter, Jimmy, 69, 159, 189
Carter, Judge Robert L., 36
cases: and aircraft/airlines, 125, 127, 146, 150; and auto-insurance laws, 117–18; celebrity, 65–67, 71–73; commercial speech, 220–21; copyright, 45, 51, 73, 96; corruption, 190–91, 204; criminal, 24, 49, 69–70, 98–99, 127–28, 146–47, 177, 199–200, 204–05; customs, 56–57, 215; and dairy cows, 220; and data-mining companies, 221; and death penalty, 36, 50; for discrimination, 126, 204; and the draft, 98, 161; drug-related, 69–70, 72, 74, 128, 147, 205, 221; and education, 36; electronic surveillance, 53; evasion of military duty, 215; and "fight films," 98; and firefighters, 190; fraud, 82, 107; gambling, 146, 200; insider trading, 53, 82; and labor practices, 46; for land claims, 60, 208–09; libel, 50, 73; mail-fraud, 97–98, 201; and motorcycle gangs, 146, 204; obscenity, 31, 34, 70–71; and oil/gas companies, 86–87; passenger-ship disasters, 64; piracy, 82; police misconduct, 126–27, 156, 204; prisoner rights, 49, 97–99, 156; and public health/safety, 208, 220–21; race discrimination, 87, 126–27, 135, 190; and school prayer, 51; securities fraud, 82, 201; and segregation, 36, 161; sex-abuse, 205; slave trade, 61, 175–81; and taxes, 36, 45, 72–73, 97; technology related, 82, 115; trademark, 45, 96, 109; treason, 125, 215; voting-rights, 107, 149; and welfare assistance, 201–02; white-collar crime, 34, 201; and wiretapping, 82, 199–200. *See also* admiralty cases/law; Amendments; bankruptcy cases; civil rights cases; environmental cases/law; organized crime; patent cases/law
Catalano, Salvatore, 69
Cayuga County, New York, 98–99
Cedarbaum, Judge Miriam Goldman, 73
Celler, Emanuel, 125. *See also* Emanuel Celler Federal Building and U.S. Courthouse (Brooklyn)
Central Islip, Long Island, New York, 20, 28, 120–21, 142–44, 146–47. *See also* Alfonse M. D'Amato U.S. Courthouse and Federal Building
Chambers, Whittaker, 66
Champlain, Samuel de, 209
Charles L. Brieant Jr. Federal Building and U.S. Courthouse (White Plains), 20, 28, 55; exterior of, 54, 83–85; interior of, 84–86; notable cases of, 86–87
Chase, Judge Harrie B., 45, 47
Chicago World's Fair, 26, 216
Chin, Judge Denny, 82
Chipman, Judge Nathaniel, 22, 208–10
Chittenden, Thomas, 214
City Beautiful movement, 182
Civil Rights Act of 1957, 125
civil rights cases, 36, 50–51, 86–87, 97, 125–27, 135, 156, 161, 190
Civil War, 23, 25, 62, 151, 215
Clarie, Judge T. Emmet, 199, 201–03
Clark, Judge Charles E., 47, 49
classical style, 26, 32, 54, 90–91, 94, 110, 114, 116, 123, 158, 170–71, 210, 219. *See also* "starved classicism;" Greek Revival style; neoclassical style
Claudio, Avelino Gonzalez, 199–200
Clean Water Act litigation, 220
Coath & Goss, 110
Coffrin, Judge Albert W., 207–08
Cohn, Roy, 67, 205
Cold War, 66
Colombia, 128, 147
Communists, 47, 66–67
Comprehensive Environmental Response Compensation and Liability Act (CERCLA), 158
Conrad & Cummings, 110

Conrad B. Duberstein U.S. Bankruptcy Courthouse (Brooklyn), 20, 25; exterior of, 120–21, 123–24, 135–37; interior of, 123, 138–39; notable cases of, 123, 125; restoration of, 121, 123, 138–39
Cooper, Judge Frank, 117
Cooper, Judge Irving B., 71
Corallo, Antonio "Tony Ducks", 69
Cornell University, 98, 109, 115
Cotter, William R., 192. *See also* William R. Cotter Federal Building (Hartford)
courthouses: 21st century role/image of, 147; architectural styles of, 24–28; fallout shelters in, 198; functions of, 24, 26, 79, 147; handicap access in, 198; influences on, 78; powered by wind energy, 115; practical features of, 28; and security requirements, 28, 83, 128–29, 132, 162–63; as symbols of growth, 169; as symbols of justice, 28, 121, 188–89; as symbols of patriotism, 90; of technology era, 28, 132, 162–63, 169
Covello, Judge Alfred V., 200
Covey, James, 178–79
Cox, Archibald, 202
Cregg, Frank J., 97–98
Crown Heights riots, 126–27
Curtin, Judge John T., 160
Curtiss, George B., 97
Cushing, Justice William, 23

Daly, Judge T. F., 204
D'Amato, Alfonse M., 28, 84, 142. *See also* Alfonse M. D'Amato U.S. Courthouse and Federal Building (Central Islip)
Dancis, Bruce, 98
Daniel Patrick Moynihan U.S. Courthouse (Manhattan), 20, 28, 37, 53, 55; building of, 73–74; exterior of, 54, 75–80; interior of, 78–82; notable cases of, 72–73, 82
Davis, Alexander Jackson, 61
Davis, Bankruptcy Judge Diane, 117
Defreitas, Russell, 135
Del Vecchio, Alfred, 84
Derry, Robert, 60
design competitions, 26, 28, 58, 62, 84, 90, 110, 182, 191
Design Excellence Program, 28, 74, 78, 108, 142, 146
Dhafir, Dr. Rafil A., 109
Dickens, Charles, 35
DiLieto, Biagio, 189
Dillon, Michael J., 26, 158. *See also* Michael J. Dillon U.S. Courthouse (Buffalo)
District of Connecticut: description/history of, 21–23, 171–80, 205; notable cases of, 189–91, 199–202, 204–05; three main courthouses of, 20, 27, 170–71. *See also* specific courthouses
District of Vermont: creation of, 208; description/history of, 21–23, 207–09; notable cases of, 208–09, 214–17, 219–21; three main courthouses of, 20, 206–07. *See also* specific courthouses
Dixey, John, 59
Dodd, Chris, 204

Dodd, Thomas, 189
Donovan, William J. "Wild Bill," 150
Douglas, Stephen, 215
Duane, Judge James, 22, 55, 57
Duberstein, Judge Conrad B., 139. *See also* Conrad B. Duberstein U.S. Bankruptcy Courthouse (Brooklyn)
Duberstein, Samuel C., 139
Duffy, Judge Kevin T., 68

Eastern District of New York, 28; creation of, 24, 62, 122; description/history of, 21–25, 121–23; notable cases of, 123, 125–29, 146–47; three main courthouses of, 20, 120–21. *See also* specific courthouses
Eastman, George, 150
Ebbets Field (Brooklyn), 125–26
Ebbets, Frid and Prentice, 194
École des Beaux-Arts, 26. *See also* Beaux-Arts style
Edison, Thomas A., 33
Edward B. Green & Sons, 158
Edwards, Jonathan, 171
Edwards, Judge Pierpont, 171
Eginton, Judge Warren W., 189, 204–05
Ellis, Harvey and Charles, 151
Ellsberg, Daniel, 71
Emancipator, The, 177
Emanuel Celler Federal Building and U.S. Courthouse (Brooklyn): connected to Roosevelt courthouse, 128–29; exterior of, 120–21, 125; interior of, 125, 132
Embargo Act of 1807, 215
Emergency Construction and Relief Act, 157
environmental cases/law, 49–51, 131, 158–60, 208, 220–21
Environmental Protection Act, 49, 69
espionage, 65–67, 123, 125
Espionage Act, 65, 216–17
"Evarts Act" of 1891, 24
Evarts, William, 24

federal building programs, 25–28, 31, 35, 110, 158, 180, 182
Federal Hall (New York City), 56–59
Federal Power Commission (FPC), 49
Federal style, 37–40, 56–57, 59, 123, 172–73
Feinberg, Judge Wilfred, 51
Feinberg, Kenneth, 127
Ferrer, Ramon, 175–76
First Impressions Program, 28, 108
Flegenheimer, Arthur "Dutch Schultz," 96–97
Foley, Judge James T., 26, 105. *See also* James T. Foley U.S. Courthouse and Post Office (Albany)
Foley Square (Manhattan), 26, 28, 30–31, 34–38, 65, 74–75, 85–86, 91
Foley, Thomas F., 35
Forbes, Walter, 201
Ford, Gerald, 78
Fordham, Palatial, 177
Foreign Sovereign Immunities Act, 146
France, 25, 58–59, 90, 215

Frank, Judge Jerome, 47, 49
Franklin, Benjamin, 105, 192
Freeman French Freeman, 219
French, Daniel Chester, 90
French Second Empire style, 25, 31–33, 191, 219
Freret, Will A., 110
Friedman, Stanley, 190–91
Friendly, Judge Henry J., 50, 53, 161

Gagliardi, Judge Lee P., 83
Galella, Ron, 71–72
Gambino crime family, 127
Gambino, Rosario, 117
Gander, Gander & Gander, 99, 105
Garaufis, Judge Nicholas G., 135
Gedney, Thomas R., 176–79
General Services Administration (GSA), 27–28, 74, 78, 84, 105, 107–08, 129, 132, 138–39, 142–43, 146, 163, 188–89, 198, 219
Gerena, Victor Manuel, 199–200
Germany, 58, 64, 90, 102, 105, 125
Gershon, Judge Nina, 135
Giaimo, Robert N., 189
Gibbs, Josiah W., 178
Gilbert, Cass, 26, 30–31, 35–36, 38–40, 42, 53, 74, 90
Gilbert, Cass Jr., 36
Gilpin, Henry, 179
Giordano, Philip, 205
Giuliani, Rudolph W., 191
Glasser, Judge I. Leo, 127–29
Gleeson, Judge John, 128
Glintenkamp, Henry, 64–65
Goddard, Judge Henry W., 66–67
Goldman, Emma, 65
Goodyear, Charles, 61
Gothic Revival style, 36
Gotti, John, 127–28
Grant, Cary, 73
Grasso, Ella, 189
Grasso, William, 200–201
Great Britain, 56, 84–85, 175, 210, 212, 215
Great Depression, 26, 35, 37, 110, 115, 158, 191
Greek Revival style, 60–61, 149, 173–74, 182–83
Green, Henry, 177
"Guiding Principles of Federal Architecture," 27–28, 78
Gurfein, Judge Murray, 50, 71

Hamilton, Alexander, 24, 26, 56, 58–59, 91, 209. *See also* Alexander Hamilton U.S. Custom House (Manhattan)
Hand, Judge Augustus N., 34, 45, 47
Hand, Judge Learned, 34, 45–47, 49–50, 64–65, 82
Hanley, James M., 27–28, 107–08. *See also* James M. Hanley Federal Building and Courthouse (Syracuse)
Harlan, Judge John M. II, 53
Harriman, W. Averell, 74
Hartford, Connecticut, 20, 27, 170–73, 180, 191–202. *See also* Abraham A. Ribicoff Federal Building and U.S. Courthouse; District of Connecticut; Old State House
Haskins, Kittredge, 216
Hatchett, Duane, 156
Havana, Cuba, 61, 175, 177
Hawkins, Benjamin, 100–101
Hazel, Judge John R., 150–51, 154, 158
Helmsley, Leona, 72–73
Hill, James G., 99, 116
Hinchey, Maurice, 115
Hiss, Alger, 66–67
historic preservation, 27, 49, 91, 138, 155, 182, 188–89. *See also* National Register of Historic Places
Hitchcock, Judge Samuel, 23, 210, 215
Hobart, Judge John S., 24, 57–59
Holabird, William S., 176
Holwell, Judge Richard J., 82
Hooker Chemical Company, 159–60
House Committee on Un-American Activities (HUAC), 66–67
Howe, Judge Harland, 216–17
Hoxie, Frederick, 215
Hunt, Richard Morris, 62
Hurd, Judge David N., 116

Ingersoll, Charles A., 173–74
Iraq, 109, 115
Irizarry, Judge Dora L., 135
Ismoil, Eyad, 67–68
Italianate style, 182, 194, 208–09. *See also* Second Renaissance Revival style

Jackson, Justice Robert, 162
Jackson, Robert H., 20, 28
Jacobs, Judge Dennis, 40, 51, 53
James M. Hanley Federal Building and Courthouse (Syracuse), 20, 27–28, 96; exterior of, 94–95, 106–08; interior of, 108–09; notable cases of, 109; plaza of, 106–09
James T. Foley U.S. Courthouse and Post Office (Albany), 20, 26, 96; exterior of, 94–95, 99–101; interior of, 102–05; notable cases of, 105–07
Jay, Justice John, 22–23
Jefferson, Thomas, 23, 192
John Cox Stevens House, 60–62
John F. Kennedy International Airport, 125, 135
Johnson, Judge Sterling Jr., 126, 128
Johnson, Lyndon, 27, 36, 74
Jones, Judge Barbara S., 82
Joyce, James, 34, 70
Judd, Judge Orrin G., 125–26
Judicial Code of 1911, 24
Judiciary Act of 1789, 22, 24, 55, 171
Judiciary Act of 1801, 22–23, 214–15
Judson, Judge Andrew T., 176, 178–79

Kadir, Abdul, 135
Kaskey, Raymond, 28, 80–82

258 | INDEX

Katzmann, Judge Robert A., 51
Kaufman, Judge Irving R., 47, 49–51, 66–67, 72
Kaufman, Judge Samuel H., 66
Keating, Kenneth B., 20, 27, 155. *See also* Kenneth B. Keating Federal Building (Rochester)
Kennedy, John F., 27, 36, 71, 74, 125, 199
Kenneth B. Keating Federal Building (Rochester), 20, 27, 149; exterior of, 148, 155–56; interior of, 157; notable cases of, 156–57
Keyes-Elliott Bill of 1930, 26, 110, 191
Kimberly, Dennis, 173–74
Knapp, Judge Whitman, 190
Knight, Judge John, 151
Kodak, 51, 150, 156–57
Kohn Pederson Fox, 28, 79, 162–63
Kunstler, Bill, 205

Lady Chatterly's Lover, 70–71
Lake Champlain (Vermont), 215, 218–20
Lang, Herman, 125
Laurance, Judge John, 57
Law, Judge Richard, 22, 171
Le Corbusier, 28
Leavitt, Joshua, 177
LeBrun, Napoleon, 62
Leddy, Judge Bernard, 219–20
Lee, Richard C., 20, 26–27, 189. *See also* Richard C. Lee U.S. Courthouse (New Haven)
Lehman Brothers, 93
L'Enfant, Pierre Charles, 56–57
Lennon, John, 72
Leval, Judge Pierre, 69, 72
LeWitt, Sol, 28, 106, 108
Libya, 146
Life magazine, 45
Lima, Joseph, 117
Lin, Maya, 28, 80
Lincoln, Abraham, 24, 90, 105, 122, 192
Litchfield, Electus, 99, 105
Litchfield Law School, 171
Livingston, Judge Debra Ann, 221
Livingston, Justice Brockholst, 215
Long Island, 120–22, 132, 138, 142–43, 146, 175. *See also* Central Islip, Long Island, New York
Los Macheteros, 199–200
Louima, Abner, 126–27
Love Canal case, 158–60
Love, William T., 158
Ludington, Sybil, 84–85
Lumbard, Judge J. Edward, 49
Lyon, Matthew, 210–11, 214

Madoff, Bernard, 82, 93
mafia. *See* organized crime
Malmfeldt, Adams & Prentice, 191
Malone, New York, 97–98

Mangin, Joseph Francois, 58–59
Mangold, Robert, 28, 165, 169
Manton, Judge Martin T., 34, 37, 45
Marcus, James, 69
Marshall, Justice Thurgood, 36, 53, 58, 106–07, 222. *See also* Thurgood Marshall U.S. Courthouse (Manhattan)
Marx Brothers, 73
Mason, James, 211
Massachusetts, 23, 28, 200
Masses, The, 64–65
Mayer, Judge Julius, 64–65
McAvoy, Judge Thomas J., 115
McComb, John Jr., 58–59
McKinley, William, 150–51
McMahon, Brien, 27, 171, 203–04. *See also* Brien McMahon Federal Building and U.S. Courthouse (Bridgeport)
Meade, Richard W., 177
media/press, 46, 50, 71–73, 97, 106, 162, 177. *See also* specific publications
Medina, Judge Harold R., 69
Meier, Richard, 28, 121, 142–43, 147
Melville, Herman, 90
Meskill, Judge Thomas J., 51
metalwork. *See* building details
Michael J. Dillon U.S. Courthouse (Buffalo), 26, 150, 157; exterior of, 158–59; interior of, 158, 162; notable cases of, 158–62
Milano, Gaetano, 201
Mishler, Judge Jacob, 147
Moby Dick (Melville), 90
"modern classical" style, 99, 101, 110
modern style, 27, 54, 94, 96, 120–21, 125, 128, 140–48, 155, 162–67, 170–71, 200, 203, 217, 219. *See also* Art Moderne
Montez, Pedro, 175–79
Montpelier, Vermont, 213, 215, 219
Moore, Judge Leonard P., 70
Morgenthau, Robert, 67
Morris, Gouverneur, 23
Morse, Charles W., 34
Morton, W. T. G., 61
Moynihan, Daniel P., 25, 27–28, 37, 74, 78, 84, 131, 138. *See also* Daniel Patrick Moynihan U.S. Courthouse (Manhattan)
Mullett, Alfred B., 25, 32, 62, 65, 191, 219
Mullett Post Office (Manhattan), 25, 32–35, 62–65
Mumford, Lewis, 40
Munoz-Mosquera, Dandeny, 128
Munson, Judge Howard G., 106
murals, 27, 91, 102, 105, 114–15, 176, 178–79, 210, 212
Murtha, Judge J. Garvan, 220–21
Muse, Abdiwali Abdiqadir, 82

National Historic Landmarks, 87, 173
National Labor Relations Act/Board, 46
National Museum of the American Indian, New York, 87–89
National Prohibition Act, 51, 65, 117, 123
National Register of Historic Places, 87, 99, 105, 115, 121, 139, 158, 192

naturalization proceedings, 109, 125–26, 142
Nearing, Scott, 65
Nelson, Lemrick Jr., 126–27
neoclassical style, 26, 37, 42, 116, 183–87, 191–92
Nevas, Judge Alan H., 200–201, 205
New Deal, 34, 46, 96, 157–58
New Hampshire, 22–23, 209
New Haven, Connecticut, 20, 26–27, 170–91, 194. *See also* Richard C. Lee U.S. Courthouse
New Haven Landmarks, 188–89
New Haven Preservation Trust, 188–89
New Haven Redevelopment Agency, 184, 189
New Jersey, 22
New London, Connecticut, 176
New York, 21–26, 31, 125, 209. *See also* Eastern District; Northern District; Second Circuit; Southern District; Western District
New York City: City Hall Park in, 32, 35, 58, 61–63; Collect Pond in, 34–35; fire department of, 126, 135; Five Points District in, 34–35, 37, 78; mafia in, 69–70; main courthouses of, 20, 28, 30–31, 55; as mercantile/financial center, 33–34, 56; parades in, 93; phenomenal growth of, 59–60; as sea trade/commerce center, 87, 90. *See also* specific courthouses
New York City Hall, 56, 58–60
New York City Landmarks, 87
New York City Landmarks Preservation Commission, 138
New York County Almshouse, 59–61
New York Royal Exchange, 56–57
New York Times, The, 45, 50, 61–62, 65, 69–71, 82, 84
New York Tribune, 97
New Yorker, 40, 45
Newman, Judge Jon O., 51, 190
Newport, Vermont, 213, 215
Niagara, New York, 159–60
Nickerson, Judge Eugene H., 126–27
Nixon, Richard, 27, 67, 71–72, 74
Northern District of New York, 149, 157; creation of, 24, 95; description/history of, 21, 24–25, 59, 61, 95–96; first session of, 115; four main courthouses of, 20, 94–95; notable cases of, 96–99, 105–07, 109, 115, 117–18. *See also* specific courthouses
Norvell, Patsy, 28, 202

Oakes, Judge James L., 51, 217, 219, 221
Obama, Michelle, 108
Oklahoma City, 92–93, 129
Old Post Office and Courthouse (Auburn), 96–99
Old State House (Hartford), 172–73, 175–78
Old State House (New Haven), 173–81
Olmsted, Frederick Law Jr., 182
Onassis, Jacqueline Kennedy, 71
organized crime, 65, 69–70, 127–28, 200–201
O'Rourke, Jeremiah, 157
Orr, Douglas, 194
Osborne, Arthur D., 174
Ossining, New York, 174

Paine, Judge Elijah, 215
Parker, Judge Barrington D., 87
Parsons, Ethel M., 102, 105
PATCO union cases, 127
patent cases/law, 33–34, 45, 61, 96, 109, 115, 150, 154, 156–57, 189–90
Patiño Restrepo, Carlos Arturo, 147
Patterson, Judge Robert P. Jr., 131
Patterson, Judge William, 210
Pederson, Bill, 163. *See also* Kohn Pederson Fox
Pei, I. M., 184, 189
Pelli, Cesar, 28, 121, 129, 132, 189
Pentagon Papers case, 50, 70–71
Pierce, Franklin, 215
Pierce, Judge Lawrence W., 71
Pirnie, Congressman Alexander, 116. *See also* Alexander Pirnie U.S. Courthouse and Federal Building (Utica)
Platt, Judge Thomas C., 127
plazas, 28, 80, 82, 106–09, 138, 142
Pollak, Magistrate Judge Cheryl L., 128
Port, Judge Edmund, 98–99
postmodern style, 83–84
Powers, Gary T., 125
Preska, Judge Loretta A., 82
Price, Charles, 126–27
Prohibition, 51, 65, 96–97, 117, 123, 150, 154, 217
Public Buildings Act of 1926, 26, 110, 191
Public Buildings Cooperative Use Act (1978), 91
public-works programs, 37. *See also* New Deal
Puerto Rican Armed Forces of National Liberation (FALN), 128
Puerto Rico, 199–200

R. M. Kliment & Frances Halsband Architects, 121, 138
Rader, Judge Randall Ray, 109
Rahman, Omar Adel, 68
Rajaratnam, Raj, 82
Rakoff, Judge Jed S., 82
Ray, Judge George W., 97
Reader's Digest, 45
Reagan, Ronald, 127
Reeve, Tapping, 171
Reilly, Peter, 204
Reitz, George C., 118
Renaissance Revival style, 26
Revolutionary War, 56, 84–85, 209–10, 212
Ribicoff, Abraham A., 27, 170, 189, 192, 198–99. *See also* Abraham A. Ribicoff Federal Building and U.S. Courthouse (Hartford)
Richard C. Lee U.S. Courthouse (New Haven), 26–27; exterior of, 170–71, 182–83; interior of, 182–87; notable cases of, 189–91; saved from demolition, 184, 188–89
Richardson, Henry Hobson, 25
Richardsonian Romanesque, 25, 96–97, 99, 151–54, 194
RICO, 200, 205
Rippey, Judge Harlan W., 151

Robert H. Jackson U.S. Courthouse (Buffalo), 20, 28, 148–50, 157–58, 162–69
Roberts, Justice John, 53
Rochester, New York, 20, 25, 27, 148–58
Rochester U.S. Post Office and Courthouse Building, 149–55
Rockefeller, Nelson, 156
Rogers, James Gamble, 26, 182
Rolling Stone, 72
Romanesque Revival style, 25, 120–21, 123–24, 135–37, 151, 157. *See also* Richardsonian Romanesque
Roosevelt, Franklin D., 26, 47, 49, 158
Roosevelt, Theodore, 28, 135, 150–51. *See also* Theodore Roosevelt U.S. Courthouse (Brooklyn)
Rosenbaum, Yankel, 126–27
Rosenberg, Julius and Ethel, 50, 66–67
Rowling, J. K., 73
Ruiz, Jose, 175–79
Rutland U.S. Courthouse and Post Office, 20, 27, 206–07, 210–12, 214–15
Rutland, Vermont, 20, 27, 206–07, 209–12, 214

Sand, Judge Leonard B., 82
Sargent, Webster, Crenshaw & Folley, 107
Saypol, Irving, 66
Scenic Hudson Preservation Conference, 49
Scheer, Lisa, 28, 128, 131
Schumer, Charles E., 74, 135
Scullin, Judge Frederick J. Jr., 109
Scully, Vincent J. Jr., 188
sculptural details, 57, 111; friezes, 26, 97, 101, 105, 116, 183, 191–92, 194; medallions, 26–27, 39–40, 84, 158, 192
sculptures, 88–89, 91, 158; aluminum eagles, 191–94; *America* (French), 90; *Beacon* (Scheer), 128, 131; *Citizen* (Woodman), 199; *Eagle* (Stewart), 100–101; *Equilateral Six* (Hatchett), 156; *Justice* (Dixey), 59; *Justice* (Kaskey), 80–82; *Justice* (Stanwood), 172–73; *One, Two, Three* (LeWitt), 106, 108; *Sounding Stones* (Lin), 80; *Symbols of Government*, 90; *Untitled* (Norvell), 202
Searle, Henry, 149
Second Circuit, 20, 204, 215, 221; affirming decisions, 98, 190, 219–20; description/history of, 21–25, 31, 33, 64; influential role of, 31, 33–34, 51; notable cases of, 71, 106–07, 109, 126–27, 150. *See also* specific courthouses
Second Renaissance Revival style, 214, 216
Securities and Exchange Commission, 46–47, 201
Sedition Act trial, 210–11, 214
Seeger, Pete, 107
September 11, 2001, 85, 92, 127, 131–32, 162–63
Sharon, Ariel, 73
Sharpe, Judge Gary L., 107
Shelton, Kirk, 201
Sherman Antitrust Act, 46, 50–51, 189
Shinnecock Indian Nation, 146
Sifton, Judge Charles P., 126, 132, 135
Simon, Louis A., 110, 114, 116
Sims Act of 1912, 98

Skidmore, Owings and Merrill, 28, 83–84
Skretny, Judge William M., 162–63, 165, 169
skyscrapers, 36, 39, 131, 189
slavery, 61, 210, 212. *See also* Amistad Case
Smalley, Judge David A., 215
Smith, Abel I., 97
Smith Act, 47
Smith, Judge J. Joseph, 71–72, 201–02
Sobell, Morton, 66–67
Socialists, 64–65
Sontag, Susan, 162
Sotomayor, Justice Sonia, 53, 190
South Africa, 105–07
Southern District of New York, 28, 96, 122; creation of, 24, 95; description/history of, 21–22, 24–26, 55–62; four main courthouses of, 20, 54–55; notable cases of, 64–73, 82, 129. *See also* specific courthouses
Spain, 175, 177–79
Stafford, Robert T., 210
Stanwood, John, 173
"starved classicism," 26, 116
state courts, 60–61
Staten Island, 122, 125–26
Stella, Frank, 28, 142, 144–45
Stevens, John Cox, 60–62
Stewart, Albert T., 100–101, 105
Stewart, Martha, 66, 73
Story, Justice Joseph, 60, 180
Sturgis, Norman R., 99, 105
Supervising Architects, 25–26, 62, 97, 99, 110, 116, 123, 157, 180, 191, 209
Swan, Judge Thomas W., 45, 47
Swango, Michael, 146–47
Syracuse Herald-Journal, 107
Syracuse, New York, 20, 27–28, 94–96, 98, 106–09. *See also* James M. Hanley Federal Building and Courthouse
Syracuse Post-Standard, 107

Taft, William Howard, 34, 182
Tallmadge, Judge Matthias B., 24, 59, 95, 115
Tappan, Lewis, 177, 179
Tarsney Act, 25–26, 182
Tarsney, John C., 25–26
Task Force on Federal Architecture, 27
Telesca, Judge Michael A., 156–57
terrorism trials, 65, 67–69, 127, 135, 162
terrorist acts, 128–29, 131–32, 135. *See also* Alfred P. Murrah Federal Building (Oklahoma City); September 11, 2001
Thai, David, 127
Theodore Roosevelt U.S. Courthouse (Brooklyn), 20, 28; art gallery in, 135; exterior of, 120–21, 128–31, 136–37; interior of, 129, 132–35. *See also* Emanuel Celler Federal Building and U.S. Courthouse (Brooklyn)
Thomas, Isaiah, 73
Thompson, Isaac and Charles, 174
Thompson, Judge Alvin W., 201

Thompson, Justice Smith, 60–61, 177
Thompson, Vivian, 201–02
Thurgood Marshall U.S. Courthouse (Manhattan), 20, 25–27, 30–31, 55, 73–74, 78–79; architect of, 90; building of, 35–39; exterior of, 36–41, 52–54, 75–77; interior of, 40, 42–44, 46–48, 52–53, 66; notable cases of, 45–51, 53, 65–73; renovations of, 51–53
Timbers, Judge William H., 188–89, 203–04
Time magazine, 66, 73
Touro Law School, 143
Town & Davis, 174
Town, Ithiel, 174
Trager, Judge David G., 126–27, 135
Treasury Relief Art Project, 27, 210
Troup, Judge Robert, 57–58
Truman, Harry S., 27, 105

Ulysses (Joyce), 34, 70
U.S. Bill of Rights, 117
U.S. Bureau of Alcohol, Tobacco, and Explosives, 127
U.S. Congress, 33, 46–47, 58, 64, 73–74; appropriates funds for courthouses, 35, 62, 83–84, 151, 182, 189; authorizes restoration projects, 91; creates courts/districts, 22–24, 59, 149; earliest meeting places of, 56–57; and Sedition Law, 210–11, 214
U.S. Constitution, 22, 28, 56, 165, 168, 201–02, 204
U.S. Custom House and Post Office (New Haven), 180, 182
U.S. Customs Service, 87, 90–91. *See also* Alexander Hamilton U.S. Custom House (Manhattan)
U.S. Department of Defense, 50
U.S. embassies, 68–69
U.S. Food and Drug Administration, 98
U.S. Immigration and Naturalization Services, 72
U.S. Justice Department, 66
U.S. Post Office, 25, 189
U.S. Post Office and Customhouse (Hartford), 191
U.S. Postmaster General, 64–65, 70
U.S. Supreme Court, 22–24, 36–37, 42, 46–47, 49, 53, 55, 57–58, 60, 71, 90, 106–07, 117–18, 179–81, 190, 199, 202, 204, 220–21
U.S. Treasury Department, 25, 35, 37, 62, 90, 97, 105, 110, 116, 123, 157, 182, 209
Utica, New York, 20, 94–96, 98, 115–19. *See also* Alexander Pirnie U.S. Courthouse and Federal Building

Van Buren, Martin, 177–79
Van Ness, Judge William P., 24, 59
Vermont, 31, 213, 215, 221. *See also* District of Vermont; specific courthouses; specific towns
Vietnam, 50, 70–73, 116, 127, 161–62
Volstead Act. *See* National Prohibition Act; Prohibition

Waldron, Clarence, 216–17
Walker, Judge John M. Jr., 51, 72
Ward, Jim, 132
Washburn, Kenneth Leland, 114–15

Washington, George, 22–23, 56–57, 84, 105, 192, 208, 210, 215
Washington, Justice Bushrod, 23
Waterbury, Connecticut, 205
Watts, John, 56
Weicker, Lowell P., 198
Weinstein, Judge Jack B., 127
Wells Fargo robbery, 199–200
Werker, Judge Henry F., 69
West Africa, 180
Western District of New York, 28; creation of, 24, 95, 150; description/history of, 21, 25–26, 149–51; notable cases of, 150, 154, 156–62; two main courthouses of, 20, 148–49. *See also* specific courthouses
Westmoreland, William C., 72–73
Wetmore, James A., 116
White Plains, New York, 20, 28, 55, 83–87. *See also* Charles L. Brieant Jr. Federal Building and U.S. Courthouse (White Plains)
Wilcox Mansion Museum, 150
Wiley, Dr. Harvey, 97–98
William R. Cotter Federal Building (Hartford), 191–95
Willowbrook State Development Center (Staten Island), 125–26
Wilson, Woodrow, 217
Windsor, Vermont, 25, 208–09, 216
Winter, Judge Ralph K. Jr., 36, 51
Wisdom, Judge John M., 50
Wolcott, Judge Oliver Jr., 23
wood details, 154, 172, 174, 182; decorative doors, 204; inlay, 104–05; paneling, 27, 43, 82, 115, 119, 143, 147, 158, 169, 184
Woodman, Timothy, 199
Woodruff, Hale, 176, 178–79
Woodruff, Judge Lewis B., 23
Woolsey, Judge John M., 34
Woolworth Building, 36, 63, 65, 90
World Trade Center, 67–68, 85, 90, 92, 131
World War I, 26, 34, 65, 110, 123, 216–17
World War II, 27, 45, 102, 105, 116, 125, 139
Wright brothers, 33–34, 150
Wyatt, Judge Inzer B., 67

Yale Law School, 171, 182, 188, 203, 208
Young, Ammi B., 25, 157, 182, 209–10
Yousef, Ramzi, 67–68

Zampano, Judge Robert C., 189